DIGITAL TYPE DESIGN GUIDE
THE PAGE DESIGNER'S GUIDE TO WORKING WITH TYPE

SEAN CAVANAUGH

with
**Adobe Photoshop and
Illustrator techniques
by Ken Oyer**

Hayden
Books

Library of Congress Catalog Number: 95-77735

ISBN 1-56830-190-1

97 96 95   4 3 2 1

Interpretation of the printing code: the rightmost double-digit number is the year of the book's printing; the rightmost single-digit number is the number of the book's printing. For example, a printing code of 95-1 shows that the first printing of the book occurred in 1995.

Trademark Acknowledgments: TrueType is a trademark and Apple and Macintosh are registered trademarks of Apple Computer, Inc. Windows is a trademark of Microsoft Corporation. Adobe, Adobe Acrobat, Adobe Illustrator, Adobe Photoshop, Adobe PageMaker, Adobe Type Manager and ATM, Mezz, Minion, Myriad, Nueva, PostScript, Tekton, and Type On Call are registered trademarks of Adobe Systems Incorporated. FontMinder is a registered trademark of Ares Software Corporation. Futura is a registered trademark of Fundicion Tipografica Neufville S.A. ITC Avant Garde Gothic, ITC Galliard, ITC Zapf Chancery and ITC Zapf Dingbats are registered trademarks of International Typeface Corporation. Ad Lib, American Typewriter, Caslon Antique, Commercial Script, Copperplate Gothic, Franklin Gothic, Goudy Handtooled, Goudy Sans, Hobo, OCR-A, Olde English and Walbaum are trademarks, and Park Avenue is a registered trademark of Kingsley/ATF Type Corporation. University Roman is a trademark of Esselte Pendaflex Corporation. Glypha, Helvetica, Optima, Palatino, Sabon, Times, and Univers are trademarks of Linotype-Hell AG. URW Palladio and URW Antiqua are trademarks of URW GmbH. Bembo, Gill Sans, and Times New Roman are trademarks of The Monotype Corporation. Monotype is a trademark of Monotype Typography Limited. All other brand or product names are trademarks or registered trademarks of their respective holders.

CREDITS

PUBLISHER
Don Fowley

EDITOR-IN-CHIEF
Michael Nolan

PROJECT MANAGER
Robin Graham

DEVELOPMENT EDITOR
Jan B. Seymour

TECHNICAL EDITORS
Ellen Wixted
Deanna Bebb

BOOK DESIGN & TYPOGRAPHY
Ken Oyer
Sean Cavanaugh

COVER DESIGN
Ken Oyer

PRODUCTION
Ken Oyer
Sean Cavanaugh

INDEXER
Leslie Leland Frank

INSPIRATION
Homer Simpson
Richard Brautigan
Robert Bringhurst

for Rosie and Mrs. Flynn…

ACKNOWLEDGMENTS

This book would not have been possible without the effort of many people. First among them is Ken Oyer. I asked Ken over a year ago whether he'd be interested in coming up with some neat-o Illustrator and Photoshop techniques for a book I was then just thinking about writing. Well, he came up with the neat-o techniques and then some. Ken wound up designing and producing this book with me, and is responsible for most of the graphics you'll see in it. The cover is also a Ken Oyer original. He is not only one of the best designers and production artists I know, but a great friend as well ("Oh, wait…"). I thank him from the bottom of my heart. Secondly I want to thank Jan Seymour for providing the structure of this book. Jan was the "development editor," which basically means she took a bunch of words from me and molded them into chapters. For a while there I felt like Mr. Kurtz in *Heart of Darkness*—living in the bowels of the Belgian Congo, aimlessly cranking out pages on my word processor—until she joined the project. Of course, there are others: Michael Nolan and Robin Graham at Hayden for believing in this project and providing me with more understanding and support than I ever expected from a publisher; Deanna Bebb for her wonderful eye for editing (and for going through all the text and making sure it applied to Windows as well as to Macs); Ellen Wixted for her thoughtful comments and technical review; Paul Celestin for producing the companion CD; K.C. Ennis for the author photos; Dennis Harrington for his technical advice; Sage Osterfeld and SoftMaker, Inc. for providing the typefaces on the companion CD; Jim Mayall and the crew at MicroVision for providing *WordExpress*; all the folks at Adobe, Ares, Nisus, Macromedia, MetaTools (formerly HSC Software), and Xaos Tools for providing product information, assistance and, of course, really cool products; and last, but not least, my wonderful agent Margot Maley at Waterside Productions.

TABLE OF CONTENTS

Foreword   ix

Introduction   xi

1 PostScript and TrueType Fonts: The Basics   1
  Bitmap fonts   2
  Font scaling   2
  Hinting   4
  Printing issues   6
  Difference between PC and Macintosh fonts   7

2 PostScript and TrueType Fonts on the Macintosh   9
  Recognizing PostScript and TrueType fonts   10
  Under the Hood of PostScript and TrueType   13
  Macintosh TrueType fonts   14
  Suitcases on your Macintosh system   14
  Installing fonts with System 7.5   15
  Managing Font Files on the Macintosh   16
  Dueling Font Managers   18
    Sean Cavanaugh Using MasterJuggler   19
    Ken Oyer Using Suitcase   23
  Font management summary   27
  New technology: QuickDraw GX   27

3 PostScript and TrueType Fonts with Microsoft Windows   31
  Font files on the PC   32
    TrueType fonts   32
    Bitmap fonts   33
    Vector fonts   33
    PostScript fonts   34
  Installing and working with fonts on your PC   34
  Removing or deleting TrueType fonts in Windows 3.1   35
  Deleting TrueType and bitmap fonts in Windows 95   37
  Previewing TrueType fonts in Windows 95   38
  Managing font files in Windows   39
  Managing Fonts with Ares FontMinder   42

4 Cross Platform Issues   47
  Using PostScript and TrueType fonts together   48
  Converting fonts   49
  Font substitution   53
  Printer resident fonts   55
  Downloading fonts   57
  Adobe Type Reunion   59
  Family-ized fonts   60
  Multiple Master typefaces   62

5 Working with Characters   65
  ASCII Shmascii, what does it mean?   67
  Macintosh character chart   68
  Windows character chart   69

Typing extended characters in Windows   70
Typing extended characters on the Macintosh   72
Key combinations for extended characters   74
Rearranging characters with FontMonger   78

6 Ligatures and Expert Set Characters   83
Ligatures   84
    Non-English ligatures   86
Ampersands   86
Using expert set typefaces   87
Fractions   88
    Creating fractions without expert sets   89

7 The Rules of Digital Typography   93

8 E-mail Typography   113

9 Type as Graphic Element   121
Drop shadows   124
Type on a path   126
Type with a neon glow   128
Bevel type   130
Quilted type   132
Ghosted type   134
Interlapping type   136
Engraved type   138

Reflecting type   141
Embossed type   144
Debossed type   146
Type in flames   150
Plug-ins & filters   154

10 Choosing Typefaces   159

11 Typefaces   165
Typeface classification   166
    Parts of a letter   167
Oldstyles   172
Transitionals   188
Moderns   196
Slab serifs   204
Sans serifs   210
Script faces   234
Uncials   238
Black Letter   240
Symbols & borders   242
Decorative type   248

Bibliography   259

Index   265

FOREWORD

by Sage Osterfeld

I've been working in the type and design field for the better part of a decade, and over the years I've had the opportunity to read a lot of books on the subject. Many of these books are nice to look at. But reading them, well, that's quite often a different story. The text is either of such secondary concern that reading it, obviously, was not really the author's intent, or so incoherent and full of jargon that you wonder if the author was actually writing in a known language.

Of course, that should come as no surprise. Typography and design are visual media, and typographers and designers communicate with objects and space, not with words. As a result, many find it extremely difficult, if not impossible, to write a book about their craft. (Ask one how it is that he does what he does. I guarantee that 90 percent of the time you'll get one or two words and a whole lot of grunts and gestures as an answer. Sure, it's interesting stuff to watch, but not very informative unless you've seen *Gorillas in the Mist* a dozen times.)

I'm pleased to report that this book is not more of the usual — primarily because the author, Sean Cavanaugh, is most unusual. Oh, he's no stark, raving lunatic. You won't find him running around in a loincloth and carrying a spear at the grocery store or anything. (At least I think you won't.) But anyone who's spent more than a few minutes with him knows without a doubt that there's something different about him.

I've known Sean for a little more than five years now, and have never ceased to be amazed by his seemingly limitless talents. He is funny, articulate, and an avid motorcycle adventurer. An expert with the Mac and PC as well as a raft of software packages, he's also a gifted (and self-taught) computer-based graphic designer. Perhaps most importantly, he's one of the best writers I know.

There is a tendency among writers of books like this one to present the material in a staid, straightforward manner that makes them about as interesting as your high school history textbook. This isn't Sean's way. Rather, I've always found that he treats his books as a sort of personal sandbox where every page is a fresh source of amusement. With his lively and down-to-earth style, he twists dry and boring subjects into funny and fascinating material the way a birthday party clown turns a plain old balloon into a dachshund or hat with antlers. If you're observant you'll also find many a surprise tucked into his examples and captions. Some will make you raise an eyebrow; others will probably make you laugh out loud. All of it combines to make a great, one-of-a-kind book.

As a bonus, Cavanaugh has enhanced a number of chapters by enlisting the talented Ken Oyer for some of the more advanced design techniques. Oyer is an accomplished designer and musician whose work has received national attention. Less prone to grunts and

gestures than most designers, Oyer teaches design
and computer graphics at Platt College. Many of his
Illustrator and Photoshop techniques and shortcuts
are detailed for the first time in these pages.

Take your time with this book. Browse through
the examples and give the text a good read. I think that
you'll find this book to be one of the most fun and
interesting "how-to" books you've ever laid eyes on.
Of two things I am certain: first, when you've finished
this book you'll definitely come away with more typographical and design ability than you ever thought you
had. And second, you'll probably never look at a page
of text the same way again.

Really, the book is that good. Enjoy it.

— Sage Osterfeld
August 1995

Mr. Osterfeld is the former president of SoftMaker, Inc.

INTRODUCTION

Hi, and thanks for buying this book. (If you're just browsing it in a store, thanks for thinking about buying this book.)

This brief introduction serves a couple of purposes: 1) to explain my reasons for writing this book, as well as the philosophy behind it, and 2) to provide a chapter-by-chapter synopsis, since you don't have to, and may not even want to (ouch), read the whole book from cover to cover.

Who should buy this book?

Anyone who uses type and loves it; Anyone who uses type and hates it; Anyone who uses type and doesn't understand it; Anyone who uses type...

Why I wrote this book...

When you plop down cash money for a software program — doesn't matter what kind: a word processor, contact manager, arcade game, even a shareware utility, for example — you expect a user manual to come along with it. All software comes with user manuals. This is just the way things are. Except for fonts, which rarely, if ever, come with user manuals. Usually the publishers include some bare-bones instructions for *installing* the fonts, maybe even some printouts showing you what

they look like, if you're lucky, but that's about it. This is ironic, especially when you consider that word processing has a history of about 25 years, desktop publishing less than half of that, but typography, well, it's been around for about 500 years. It might seem obvious, but a lot has happened in 500 years. There's a lot to learn. Where are the manuals?

And if that weren't enough, most word processors come with integrated spelling and grammar checkers; graphics programs are bundled with sophisticated filters and plug-ins; desktop publishing programs come with templates and layout wizards. But what do fonts come with? Nothing. You're just supposed to know what to do with them when you buy them. The design philosophy behind a typeface such as *Fette Fraktur,* for example, is over four centuries removed from one such as *Futura,* yet at most a few pixels will separate them on a font menu. Those 500 years of typographic evolution should be ingrained in our collective unconscious by now, right? Well, that doesn't appear to be the case. Most of the problems I see in documents created on the desktop aren't due to a lack of creativity, or some dearth of artistic inspiration, or even technical ineptitude. Most design problems (read: ugly, unattractive documents) exist at the typographic level; poor font choice, inappropriate sizes, too many fonts, wrong characters, and bad spacing are chief among them.

Not too long ago I worked for a company that published a product called *defi_niType Plus*. As its name suggests, *definiType Plus* was a typeface package for Macs and PCs. It came with a manual. And people absolutely loved it. I mean, they wrote us letters just to let us know how much they loved it. Good looking letters at that. We received more praise from end-users and the press for the manual than we did the typefaces themselves. We covered entire walls with those letters.

It was a big ego boost for me because I wrote that manual. But as manuals go, it really wasn't that special. I didn't come up with the typographic and design principles I wrote about. I simply shared what I had learned about these things over the years. And as well-received as that manual was, I always thought I could have improved upon it, could have provided more information, more tips and tricks, more neat-o designs that just might inspire others to create, um, neat-o designs.

Enter the *Digital Type Design Guide*. In a very real sense, this book is my second crack at writing about type, at sharing what I know about working and playing with fonts, and creating good-looking documents. And of course, second cracks are usually better because the cracker gets to go back and improve things from the first go around. That's what I want this book to be, an improvement over that first manual.

How this book is organized

The first four chapters aren't really about typography at all, but rather the technical details of identifying, installing, and managing font files. Chapter 1 introduces some basic concepts about PostScript and TrueType. Chapter 2 deals with font installation and management for Mac users, while Chapter 3 is for Windows users. Chapter 4 discusses some cross-platform issues.

Chapters 5 and 6 are about *characters*. While these chapters are still somewhat technical in nature, they are also about the intersection of typography and technology. Issues such as character encoding and how fonts are accessed by software and operating systems are discussed. Charts and tables abound.

Chapter 7 is about the rules of type. I've presented those I consider most important. These are the rules I adhere to, the reason people come to me and say, "How can I make my documents look like yours?" My approach is practical, and I've tried to be as thorough as possible without getting too deep in arcana. I consider this chapter the heart of the book, and it is one I spent the most time writing and fretting over. The information here will help you produce better looking letters, memos, reports, packaging, advertisements, résumés, newsletters, brochures — heck, any document that's made up of words. Chapter 8 is a brief examination of how these rules apply to an area generally considered out of bounds from them: e-mail.

Chapter 9 takes a 90-degree turn and examines type not as type, but as graphic element. If the previous chapters are about *working* with type, this one is about *playing* with it. It's packed with Adobe Illustrator and Photoshop techniques for creating exciting type-based designs. Even if you don't own or use one of these programs, I suggest taking a look at this chapter anyway, as it really exemplifies what it means to be digital. (For a long time I thought a digital artist was a finger painter.)

Chapter 11 is a detailed look at several typeface designs and categories of designs. It examines typefaces from both a historical as well as a functional perspective. I've included suggestions on which fonts are best suited for which types of documents (but keep in mind they're just suggestions, not rules).

Hey, what happened to Chapter 10? Chapter 10 is really a subset of Chapter 7, "The Rules of Digital Typography," but because it offers advice on choosing typefaces, I thought it should appear immediately before Chapter 11, "Typefaces."

About the Companion CD

Although the typefaces I discuss are available from various vendors, they also happen to be the same ones included on the companion CD. When I licensed these fonts from SoftMaker, Inc., I had several thousand to choose from. I assembled this particular collection because I think it provides a core set of fonts from all the major historical categories of text fonts, the primary functional categories of sans serif fonts, and enough decorative and script fonts to keep it flexible and interesting. Every font was chosen for a purpose: to create what I consider an essential type library.

So that's it, then.

In his book *The Elements of Typographic Style*, Robert Bringhurst makes a distinction between *macro* typography and *micro* typography. These terms do not refer to point sizes. The former is primarily concerned with what we generally consider desktop publishing: page layout and design. The latter is that ill-documented (in terms of software user manuals) world of type. This book, when it's about typography (and it's not always), is really about micro typography. It's about the detail stuff. I'll tell you again that my approach is practical. Simple techniques you can use at the typographic level to improve the appearance of your documents, and make working with fonts easier and maybe even fun.

Enjoy.

— S.C.

*PostScript and
TrueType Fonts*

The Basics

PostScript and TrueType Fonts

The Basics

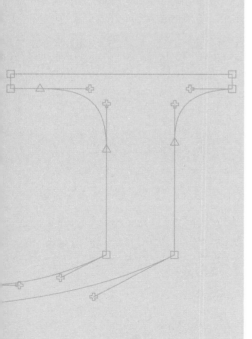

OVER THE YEARS, MANY DIFFERENT FONT FORMATS HAVE appeared on the scene; only two — PostScript Type 1 and TrueType — have remained. TrueType is the relative newcomer, introduced in 1991 by Apple Computer and Microsoft Corporation, nearly seven years after PostScript typefaces were first released by Adobe Systems. (Many Darwinian theories have been offered explaining the rise of these two formats as well as the demise of the others, but I'll save this interesting topic for my next book.) It is nearly inconceivable that PostScript or TrueType will fade away, although they will change somewhat to accommodate new operating systems. So rest assured your investment in typefaces of either one of these formats is a safe one; obsolescence does not loom around the corner.

People ask me all the time which format they should use, and there's no perfect answer. Fortunately it's not an either/or proposition. It's perfectly acceptable to use both formats concurrently if you make certain considerations to ensure it's smooth and trouble-free (such as not installing the same font in both formats, a situation that will cause you endless grief). But we'll get to that a bit later. My objective first is to discuss the differences and similarities of the formats. Then you can make an informed decision as to which format best suits you or your situation.

BITMAP FONTS

In discussing the two formats, I need to mention a third item: bitmap fonts. Bitmap fonts don't fall under the font *format* category per se; instead bitmap fonts are things, actual representations of a font, or better yet, pictures of a font. They are really only intended for two things: screen display (where resolution is substantially lower than even a modest laser printer), and printing

on old dot-matrix printers (where resolution is normally low as well).

Bitmap fonts are of fixed resolution (e.g., 72 dots per inch) and fixed size (e.g., 12 points); you can't really change their resolution or their size. Well, you can but with negligible or poor results. For example, if you print a 72-dpi bitmap font to a 600-dpi printer, it still only produces a 72-dpi bitmap. If you scale a bitmap font, that is, change its size from 12 points, for example, to 24 points, it will look bad. Very bad.

FONT SCALING

The bitmap font shown here is Times 12 point with a resolution of 72 dots per inch. For low-resolution screen display, it's not bad. On your monitor, it looks good and is quite easy to read. Scaling it to 24 points, however, degrades its appearance considerably, and at 41 points it looks awful, not to mention the fact that it no longer bears any resemblance to Times:

Rosebud   Rosebud   Rosebud

In terms of digital typography, this concept of *scaling* is what it's all about, and is the reason PostScript and TrueType exist. These formats are also referred to as *outline fonts* or *scalable fonts*. A PostScript or TrueType font isn't simply a representation of a font at a fixed size and resolution like a bitmap font is, but a mathematical description of a font, a set of instructions telling your computer and printer how to draw its characters at any size or resolution. The mathematics involved define the curves, or outlines, that make up a font. So it doesn't really matter if the font is 12 points or 112 points — it will be drawn proportionally on your screen and printed proportionally to your printer.

PostScript and TrueType fonts are always scalable, and are based on a relative measurement system called an *em-square*. An *em* is a unit of distance equal to the point size. In 12-pt type, an em is 12 points (0.167 inches) wide; in 72-pt type it is 72 points (one inch) wide. For any given typeface, an em is proportionally the same at any point size. When you scale or print a font, a transformation is made from relative measurements to absolute ones. The absolute values are based on the resolution, in dots or pixels, of the device, which might be a computer monitor (typically 72 dpi), a printer (which could be 300 dpi or 600 dpi or 2540 dpi), or a film recorder (generally 4000 or 8000 dpi). Neither PostScript nor TrueType have any built-in resolution or dpi limitations—they are capable of infinite scaling, of translating from relative coordinates to any absolute coordinate system. In font terms, this is what is meant by *device independence*.

For TrueType fonts, the mathematical wizardry required to do this scaling is built into the Macintosh and Microsoft Windows operating systems. You don't have to purchase or install any special "scaling" programs. For PostScript fonts, however, you need to install Adobe Type Manager (ATM) to enable your system to scale PostScript fonts to any size for screen display. ATM is not capable of scaling TrueType fonts, nor are the Macintosh and Windows operating systems capable of scaling PostScript fonts without ATM installed. An added advantage of ATM is that it lets you print PostScript fonts to any non-PostScript printer or output device. But even if you have a PostScript printer, you'll still need ATM to scale fonts for screen display. Although it is technically possible, nobody uses Post-Script fonts without also using Adobe Type Manager.

NOTE Technically, ATM is not a requirement for using PostScript Type 1 fonts on the Macintosh. You can install and print Type 1 fonts without ATM, but they may look jagged on your monitor. And while it is technically not required for Windows, it is damned near impossible to use Type 1 fonts without it. The procedure is so difficult, in fact, that it's not even worth discussing—the effort and limitations involved more than justify the price of ATM…even at full retail. And as further reason to use ATM, for both the Macintosh and Windows, it lets you print Type 1 fonts to any printer, not just genuine PostScript printers.

With TrueType or with PostScript (using ATM), fonts can be scaled to any size and still look good. This example is 72-dpi screen display just like before, but notice how much nicer the text is scaled:

Rosebud Rosebud Rosebud

One significant difference between PostScript and TrueType is the way each defines its curves. When you think about it, it's relatively easy to define a straight line: determine the coordinates of the two endpoints and connect the dots. But the math involved in describing curves is considerably more complex. PostScript uses what is referred to as *Bézier curves*, and TrueType uses *quadratic B-splines*. The primary functional difference is that Bézier curves rely on control points that are not on the curve itself to define it, while the quadratic B-spline uses points that are all positioned directly on the curve to define it. So in the PostScript language, a minimum of four points is required to define a curve—two end-points and two control points—but with TrueType, only three points are

ADOBE TYPE MANAGER (ATM)

The retail version of ATM is available for about $40, but it comes free with most Adobe products—Illustrator, Photoshop, PageMaker, and all Adobe PostScript Type 1 fonts. It's simply a must-have addition to any Macintosh or Windows system. Updates to ATM are free, and can be downloaded from the Adobe Systems electronic bulletin board (206.623.6984), the Adobe web site (http://www.adobe.com), or from the Adobe Applications Forum on CompuServe (GO ADOBEAPP).

On the Macintosh, ATM consists of a single startup file you need to place in the Control Panel folder within your System Folder. For Windows users, ATM is a system driver you should install with the setup program provided by Adobe (the installation program makes changes to your SYSTEM.INI and WIN.INI files, in addition to creating its own .INI file, ATM.INI).

The Windows version of ATM differs from the Macintosh version in that it is an actual type *management* program, that is, the Windows version actually manages the installation of fonts, as well as provides some other functions. The Mac version, on the other hand, does not manage the installation and removal of typefaces, or do anything besides provide your Mac with the capability to display PostScript fonts at any size, smoothly and without jaggies, and print them to any printer. No small feat, but I still believe the name *Adobe Type Manager* is somewhat misleading. For you Mac users unfamiliar with the ways of Windows, think of Windows ATM as a cross between Mac ATM and the popular font manager Suitcase.

Both the Windows and Mac versions of ATM are available on the companion CD. To install them, simply install the Adobe Acrobat Reader application located in the "Demos" folder (Mac), or in the \TRYOUTS directory (Windows).

required. I suppose in theory it would be somewhat faster for a computer or printer to draw a curve using quadratic B-splines, but in reality there is very little difference. Perfectly clear?

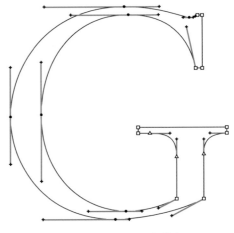

Bézier curves in a more recognizable form

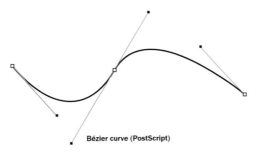

Bézier curve (PostScript)

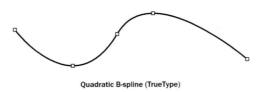

Quadratic B-spline (TrueType)

Bézier curves are self-contained such that each curve segment can exist on its own. Quadratic B-splines, on the other hand, are progressive, that is, the function of one point on a curve is used to determine the function of the next point.

Theoretically, the two formats have their mathematical nuances, and TrueType might well have more fans among rocket scientists and graphics gurus, but in terms of practical considerations, the bottom line is that the two formats are similar and have more or less the same capabilities.

HINTING

Hints are special instructions in PostScript and True-Type fonts used to improve the display or output of fonts at lower resolutions. The goal of hinting is to reduce the distortions that arise when there aren't enough pixels to draw a character accurately. These instructions are algorithms, programs actually, that help "gridfit" characters to low resolution devices (monitors, laser printers, etc.), thus improving their appearance without permanently altering the actual typeface design or character outlines. Hints are very important at lower resolutions (300 dpi and below), less so at medium resolution (600 dpi), and unnecessary at high resolutions where there are ample pixels to faithfully render the character outlines.

A hint might shift a character, or just part of a character, such as the stems in the letter *H* ever so slightly to make it appear more natural under poor conditions (low resolution). For example, suppose pixels must be added to make bold characters appear bold, or removed to prevent normal characters from appearing bold. If a character outline were to fall between two pixels, such as in this illustration, both pixels would be turned on, and the stem would appear bold when it shouldn't.

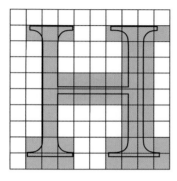

Unhinted

Hints in a well-produced font prevent this from happening. Notice how in the second example the pixels have been shifted to better represent the outline.

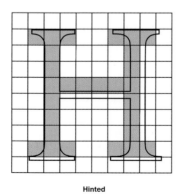

Hinted

Hinting is not an automatic feature of the True-Type or PostScript rasterizers, and so must be done by the font manufacturer. As such, not all fonts are hinted equally. Adding hints to a font is a time-consuming and expensive process, and generally speaking is something only the larger type manufacturers do well—Adobe, Bitstream, Agfa, Monotype, URW (the source of most of the fonts on the companion CD), Fontek, and Emigre. In the illustration below, the font designer places hints (the arrows) at key locations, and in certain directions, to instruct ATM how to draw characters more legibly at low resolutions. The process can greatly improve screen display at small sizes (below 14 points, for example) where no hand-tuned bitmaps exist, and also improves the appearance of text printed on lower resolution, e.g., 300-dpi, laser printers.

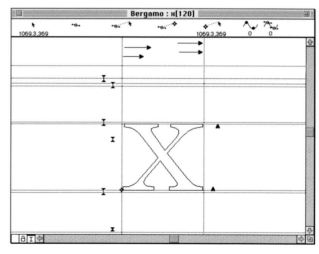

A hinted character in Macromedia's Fontographer

Like the differences between Bézier curves and quadratic B-splines, PostScript and TrueType use different types of algorithms to hint characters and fonts, but the results are roughly equivalent. In theory,

WHAT KIND OF PRINTER SHOULD I BUY?

Buy a laser printer of the highest resolution you can afford, with as much extra RAM as you can afford. If you're doing any kind of serious graphic work, PostScript is a necessity. Non-PostScript printers are considerably less expensive, but I only recommend them if you're really just concerned with word processing. That is, if you don't plan on working with more sophisticated graphics and page layout applications such as Illustrator, FreeHand, PageMaker, QuarkXPress, etc., you may not need a PostScript printer.

Regarding resolution, the standard is 600 dpi, and I don't recommend purchasing a printer with anything less. 300 dpi is sufficient for office and personal correspondence, but professional documents (newsletters and instruction manuals, for example) require a minimum of 600 dpi. Also consider that several type designs (Bembo, Bodoni, Garamond, and Optima, to name a few) look considerably better at 600 dpi. This isn't to say that they look bad at lower resolutions, but they lack many of the characteristics present at higher resolutions — cupped serifs, gentle variations in stroke width, fine lines, etc.

I recommend at least 2 mb of memory, but this is usually quite easy to add later.

For the money, I think the Hewlett-Packard Laser-Jet 5MP is the best laser printer available. It is a 600-dpi PostScript printer with 3 mb of RAM and 35 resident (built-in) Adobe Type 1 fonts. It accepts the same memory chips (SIMMs) that you use in your computer, so upgrading memory is easy and inexpensive.

the TrueType format is capable of more sophisticated hinting, just like quadratic B-splines are capable of using fewer points than Bézier curves. However, there are few development tools available to font designers for producing these über hints. PostScript tools, on the other hand, are widely available. So in reality, most font houses that produce both PostScript and TrueType fonts usually do the primary development on their PostScript fonts, and then convert them to TrueType, tweaking them as needed. It's not uncommon to see PostScript fonts that are of higher hinted quality than their TrueType counterparts of the same design. The exceptions are the TrueType fonts that ship with Microsoft Windows — Arial and Times New Roman — developed by Monotype Corporation. These typefaces live up to the potential inherent in the TrueType format, but does the world really need these great looking reworks of Helvetica and Times?

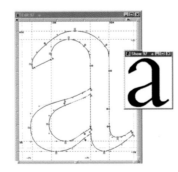

A postscript font opened for editing in FontLab for Windows

PRINTING ISSUES

PostScript is a page description language (PDL) as well as a font format, whereas TrueType is really only a font technology. In addition to describing the curves and lines that make up the characters in a font, the PostScript language also describes graphics and digitized images — virtually everything on a page — for printing. As a full-fledged language, it is loaded in ROM on many printers, and this is what is meant by "PostScript printers" — printers that natively speak the PostScript language. When printing to a PostScript printer, everything on the page is sent to the printer in PostScript language, even TrueType fonts which the printer must translate into PostScript (not that big a deal, but it still has to convert them). And very importantly, PostScript printers print PostScript fonts faster than they do TrueType fonts. If you own a PostScript printer, this very fact should convince you to use PostScript fonts whenever there is a choice.

Also consider whether you will be sending any of your documents to a service bureau for high-resolution output. Virtually all imagesetters use PostScript RIPs (Raster Image Processors), which are basically PostScript laser printers capable of very high resolutions (1200 dpi and higher). I've worked with several service bureaus, and not a single one of them *recommends* using TrueType fonts. Some will accept them, but they do so grudgingly, for problems will inevitably pop up. Perhaps I'm biased, but when you consider that in terms of professional imagesetting TrueType offers no advantage over PostScript, and in the best scenario can only perform equally with it, why even take the chance? My advice: stick with PostScript fonts if you work with service bureaus.

Choosing the Best Font Format

SITUATION:	RECOMMENDED FONT FORMAT:	COMMENTS:
PostScript printer	PostScript	A no-brainer
Creating documents you'll send to a service bureau for hi-resolution output	PostScript	Your service bureau will accuse you of having no brain if you bring them TrueType fonts
Non-PostScript laser printer	PostScript or TrueType	Must use ATM with PostScript
Low-res printer	PostScript	Fonts are generally of higher quality*
Illustration programs (e.g., Illustrator, FreeHand)	PostScript	Later versions of these programs work with TrueType fonts
Image processing (e.g., Photoshop)	PostScript or TrueType	
General use	PostScript or TrueType	
What Sean uses	PostScript	

* The TrueType fonts Arial, Times New Roman and New Courier, as well as the fonts available in the Apple TrueType Font Pack, and just about any TrueType font from Monotype Corporation, are of exceptionally high quality. Unfortunately these fonts are not indicative of the majority of TrueType fonts on the market. Most TrueType fonts are sold in huge collections, with little or no attention paid to quality. On a cost per font basis, such collections look pretty good…but you get what you pay for. My suggestion is to avoid them.

DIFFERENCES BETWEEN PC AND MACINTOSH FONTS

With one exception, PostScript and TrueType are the same on the Macintosh as they are on the PC. They print the same. They look the same. They smell the same. There are no quality differences whatsoever (contrary to what some Mac users might like to believe). These formats are not tied to any operating systems, so if you have a PostScript printer hooked up to your Macintosh, for example, as long as it has the right kind of printer port, it is also a PostScript printer for the PC.

But that one exception — character encoding — is a biggie. Character encoding has significant differences across platforms. And it goes beyond the mere "You say tuh-MAY-toe, I say tuh-MAH-toe" level. More like "You say tuh-MAY-toe, I say zucchini." But we'll cover that issue in Chapter 5. We'll also discuss another cross platform concern in Chapter 4: sharing documents between platforms, specifically focusing on issues at the typographical level. ∎

POSTSCRIPT TYPE 1 VS. TYPE 3

There are two types of PostScript fonts: Type 1 and Type 3. PostScript Type 1 is the industry standard, and when people talk about "PostScript fonts," they're really talking about PostScript Type 1 fonts. The Type 3 format is to desktop publishing what the eight-track format is to hi-fi. It experienced a mild surge in popularity a few years back but is basically dead in the water. Adobe developed the Type 3 font specification because they didn't want the rest of the world to make Type 1 fonts, apparently in an attempt to keep the high-end type market to themselves and other select manufacturers. Type 3, then, was really just a bone Adobe tossed out to keep developers happy. It didn't work, however, or at least it didn't work for very long. The Type 3 format is inadequate at many levels. While Type 1 fonts contain hinting, Type 3 fonts do not and so will always look worse at small sizes or low resolution. And unlike Type 1 fonts, Type 3 fonts cannot be encrypted or compressed, making them larger than comparable Type 1 fonts. The only real benefit of Type 3 fonts is that they can contain fill patterns (greyscales, cross hatching, etc.), whereas Type 1 fonts can only be solid colors, for example, black. Of course, you can open any font — Type 1 included — in an illustration program and change its fill pattern, adding things like color gradients, patterns, or pictures of kittens, for example, but doing so requires converting it to a graphic first, that is, it's then no longer a font.

I occasionally run across interesting shareware or freeware Type 3 fonts on computer bulletin boards and online services, but for the most part they're more trouble than they're worth. And in fact many applications are incompatible with them. Adobe has long since abandoned the format, and ATM only supports Type 1 fonts. Type 3, see ya.

PostScript and
TrueType Fonts
on the Macintosh

PostScript and TrueType Fonts on the Macintosh

CHAPTER 1 PROVIDED YOU WITH ENOUGH BACKGROUND information to help you decide whether you should use PostScript with ATM or TrueType as your primary font system. And even if you haven't yet made such a decision, don't worry: you don't have to. As we discussed, it's not an either/or proposition. Chapter 1 compared the formats without being specific to any operating system. Now let's analyze these font formats at a functional level, to show you how they're the same and how they're different, and guide you through the process of managing font files on the Macintosh.

RECOGNIZING POSTSCRIPT AND TRUETYPE FONTS

PostScript fonts on the Macintosh are made up of two separate files: the suitcase file containing the screen bitmaps (at least one point size is required) and the corresponding printer font. TrueType fonts are comprised of a single suitcase file, which is *outwardly* identical to the bitmap suitcase used by PostScript fonts. Here's what they look like:

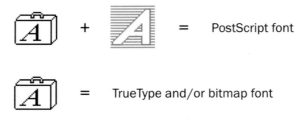

On the Mac, suitcase files can contain both screen bitmaps and TrueType fonts. The suitcase metaphor is a very good one in this regard. The order and amount you pack the suitcase makes no difference. It is simply a container for bitmap and TrueType fonts. It doesn't matter whether these bitmaps are required for Post-

Script fonts (and optionally used by TrueType fonts), or for TrueType fonts themselves. As far as the Mac is concerned, there is no distinction between a suitcase that just contains bitmap fonts or one that contains TrueType fonts. In fact, the suitcases themselves aren't even required. You could actually install the *contents* of a suitcase file directly into the Fonts folder without including the suitcase file. Although I wouldn't recommend doing this for two reasons:

1. You'll have too many font files to keep track of. Grouping them into convenient suitcase files greatly simplifies the task of installing/un-installing them.

2. It takes more System resources and memory to manage font files that aren't kept within suitcases.

TrueType fonts do not require separate bitmaps (unlike PostScript fonts), but can utilize them. In other words, if you have a TrueType font named "Janbee" and a bitmap font named "Janbee 12," whenever you select the Janbee font at a size of 12 points within your word processor or page layout program, for example, the bitmap font "Janbee 12" will be used for screen display. When you print the font, however, the TrueType font will be used in place of the bitmap.

Depending on the font and the font designer, hand-tuned bitmaps often look better on screen and are more easily readable than TrueType fonts by themselves, even though the same bitmap would look terrible when printed. To try this out, install the font Bergamo in TrueType and examine how it looks on screen when you type 10- or 12-point text. Now install the PostScript version and its associated suitcase file. The PostScript version, in this particular example, has hand-tuned screen bitmaps for 10 and 12 points. These bitmaps were designed for maximum legibility on screen. For this reason, if you plan on using TrueType fonts, you might want to copy some of the hand-tuned bitmaps from the PostScript fonts to your TrueType suitcases. To do this, open the suitcase file provided with the PostScript font by double-clicking it, select some bitmaps (Bergamo 10, Bergamo 12, Bergamo Italic 10, etc.) and drag them to the suitcase containing the TrueType font. Now, whenever you use the Bergamo TrueType font, the bitmaps you copied will be used for screen display.

When you look at suitcases, outwardly they are identical so it's important to know the distinction by looking inside the suitcase file. People sometimes ask why when they print a font, it prints jagged and ugly. The reason is often that they assumed they were using a TrueType font because they noticed the suitcase file, but the suitcase only contained bitmap fonts.

A standard suitcase file

The suitcase file shown here contains a TrueType font (Geneva) and several screen bitmaps (including Geneva 10, Geneva 14). I opened it by double-clicking its icon in the Finder, and then choosing the "by Icon" command from the View menu.

TrueType font

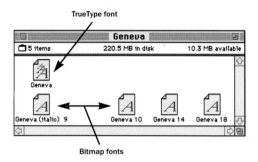

Bitmap fonts

It is quite simple to tell bitmap from TrueType fonts once you look inside the suitcase: bitmap fonts come in certain point sizes, and their names are always followed by a number, such as "Geneva 10" or "Bergamo 12." The number, of course, is the point size of the bitmap, and determines what point sizes are displayed in your applications' font Size menus and dialog boxes. TrueType fonts, on the other hand, never have a number following the typeface name (unless, for some reason a number is part of the font's name, such as the typeface "Modern 216"). They are simply listed as "Geneva" or "Bergamo." Another way to tell the difference between bitmap and TrueType fonts is that the icon for a bitmap contains a single letter *A*, whereas TrueType fonts contain three *As* in a scale.

Fonts folder viewed by name

Likewise, you can see a distinction on the Size menu between bitmap and TrueType fonts. Bitmap font sizes appear outlined on the menu to show which sizes are installed in the suitcase, whereas TrueType fonts have this outlined appearance for all font sizes whether they're installed or not. This is somewhat misleading since Adobe Type Manager is going to display the font at any size, regardless of which bitmaps are installed in the suitcase. This convention of outlining font sizes in menus is a remnant of the days before ATM and TrueType.

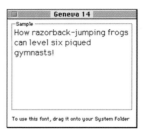

Bitmap font sample

TrueType font sample

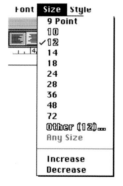

Bitmap fonts clearly display installed font sizes (10 and 12 points in this example).

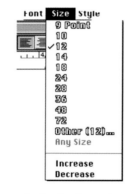

TrueType fonts have no visual distinction of installed fonts sizes.

When you double-click one of the icons in a suitcase file, it displays a sample of that typeface. Of course, it's shown at screen resolution (72 dpi), so is not a definitive sample — you'd have to print the font out for that — but it gives you a rough idea of what the font looks like.

Unless you're using a font manager such as Master-Juggler or Suitcase that lets you keep your fonts wherever you like (discussed later in this chapter), the Macintosh operating system requires bitmap and TrueType font files to be installed in the Fonts folder in the System Folder.

Unlike suitcase files that usually have the same icon, PostScript printer fonts come in all sorts of different icons. In the example below, the icon at top left is the one Adobe uses for all of its printer fonts. The one shown immediately to its right is the icon used for the Type 1 fonts on the companion CD. The icon in the upper right is the generic icon for Type 1 fonts, and is quite common among shareware fonts. The bottom row of icons are from SoftMaker and URW. The default location for PostScript printer fonts is the Fonts folder located inside the System Folder.

Some familiar PostScript Type 1 printer font icons

UNDER THE HOOD OF POSTSCRIPT AND TRUETYPE

Before proceeding, let me just note that none of what follows is required reading. If you have a desire to learn more about fonts and font editing, this stuff might very well be of interest to you, and will provide a good primer for jumping off into some of the more technical aspects; but if you're not into this, or don't plan on getting into this, then what follows is pure eyeball glaze.

Macintosh PostScript Fonts

There are three elements that make up a Macintosh PostScript font: The NFNT resource, the FOND resource, and the printer outline file. The first two items, for all practical purposes, can be considered a single entity because the Macintosh operating system maintains them as one unit, usually stored within a suitcase file. In fact, the only way to view them separately is by using a program such as ResEdit, an Apple Computer development utility that lets you manipulate the many different types of resources contained in a Macintosh file — any Macintosh file. The NFNT resource stores the actual bitmaps for each character in the font, and for each size. You can determine which sizes are available by opening a suitcase. For example, a suitcase file might list "Macfont 10" and "Macfont 12." Each size — in this example 10 point and 12 point — constitutes a single NFNT resource. The NFNT resource additionally stores metric information for the font, such as character height, width, and available kerning pairs (if any).

The FOND resource is the central nervous system of a Mac font. It keeps track of all the available NFNT resources, and determines the font names and sizes displayed in Font menus and Character formatting dialog boxes. The FOND resource also maintains the link between the suitcase file and the printer outline files, and stores information about the font used by the operating system and applications such as Font ID codes. (Even though we humans refer to fonts by name, the Mac identifies them numerically, and these numbers are stored in the FOND.)

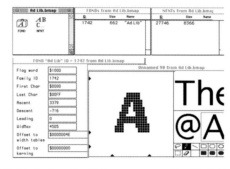

A Macintosh suitcase file with its resources opened for editing in ResEdit

The printer outline files contain all of the PostScript outline data — the lines, curves, points, and hinting instructions that your Mac, in conjunction with ATM, needs to correctly display and print the font. The Mac can display on screen the bitmap fonts contained in the suitcase file without having the printer outline files, but only at the sizes specified by the NFNT resource. In other words, without the printer outline files, ATM cannot scale the font, and choosing any font size not listed in the suitcase file will result in a rough screen display referred to as the "jaggies." The printer outline files are required for printing as well (duh). When you *download* a font to a printer, for instance, you are downloading the printer outline file.

NOTE One more thing about Macintosh PostScript fonts. You will occasionally see AFM files on the Mac.

MACINTOSH FONT NAMES

You've probably noticed that you can change the name of a suitcase file containing TrueType fonts or bitmap fonts to any name you like — for example, you could change "Bergamo.bmap" to just plain "Bergamo," or "SoftMaker Bergamo" — and it does not affect the font's name as it appears in font menus and dialog boxes. This is because the actual font's name as used by the Macintosh is stored in the FOND resource. You can change the name stored in this resource by using ResEdit, but I don't recommend doing so. I also don't recommend that you change the name of printer outline files. Doing so can lead to printing problems.

These are text files with the extension ".AFM," an acronym for Adobe Font Metrics. AFM files contain the metrics information stored in the NFNT resource (character widths and kern pairs), but in a text file format that you can open and edit with a word processor. AFM files are not required on the Mac, nor are they even used by the Mac or any current Mac applications, but if you plan on converting Mac PostScript fonts to the PC, you will need the AFM file to create the PFM file required by Adobe Type Manager for Windows.

Macintosh TrueType Fonts

Macintosh TrueType fonts are comprised of two elements — an SFNT resource, and a FOND resource — which are stored together in a single file. That is, from the outside, TrueType fonts appear as one file (as opposed to PostScript fonts which are made up of a minimum of two files).

The SFNT resource contains all of the TrueType outline data, character metrics, and kerning pairs. Think of it as a combination of a PostScript printer outline file and an NFNT resource all in one. The FOND resource is more or less the same in a TrueType font as it is in a PostScript font: it determines the font name your Mac displays in its font menus and dialog boxes, and maintains the link between the various SFNT resources.

Suitcases on your Macintosh System

The suitcase metaphor is a good one because it illustrates a key concept: the contents are more important than the container. And that's all suitcase files really are — containers. They can contain either bitmap fonts or TrueType fonts, or both.

One suitcase file typically contains the bitmaps for an entire family of outline fonts — for example, the suitcase file "Bergamo.bmap" on the companion CD contains the bitmaps in various sizes for Bergamo Regular, Bergamo Italic, Bergamo Bold, and Bergamo Bold Italic. Although you could have a separate suitcase file for Bergamo Regular, another for Bergamo Italic, and so on, I don't recommended setting them up this way. The fewer the suitcases, the easier it is for you to keep track of them, and the easier it is for the Macintosh operating system to manage them.

The font family is a good basic unit in terms of font suitcases, and one suitcase per family is the organization method I recommend. When I use the term *family*, I'm talking about the variations of a typeface — normal, italic, bold, bold italic, etc. Font managers, as well as the Mac OS itself, regard the suitcase as a basic unit. You can't, for example, install *part* of a suitcase — it's all or nothing. You could split a single suitcase into two suitcases, dividing its contents however you like, and then install one or the other. Also consider that not all font families contain four members — some may have more, some may have less, some may be a family of one. Occasionally I'll create suitcases to contain an extended family, lumping in the expert sets or small caps suitcases with the normal suitcase.

Combining Suitcases

You combine suitcases simply by dragging one onto another. This merges the contents of the one you are dragging with the one you dragged it to — burp! — keeping the filename of the one you dragged it to. The names of the individual bitmaps or TrueType fonts contained within the suitcases are unaffected. In fact, you cannot rename these fonts from the Finder at all (ResEdit is required to rename them). If the two suitcases contain fonts with the same name, a dialog box asks if you want to replace the fonts in the suitcase you are dragging them to with the fonts from the suitcase you are dragging them from.

The above procedure merges entire suitcases. You can also move and copy items from one suitcase to another without actually merging them into a single file. To move fonts from one suitcase to another, first open the suitcase containing the fonts you want to move by double-clicking it. Select the fonts you want to move and drag them to the suitcase you want to move them to. The fonts are removed from their original suitcase, and placed in the destination suitcase. To copy them without removing them from the original suitcase, hold down the Option key when you drag.

Creating New Suitcases

You might find it necessary at some point to create a new empty suitcase file. Say you're sending a document and the fonts you used to create it to your service bureau. It's always a good idea (and in many cases a necessity) to give your service bureau not only the document files and any linked graphics such as TIFF or EPS images, but the fonts you used. You've carefully selected all the PostScript outline fonts and copied them to a diskette, and now you need to round up the corresponding bitmaps, which might be distributed across several suitcase files. I suggest creating a single suitcase and giving it a name your service bureau will recognize as being part of your project (e.g., "Sean's Brochure Fonts"), and then copying the various bitmap fonts into that one suitcase.

There are a couple of ways to create a new suitcase file. Perhaps the easiest method is to simply duplicate an existing one (select it in the Finder and choose the Duplicate command from the File menu), and then drag the contents of the duplicate into the Trash and empty it. If this is something you'll be doing frequently, consider renaming this empty suitcase something along the lines of "Empty Suitcase" and storing it on your hard disk in a place you won't forget it. The next time you need an empty suitcase, just duplicate this one and there you have it.

Otherwise, to create new empty suitcases, you'll need a utility such as Apple's Font/DA Mover. The process is fairly straightforward — clicking the "New" button creates a new suitcase as you'd expect — but it has a curious drawback: after creating a new empty suitcase, unless you actually use the Font/DA Mover to copy a font from another suitcase into it, it doesn't save it. So you wind up copying a font into it in order to save it, and then removing the font from the Finder…just like the previous method.

Now that you have this new empty suitcase, you can combine other suitcases into it, or selectively copy the contents of other suitcases. If you're sending font files to a service bureau, for example, be sure to hold down the Option key as you drag fonts into it. Otherwise, you'll be moving the original font files, not duplicates.

Installing fonts with System 7.5

Beginning with System 7.1, Apple introduced the concept of the Fonts folder. Before that, you had to install bitmap and TrueType fonts directly into the System file (along with sound files and keyboard resources), and PostScript printer fonts into the Extensions folder.

RENAMING FONTS WITH RESEDIT

You can change a font's name by opening the suitcase file with ResEdit, double-clicking the FOND resource, selecting the specific font you want to change, and choosing "Get Resource Info" from the Resource menu. Enter a new font name and choose "Save" from the File menu. The next time you open the suitcase file, the font names contained in it will reflect your changes. This procedure applies to both bitmaps and TrueType files.

⚠ WARNING: If you're not familiar with ResEdit, or the damage you can inflict on files by using it incorrectly, disregard the above.

MAKE SURE ATM HAS ENOUGH MEMORY

The Font Cache setting in the ATM control panel determines the amount of RAM reserved for Adobe Type Manager to display PostScript fonts.

Generally speaking, the more fonts you have installed, the higher this value needs to be. If it is too low, ATM won't be able to efficiently rasterize fonts and display them on your screen. If it's too high, you're wasting RAM that could be put to better use by your applications.

How do you know if it's too low?

If ATM needs more memory, your documents will scroll considerably slower than normal, and it will take longer to display text on screen. If this happens, open the ATM control panel and increase the size of the font cache. Adobe recommends setting aside 50k for each outline font you use frequently, but this could turn out to be an incredibly large number. My rule of thumb is, if you need to increase this setting above 512k to avoid display problems and slow text scrolling, you have installed far too many fonts, and really should be using a type manager such as MasterJuggler or Suitcase. Of course, if you have gobs of free RAM available, go ahead and reserve 50k per outline. But think about it. If you frequently use four weights of a single typeface — for example, Times, Times Italic, Times Bold, and Times Bold Italic — that's 200k right there.

(continued on page 17 sidebar)

An ugly solution to be sure, and only marginally better than the dark ages of System 6 font management (Font/DA Mover…ugh!), but the Fonts folder simplified this. This is a much needed improvement, and leaves one to wonder what took Apple so long.

If you're not using *at least* System 7.1 (the latest as of this writing is 7.5.2), I have to ask, Why not? Apple has made significant improvements to its system software at several levels, and it simply does not make sense to continue using older versions.

The Fonts folder stores both printer outline fonts and suitcase files (bitmap and TrueType). If it looks like a font, put it in there.

To install fonts in System 7.5:

1. Select the folder containing the fonts you want to install, if they are in a folder, or select the individual printer outline and suitcase files (PostScript) or the suitcase files by themselves (TrueType).

2. Drag them to the icon of the System Folder.

When you let go of the mouse, a dialog box asks if you want to put the fonts into the Fonts folder. Click OK and they are installed automatically.

You could also drag the fonts directly into the Fonts folder, but I like the automatic method because if you drag a folder containing fonts onto the System Folder, not only does it install all the fonts in that folder, but it deletes that folder for you when it's done.

Installing and Un-installing Fonts While Applications are Open

You can install fonts with the traditional method — dragging the font files to the System Folder — while applications are loaded, but the applications won't know about them until you restart. Some font managers, however, such as MasterJuggler program from Alsoft, allow you to install fonts and immediately use them while applications are loaded without forcing you to restart the application. But even this doesn't always work — it depends on the application. Adobe Page-Maker, Adobe Illustrator, and QuarkXPress let you install fonts with MasterJuggler while they're open. Microsoft Word, Nisus Writer, and Adobe Photoshop do not. Since I use Illustrator and PageMaker for the bulk of my work, I install and remove fonts all the time without having to restart.

MANAGING FONT FILES ON THE MACINTOSH

Everyone likes typefaces and the design flexibility that a large type collection brings. It's great to have lots of type on hand, but font files require system resources, and installing too many at once can degrade system performance, that is, slow your Macintosh down. There is a temptation to install every typeface you might ever need — and I've known a few people who have installed so many fonts that it takes a few seconds for them to scroll from the top of their font menu to the bottom — but when you consider that you rarely use more than a handful of fonts in any given document, you need to reevaluate this temptation. The goal of this section is to provide you with information to maximize performance and run with a lean system.

**Installing too many fonts can make locating them difficult,
and can slow application startup times**

1. Install a font manager and use it religiously

I recommend MasterJuggler from Alsoft. MasterJuggler is a system extension that you place in the Extensions folder. It only takes about 75k of RAM, and considering the benefits it provides, is well worth it. Another popular (perhaps more widely known) font manager is Suitcase from Symantec (which is also a system extension). Both programs provide more or less the same functionality—allowing you to install and un-install fonts and groups of fonts, as well as other miscellaneous functions—and both handle PostScript and TrueType, but I prefer MasterJuggler's simpler interface. Both programs are discussed in the section "Dueling Font Managers" later in this chapter.

2. Keep only a few fonts (the system fonts Chicago, Geneva, and Monaco) in the Fonts folder

Font managers such as MasterJuggler allow you to store your fonts wherever you like. You can place them in different folders, or on network or CD-ROM drives, for example. With a font manager, then, I suggest keeping only three font files in your Fonts folder in the

System Folder: the Chicago, Geneva, and Monaco font suitcases Apple provides with its system software. These suitcases contain not only the bitmap sizes your Mac needs, but TrueType files as well (in case you ever need to print them). But the main reason to have these fonts installed is that many applications rely on them for the display of text in menus and dialog boxes; thus I consider them system fonts (as opposed to desktop publishing fonts).

If you are using a font manager, I recommend keeping your fonts in a folder at the root level of your hard drive named something like "Fonts." Within this folder you might want to group your fonts by category (e.g., text fonts, display fonts, sans serif fonts, etc.) by creating a separate sub-folder for each; by vendor (e.g., Adobe fonts, SoftMaker fonts, Monotype fonts, etc.); or do as I do and simply dump them all at the same level (no sub-folders) alphabetically.

Without a font manager such as MasterJuggler, fonts must be placed in the Fonts folder in your System Folder before they will appear in any of your applications' font menus, that is, before you can use them. If you ignore Step 1 and opt not to use a font management system, I still recommend keeping your Fonts folder as lean as possible. So place in it only the three fonts I mentioned above, plus those you use regularly. If you're using PostScript fonts, I suggest creating a single suitcase for the PostScript base fonts (the Courier, Helvetica, and Times families, plus Zapf Dingbats and the Symbol font). If you're using a Post-Script laser printer that contains these resident fonts plus Avant Garde, Bookman, New Century Schoolbook, Palatino, and Zapf Chancery, then you might want to create a separate suitcase file for this group as well. Name the suitcase "PS Base Fonts" (or something along those lines), put it and the corresponding

(continued from page 16)

I like to install as few fonts as possible, installing others on the fly as I need them, and then un-installing them when I don't. Of course, this isn't for the lazy, but the benefits are increased system performance and more RAM for your applications. Depending on the project, I rarely have more than 10 or 12 fonts installed at any given time. See the section "Dueling Font Managers" later in this chapter for tips on maximizing your font system using MasterJuggler or Suitcase.

Not necessarily true for Suitcase, which lets you create sets, of course, but doesn't manage them in exactly this fashion.

printer files in the Fonts folder, and forget about them. I use Bergamo, Franklin Gothic, Syntax, and Sean's Symbols all the time, so I would place these fonts in the Fonts folder as well.

For fonts you use occasionally, that is, the majority of your typeface collection, create a folder named "Fonts (disabled)" and place it in your System Folder. If you view your System Folder by name (as I do), the "Fonts (disabled)" folder will appear immediately after the "Fonts" folder. So whenever you need to install an additional font, all you need to do is open the "Fonts (disabled)" folder and drag the selected fonts to your Fonts folder. The "Fonts (disabled)" folder takes no additional memory or system resources, you can store as many fonts in it as you like, and you'll never have to worry about where on your hard disk they're located.

Store only those fonts you need and use regularly in the Fonts folder.

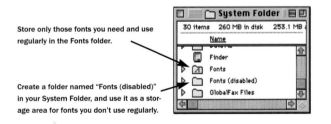

Create a folder named "Fonts (disabled)" in your System Folder, and use it as a storage area for fonts you don't use regularly.

3. Use your font manager to create *sets* or *groups* of fonts you can easily install at once

Both MasterJuggler and Suitcase let you create and edit font sets, collections of typefaces you can apply a name to and install as a single unit. For example, for this book project I created and maintained a font set containing all of the fonts needed to produce the book (barring the Typeface Descriptions part of this book, for which I created multiple sets). It doesn't matter whether the fonts in that set are located in a single

folder, or multiple folders, or even spread out over multiple volumes; by activating the set, I install all the fonts in that set.★ Considering the number of typefaces I regularly work with, I figure that this feature alone has saved me hundreds of hours of time looking for and installing individual fonts.

Font sets can be created for individual projects, or organized by any other categorization method you like—for example, alphabetically (a set for typefaces whose names begin with A through D, another for E though J, etc.), by classification (sets for text fonts, display fonts, etc.), by vendor (Adobe, SoftMaker, etc.), or more specifically ("Goofy shareware fonts I never use"), or whatever. And of course, font sets can overlap without any performance penalty. You could, for instance, install a font set named "Adobe Fonts" that contain all of the fonts you've purchased from Adobe, as well as a set named "Newsletter fonts" that might contain some of those same Adobe fonts. The fonts won't be installed twice, because the sets are really just pointers to the actual fonts.

DUELING FONT MANAGERS

In the realm of Mac DTP, have you ever noticed how we subjects seem to be divided along product lines? Are you a PageMaker or QuarkXPress user...? Illustrator or FreeHand...? The layout or graphics program we use is the queen bee of our desktop publishing system, and so we tend to be quite dedicated to her, defending her at all costs from the monotonous, ever-buzzing drones of the other camp. "Yeah, QuarkXPress is better because bzzz bzzz bzzzt." "Can you bzzz bzzz bzzz in FreeHand?" Not many other product categories have achieved such polarity, except perhaps font managers. If your page layout program is your hive, chances are the font manager you use is your axis mundi. And, of course, there are two: Suitcase and MasterJuggler.

Ken Oyer, the guy who came up with all those neat-o techniques in the "Type as Graphic Element" chapter (as well as the principal designer of this book), started buzzing most agitatedly when he discovered I was only going to use MasterJuggler in my examples. "I don't use Suitcase, Ken. I don't even like it," I informed him.

"Yeah, but bzzzzz bzzz it has more users bzzz bzzz bzzz it's quicker to build sets bzzz bzzz bzzz."

"Well, Mr. Graphic Artist, why don't *you* write about it then?" I replied, feeling pretty much assured that would be the last I'd hear of Suitcase for awhile.

The next day Ken buzzes over, does a little bee dance around my desk and hands me a disk. "It's the Suitcase section bzzz bzzz bzzz. I wrote it last night."

So here you have it. MasterJuggler *and* Suitcase.

Sean Cavanaugh Using MasterJuggler

A font management utility is a must-have for any Macintosh performing desktop publishing, and I think MasterJuggler from Alsoft is the best one available. It's not like there's a lot to choose from — the only competition, really, is Suitcase from Symantec.

The primary function of a font manager is installing and un-installing fonts, and some utilities not generally thought of as font managers (such as Casady & Greene's excellent Conflict Catcher and the less-than-excellent but adequate Extension Manager control panel that's bundled with System 7) actually perform this task. But not very well. These programs are primarily intended for managing extensions, control panels, and desk accessories. So for all

practical concerns, let's assume your only choices are MasterJuggler and Suitcase.

Even though Suitcase has a much greater installed base of users (chances are good, in fact, that you've never heard of MasterJuggler), I prefer MasterJuggler for three primary reasons:

1. It is more stable with recent versions of the Mac OS (the result of it having been updated more regularly than Suitcase)

2. Its interface is simpler and more intuitive.

3. It has an outstanding user manual.

Installing MasterJuggler

MasterJuggler consists of a single extension, so to install it, all you have to do is put it in the Extensions folder located in the System Folder, and restart your Mac. After configuring the keys I want to use to make MasterJuggler "pop-up" (⌘-Shift-click is my preference), installing and un-installing fonts and font sets is a snap.

Using MasterJuggler

When MasterJuggler is installed, it automatically places its own submenu under the Apple menu (above your desk accessories), so to run it, simply choose the MasterJuggler command from the MasterJuggler submenu (or use the MJ pop-up).

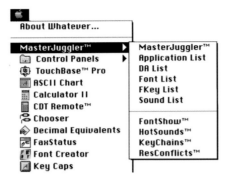

MasterJuggler menu

The MasterJuggler main window appears. The interface is exceedingly simple. Ignoring for the moment the buttons on the right, there are two selection list boxes. The list at the top is where you select from available font files (suitcase files or MasterJuggler sets). You may have your fonts stored in various folders on your hard disk. Simply select a folder from the top list. When you open a folder, any font suitcases or MasterJuggler sets in the folder appear in this list. The bottom list displays those font suitcases or sets that you have already opened.

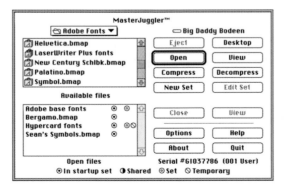

MasterJuggler main menu

MasterJuggler does not display fonts you have installed in the Fonts folder located inside your System Folder, nor can it manage them in any way. In other words, even though they are installed and available in your applications' font menus, they do not appear in MasterJuggler's "Open files" list. This is not a bug, but a necessity of the Mac operating system — any fonts placed in the Fonts folder are automatically controlled by the System and are open all the time. MasterJuggler cannot override this (nor should it attempt to). This is why I suggest placing only the fonts Chicago, Geneva, and Monaco in your Fonts folder. Keep the rest of your fonts in other folders, and use MasterJuggler to install and un-install them. I've created a folder at the root level of my hard drive named "Fonts." Within it I organize my fonts by vendor, that is, I create separate sub-folders for Adobe fonts, SoftMaker fonts, Monotype fonts, Emigre, etc. You might want to organize your fonts differently, for example, create sub-folders for the different *categories* of fonts (text fonts, display fonts, symbol fonts, etc.), or simply dump all of your fonts into one single folder with no sub-categorization. The categorization method should match your own level of anal-retentiveness. That's my rule.

NOTE PostScript outline fonts must be kept in the same folder as their corresponding suitcase, or bitmap, fonts. This is not a requirement unique to MasterJuggler, but rather a general one.

To install a font, simply select it from the top list and double-click it (or click the Open button, same dif). This places it in the bottom list, and assigns it, by default, to what is known as the "startup set." Notice the icon at the bottom of the window titled "In startup set." When you see this icon next to a font name in the Open files list, it simply means that when you restart your Mac, MasterJuggler automatically installs this font.

You don't have to remember to do it, and when you open an application, the font is available in the font menu. Again, this is the default behavior. You can also install fonts temporarily, that is, they are installed and available to all of your applications until you restart your Mac, at which point MasterJuggler forgets about them. To install a font temporarily, select it from the top list, hold down the ⌘ key, and double-click it (or hold down the ⌘ key and click the Open button). Fonts that are installed temporarily are available in all your font menus until the next time you re-start your Mac. If you know that you will only be working with a certain font for a specific instance, consider installing it temporarily.

To un-install a font, select it from the bottom list and double-click it (or click the Close button). MasterJuggler displays a warning message informing you that closing the font while an application is open might result in "improper" behavior (whatever that is). Generally speaking, it's probably best to remove fonts while no applications are loaded, that is, while only the Finder is open, but I have never had a problem un-installing a font that I was not already using in an application. I find this warning message annoying. Fortunately MasterJuggler gives you the option to suppress it. To turn off the display of this warning, as well as control other options and preferences, click the Options button.

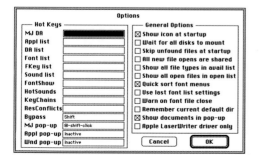

The MasterJuggler Options dialog box contains several preferences and options. The right side of the Options dialog box contains various preferences you can turn on or off. The left side of the dialog box lets you configure keyboard shortcuts, or *hot keys*, for quickly opening MasterJuggler and its various components. To assign a hot key to any of these functions, choose the appropriate box by clicking it, and then enter the key-stroke combination. To be honest, I don't use the other MasterJuggler functions such as the DA list, Sound list, KeyChains, etc. (although I've become totally dependent on the Application List pop-up to switch between open applications on my Mac) so I have not assigned hot keys to them. I occasionally use the FontShow feature, but not often enough to assign it a hot key…or remember what that hot key might have been. I do, however, use the MasterJuggler pop-up menu (MJ pop-up) all the time, and since this menu lists all the other functions, it's just as easy for me to access them from here. I have assigned the shortcut ⌘-Shift-click to open the MJ pop-up menu. It doesn't matter where I happen to be in my Mac, holding down the ⌘ and Shift keys, and clicking

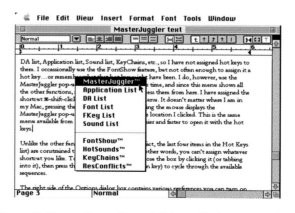

To access the MJ pop-up, there are three available key combinations you can configure:
⌘-Shift-click, ⌘-Control-click, or ⌘-Shift-Control-click

the mouse displays the MasterJuggler pop-up menu on my screen at the location I clicked. This is the same menu available from the Apple menu, but it's easier and faster to open it with the hot keys.

If you hold down the Shift key and click the Apple menu, only the MasterJuggler commands will appear. All other DAs are temporarily ignored.

Unlike the other functions, the MJ pop-up (in fact, the last four items in the Hot Keys list) is constrained to pre-defined sequences. In other words, you can't assign whatever shortcut you like. To select a sequence, first choose the box by clicking it (or tabbing into it), and then press the Enter key (not the Return key) to cycle through the available sequences.

Working with Sets

One of MasterJuggler's most important features is the ability to create and edit font *sets*. A set is simply a collection or group of fonts that you define. A set can contain any number of font suitcases. When you install a set, all the fonts that make up the set are installed at once. It doesn't matter where the fonts in the set are located — they can span multiple folders, or even disks — the set is a single entity that points to them. As I suggested earlier, you might organize font sets according to particular projects, vendors, classifications, fonts required by a certain application, etc. The organization is entirely up to you. Font sets can even overlap. For example, you might have a font set named "Adobe fonts" that contains all of your base PostScript fonts (Times, Courier, Helvetica, Palatino, etc.), and another font set named "HyperCard fonts" that contains those fonts required by HyperCard (e.g., Palatino). Even though the font Palatino appears in

both sets, installing those sets will only result in Palatino being installed once. Font sets may even contain other font sets. For example, you could create a set named "Newsletter project" that contains font sets such as "Adobe fonts" or "Symbol fonts."

To create a set, first select the drive and folder where you want the set to reside (MasterJuggler sets are actually files that resemble suitcase files), and then click the New Set button. MasterJuggler displays a dialog box where you must enter a name for the set. When you click OK, the set is created in the specified folder with the name you entered. Another dialog box appears where you select the fonts or font sets you want the set to include.

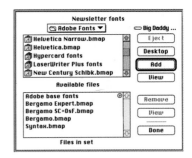

MasterJuggler Create/Edit sets menu

Select fonts or font sets from the list at top. Click the Add button to place them in the set. When you are satisfied with the files in the set, click Done. You can later add or remove files from a closed set by selecting it from the top list and clicking the Edit Set button. Note that the set must first be closed, or un-installed, before you can Edit it. If the set is currently installed, that is, if it appears in the bottom list, you must first close it before you can edit its contents.

You open and close font sets in the same manner you open and close font suitcases.

MasterJuggler font sets can be created and stored in any folder or drive on your Mac. The current folder displayed in the Available files list when you click the New Set button is where the new set will be stored. There is a disadvantage to being able to create and store sets wherever you want: you might forget where you put them. A bit earlier I recommended storing all of your PostScript Type 1 and TrueType fonts in a single folder named "Fonts" at the root level of your hard disk, and creating sub-folders within it for organizational purposes. In a similar fashion, I suggest creating and storing all of your MasterJuggler font sets in this folder. If you then turn on the "Remember current default dir" option from MasterJuggler's Options dialog box, you never have to remember where you store your font sets. MasterJuggler always opens to this folder.

It's not immediately apparent how the "Remember current default dir" option actually works, and it took me a while to find this out: Open the MasterJuggler Options dialog box and make sure the "Remember current default dir" option is off (unchecked). Quit

MasterJuggler. Open MasterJuggler again, and set the Available files list to the directory where you store your fonts and font sets. Go to Options and turn the "Remember current default dir" option on. MasterJuggler will now remember this directory shown in the Available files list, and will default to it the next time you open MasterJuggler.

Use MasterJuggler's FontShow to view installed fonts in WYSIWYG fashion. FontShow displays each of your installed fonts in its own face. You can also choose to enter sample text, and change the display size.

MasterJuggler is available from Alsoft, Inc. (713.353.4090).

KEN OYER USING SUITCASE

I use Suitcase. I've been using Suitcase ever since my font total went over a hundred or so. That was several years ago. Now I have a ton of fonts. Well, I had a ton before Sean came to me with this book idea and with it another couple of hundred fonts. Now I've got a ton of fonts plus a couple of hundred more. Thank you, Sean.

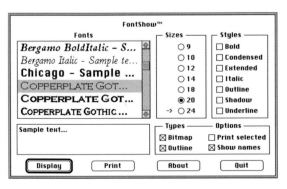

MasterJuggler's FontShow menu

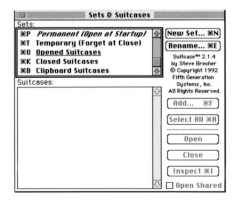

Suitcase main menu

The reasons I use Suitcase for font management are the same reasons I use any other program or utility: It's simple. I like it. It works.

Let's start with the positive things (don't worry, I have a few gripes that I'll cover later). The flexibility of managing fonts is Suitcase's strength over Master-Juggler. In both programs the user can define suitcases or sets of fonts. For example, you can define a set called "Brochure project" (the name of the set is defined by the user). This set can contain any combination of fonts you desire. Just create the set and add the fonts to it. In MasterJuggler when you turn the set on, the entire set of fonts is opened, regardless of whether you have one font or one hundred fonts in the set. And when you turn the set off, the entire set of fonts is closed. If you want to open only a portion of a set, you are out of luck.

Suitcase is different. You can still create a set of fonts called "Brochure project" and you can add any font combination to it. But unlike MasterJuggler, you can select just a portion of the fonts in any set and open just those fonts or you can select the entire set and open them too.

Another aspect of Suitcase I like is the compact interface. Information is presented to the user in a very simple and orderly fashion. The top section lists all of the sets. The bottom section lists all of the font suitcases in the currently selected set. On the right are buttons to create sets, add fonts to sets, and open and close sets or individual fonts. For you speedsters, virtually every function and button has a keyboard equivalent.

Now on to a few negative items. The program is not without its problems. First and foremost is stability. Suitcase has the tendency to bomb. And when I say bomb, I mean bomb in a big way. Usually it requires loading a fresh copy of Suitcase in your system and redefining all of your sets. This can be a tedious and frustrating chore. But it's not like it crashes all the time…just every now and again.

The other problem isn't really a problem per se, but more of a suggestion. If anyone from Symantec is out there, please take note: A re-sizable interface box would be nice (see sidebar on this page). I know I said the compact interface is one of the things I like about Suitcase, but it would be nice to be able to stretch the bottom of the box to view more sets or font suitcases. Most of my sets list fonts far below the space allotted. I am constantly scrolling through the lists looking for that special font.

Installing Suitcase

Suitcase consists of a single extension, so to install it, all you have to do is put it in the Extensions folder located in the System Folder, and restart your Mac.

Using Suitcase

Let's get into the meat of this section. The one thing I hate to do in Suitcase is to add a font to a set by using the "Add" button. When you click this button,

An example of what Suitcase could look like with a re-sizable interface

Suitcase displays the standard Open dialog box (slightly modified for Suitcase's purposes) and asks what font you want to add. You then have to navigate through your hard drive looking for one particular font among several hundred, perhaps thousands. It can be a slow process. Adding fonts in this manner may seem like a procedure you have to do quite often but, believe it or not, you can set up Suitcase so you add your fonts only once, opening and closing them later as needed.

First set up a series of sets named logically for your situation. One set will probably not do the trick so don't be afraid to set up several. I have all of my fonts set up over three sets in alphabetical order. Fonts A-C, Fonts D-M and Fonts N-Z. I then add all of my fonts to their appropriate set. Once they're added, I never use the Add button to access these fonts; I only use it when I add a new font to my system for the first time.

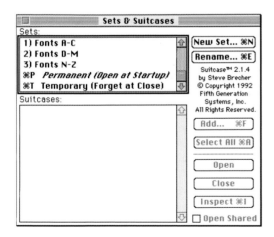

To load a font, I simply select the set it resides in, scroll through the bottom list until I find the font, and then double-click it (clicking on the name to highlight it and then clicking the Open button does the same thing, but double-clicking the name seems to be faster).

The font is loaded and I'm ready to fly. Suitcase indicates a font is loaded by underscoring its name. To close a font, simply double-click it again. You can also open or close multiple fonts at the same time by highlighting the first font and then holding down the Shift key while selecting all the other fonts. After all the fonts are highlighted, click the Open button. The same procedure can be used to close multiple fonts.

Opening and closing fonts by scrolling through lists that you have set up is much faster than using the Add button because you don't have to go through your hard drive looking for fonts. But this too can get very old. So let's take this set-building technique one step further. If you have a project that uses five font families that are spread out over three different sets, manually scrolling these sets looking for the same fonts over and over again is tiresome! When you find yourself doing this, stop, relax and then make a new set that contains just the fonts needed.

Working with Sets

To create a new set, click the New Set button and name the set. Suitcase will clear out the bottom font list where you can build any font combination you like. How do you build your font list? Don't rely on the Add button. You already have all of your fonts available to you in the original alphabetized sets. Scroll through the previously created sets and find the fonts you need. Click them one by one (after the first selection you must hold down the Shift key to add subsequent fonts to the selection) and when you have all the fonts you want out of the set, choose Copy from the Edit menu. This copies all the selected fonts to the Clipboard. (It doesn't copy the actual fonts to the Clipboard, just Suitcase's link to them.) Then select the new set and choose Paste from the Edit menu. Repeat this process until you have all the fonts needed.

NOTE If you want to permanently remove a font from any list, first select the font and then choose Cut from the Edit menu. If you want to remove an entire set from the set list, select the set and again choose Cut from the Edit menu.

Once a font is added to any set, it can be copied and pasted through the Clipboard using ⌘-C and ⌘-V. This technique allows you to move fonts around very quickly from set to set.

Suitcase comes with five sets that cannot be deleted. The following is a description of each one.

Permanent (Open at Startup) — The name is pretty much self explanatory. All fonts added or pasted into this set become permanently open in your system, and open at startup as well. This is a good place to put your most commonly used fonts, the fonts you know you will use on a daily basis. That doesn't mean to slam dunk hundreds and hundreds of fonts into this set so you can have them all available to you at all times. The main reason to have a font manager in the first place is to easily open and close fonts so you can have the least number of fonts open at any one time and still get your work done. The fewer the fonts loaded, the faster your computer will run. And who couldn't afford a faster running computer?

If you look at the Permanent (Open at Startup) name in Suitcase you will note that it's displayed in *italics*. All italicized sets in Suitcase are considered permanently opened sets. The Permanent (Open at Startup) set will always be italicized; you can't un-italicize as you can other sets. You can make any of the other sets you've defined open automatically at startup too. Just double-click the name of the set. The name will switch to italics and the set will be opened at startup. To

change it back to a standard set, double-click the name again. The name will no longer be in italics.

When I install a new system on a computer, one of the things I do to customize it is go into the Fonts folder in the System Folder and remove every font. Well, every font except those we recommend leaving in the Fonts folder: Chicago, Geneva, and Monaco. So I leave these and remove the rest. In Suitcase, under the Permanent (Open at Startup) set, I create my list of commonly used fonts. Fonts like Helvetica, Times, Courier, Symbol, and Zapf Dingbats. You can put any font you want in this set, just remember they will always be opened when start your computer. But you are not stuck with having the font opened because it is in this set. After you have started your computer, if you want to close one of these fonts, simply double-click its name and it's closed. It will automatically reopen the next time you start your computer.

Temporary (Forget at Close) — This set allows you to create a set of fonts that work like any other set. Except for one big difference. When you shut down your computer, the list of fonts is deleted. When I say deleted, I am talking about the font list itself and not the actual fonts in the list. So don't worry, Suitcase will not viciously roam your hard drive deleting font files when you turn off your computer (despite what Sean might have you believe).

I used this set quite a bit when working in a service bureau situation. Many customers would send in their oddball fonts from *Harvey's House of Fonts* for output to an imagesetter. To open their fonts, I just added them in the Temporary (Forget at Close) set, printed the job, and never admitted the fact I output a font named Scooby-Doo Demi Oblique.

Opened Suitcases — A great feature in Suitcase is the ability to mix and match fonts from several different sets. But after opening several fonts, it gets hard to remember exactly which fonts are open. Click here and Suitcase will list all the fonts that are currently open, regardless of which set they reside in.

Closed Suitcases — I rarely if ever use this set because it can be a very lengthy font list. It lists all fonts from all sets that are not currently opened. If you have a hundred fonts throughout your sets and you have ten opened, click this set and you can see the other 90 that are not opened. I'm sure there is someone out there who just cannot live without this feature, but for what reason I have not a clue.

Clipboard Suitcases — I mentioned earlier that you can copy and paste fonts to move them from one set to another. This set allows you to see which fonts are currently on the Clipboard.

There are a number of other features to Suitcase, but I'm not writing a user manual, just an overview and why I like it. I would recommend using Suitcase for professional level font management any day of the week. I hope the next version of the software finds a way to be more stable, though perhaps this is impossible given how it must interact with the system software at so many levels. Maybe it's just one of those computer things.

Suitcase is available from Symantec. (800.441.7234).

Font Management Summary

▸ Install MasterJuggler (or Suitcase) and use it to install and un-install fonts rather than doing it yourself by dragging them into and out of the Fonts folder inside the System Folder.

▸ Organize all of your fonts in a central folder, optionally creating sub-folders within it for additional categorization.

▸ Suitcase files for TrueType fonts and bitmap fonts should be organized one per family, that is, store all the Times variations, for example, in a single suitcase file (Times.bmap), and avoid combining it with other fonts.

▸ If you're using MasterJuggler, create and maintain all of your MasterJuggler sets in this central folder as well. Doing so makes editing and installing them easier, because you won't have to worry about forgetting where you put them.

▸ Place only the fonts Chicago, Geneva, and Monaco in the System Folder's Font folder. If you are using Adobe Acrobat or SuperATM, it's a good idea to keep the fonts these packages use, Adobe Sans MM and Adobe Serif MM, here too.

▸ Avoid installing too many fonts at once. Doing so eats up resources and slows down the amount of time it takes your applications to start.

New Technology: QuickDraw GX

QuickDraw GX is Apple's new graphic technology for the Macintosh. It is not so much a new typeface format, per se, as it is an extension to existing PostScript Type 1 and TrueType font technologies. GX "smart" fonts are PostScript Type 1 or TrueType fonts with an extensive set of conditional instructions, specified by the font designer, that provides automatic ligature substitution, kerning, variations in size, weight, shape, baseline positioning, and many other features. The key concept here is "automatic." A QuickDraw GX application using GX smart fonts would be able to *automatically* adjust letter and word spacing, change point size, substitute ligatures, tweak kerning and tracking values, substitute quotes, dashes, ligatures, non-lining numerals, and small caps, and make decisions about how to display the font under various conditions (considerations would be given to column width, justification, leading, type classification, size, etc.). GX fonts would also be capable of creating automatic fractions, appropriately sized and spaced automatic superscripts and subscripts, and automatic substitution of ordinals (1st, 2nd, 3rd, etc.), Oldstyle numerals, tabular numerals, and swash characters.

QuickDraw GX is available today, and a few typefaces have been developed capable of the kind of automatic features I just mentioned. However, very few applications exist that take advantage of these features. So in a manner of speaking, these wonderful typefaces are all dressed up with no place to go. Unless developers embrace the new GX technology and release GX-savvy applications, GX fonts offer little or no benefit to the user.

Until new GX-savvy versions of applications such as PageMaker, QuarkXPress, or Word are released, there is no benefit to installing the GX system software extensions. And in fact, there is a major reason not to install GX: it eats up an additional 2mb of memory! That's 2mb over and above what your system uses now, before any of your applications are loaded. 2mb just to be installed, sitting ready and waiting…

What will happen to my existing TrueType and Type 1 fonts?

You will still be able to use them as you do now, with no need to purchase upgraded fonts from the manufacturers. TrueType fonts are compatible with GX with no need for conversion. PostScript Type 1 fonts must be converted to the GX format, a process called *enabling*.

Enabling PostScript Type 1 Fonts for Use with GX

When you install QuickDraw GX, the installation program automatically enables your existing Type 1 fonts. To enable additional Type 1 fonts after you've installed QuickDraw GX, you must use an application from Adobe called the Type 1 Enabler. This program is free, and is easily obtained from electronic bulletin boards and online services.

NOTE Enabled Type 1 fonts cannot be un-enabled, nor are they backward-compatible with non-GX systems; if you install GX, and later decide to un-install it, the enabled Type 1 fonts can no longer be used. Both the GX installer and the Type 1 Enabler programs place copies of your Type 1 fonts in a folder named "• Archived Type 1 Fonts •" If you don't have backups of these fonts already, be careful not to delete this folder, as it contains all your original Type 1 fonts.

PostScript Type 3 fonts cannot be enabled, and so are incompatible with the QuickDraw GX system. If you have Type 3 fonts that you absolutely cannot live without, I suggest converting them to Type 1 fonts using a font editor such as Fontographer from Macromedia.

The nifty automatic features, however, will be rather limited in your enabled PostScript Type 1 fonts and pre-GX TrueType fonts because you can only use the automatic substitution and conditional variation features with fonts specifically developed for Quick-Draw GX: GX-savvy fonts, or "smart" fonts, such as Skia, Hoeffler Text, and new versions of Times, Helvetica, and so on. I plan someday to modify the library of fonts on the companion CD, and re-release them as bonafide, GX smart fonts, but until there is a sufficient base of GX smart applications, I cannot justify the time or resources required to do that.

Regardless of its limited acceptance and support, I think GX is the future of digital typography. It may very well make books such as mine obsolete. People won't have to spend time learning how to space or set type, or study the rules of typography because the font, in conjunction with the application, will do it for them. Before this format gains serious acceptance, not only must application developers incorporate it into their software, but Apple must provide the technology to the Windows world. ▪

PostScript and
TrueType Fonts
with Microsoft
Windows

PostScript and TrueType Fonts with Microsoft Windows

CHAPTER 1 PROVIDED YOU WITH ENOUGH BACKGROUND information to help you decide whether you should use PostScript with ATM or TrueType as your primary font system. And even if you haven't yet made such a decision, don't worry; you don't have to. As we discussed, it's not an either/or proposition. Chapter 1 compared the formats without being specific to any operating system. Now let's analyze these font formats at a functional level — to show you how they're the same and how they're different — and guide you through the process of managing font files in Windows 3.1 and Windows 95.

FONT FILES ON THE PC

Microsoft Windows 3.1 and Windows 95 handle fonts in more or less the same fashion: that is, they both use *control panels* to manage TrueType and device (bitmap) fonts, and leave the management of PostScript fonts entirely up to Adobe Type Manager or a third-party type manager such as Ares' excellent FontMinder program (discussed at the end of this chapter). In other words, Windows itself does not manage PostScript fonts.

Windows 3.1 required that TrueType font files (which have the extension TTF) be stored in the *\Windows\System* directory. New to Windows 95 is the Fonts Folder, an idea Microsoft, um, *borrowed* from Apple. Windows 95 supposedly does away with DOS and the notion of directories, but they are still there, and in fact the Fonts Folder is really just another DOS directory located inside the Windows directory (oops, I mean *folder*). Folders, directories, same diff.

TrueType

TrueType fonts all have the extension TTF, and unless you are using a font manager such as Ares FontMinder,

these files need to be located in the *\Windows\System* directory (Windows 3.1), or the Fonts Folder (Windows 95). The TTF file contains the TrueType font in its entirety (unlike PostScript fonts which are comprised of at least two files). So what about the FOT file, you ask? Short answer: don't worry about FOT files. These are files Windows creates and manages all on its own, automatically, when you install fonts. They don't contain font or design information, but rather resource information used only by Windows. If you copy or move TrueType files, only copy or move the TTF files, and ignore the FOT files.

In the Windows 95 Fonts Folder, TrueType fonts are identified by the document icon containing blue and gray *Ts*. Bitmap fonts are identified by the icon containing a red letter *A*.

Beyond the font outline data itself, TrueType fonts for Windows (and Macintosh for that matter) contain a number of tables that can be edited using program such as the shareware program FontMonster. The tables in a TrueType font let you change certain values like font name (as it appears in menus and dialog boxes), classification (used for font substitution), and copyright information. Unless you have a specific reason to use a program like FontMonster to change these values — and I don't have any suggestions as to what that might be — I don't recommend doing so.

TrueType font

Device bitmap font

Windows 95 Fonts folder

In the Windows 3.1 Fonts control panel, TrueType fonts have the word "[TrueType]" appearing after them, and screen fonts are followed with the name of the device, for example, "[8514 res]" or "[VGA res]."

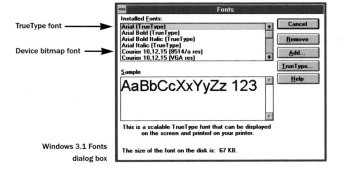

TrueType font ⟶

Device bitmap font ⟶

Windows 3.1 Fonts
dialog box

Bitmap fonts

Windows relies on bitmap fonts for certain on-screen text such as that displayed in dialog boxes, menus, and window title bars. Also known as device fonts or screen fonts, they are not intended for printing, and so do not appear in any of your applications' font menus. They are really only intended to be used by the operating system, and I'm not sure why Microsoft even grants access to them from the Fonts control panel. These bitmap fonts, which have the extension FON, are device dependent, in other words, specific to your monitor's *logical* resolution, unlike TrueType and Post-Script fonts. Your video settings determine the screen fonts Windows needs. The logical resolution is measured in dots per inch (as opposed to total screen size). The most common logical resolutions are 96 dpi (VGA) and 120 dpi (8514/a). Windows determines which set of bitmap fonts to use based on whether you chose *Large*

fonts or *Small* fonts when you set up your monitor. Choosing a video setting of 1024 x 768, for example, or 800 x 600, with *Large* fonts will result in the superior 120 dpi display, while 1024 x 768 or 800 x 600 with *Small* fonts will give you 96 dpi. If you are using a basic 640 x 480 VGA display, only the lower res 96 dpi bitmaps are available.

I've never had reason to add bitmap fonts to my system. You can't buy them. They're not available from online services. They are just part of Windows. (I have, however, removed bitmaps I knew I had no use for, such as bitmaps for video resolutions I was not using.) When you install new video cards and drivers, the appropriate screen fonts are installed for you, usually prompting you to choose either *Large* fonts or *Small* fonts for screen display. In Windows 95 this process is even more transparent. So I leave 'em alone for the most part.

Vector fonts

Vector fonts, also known as plotter fonts, are rarely seen anymore. In the early days of Windows (like version 2.0), Adobe Type Manager did not yet exist, and TrueType wasn't even an idea. So vector fonts were the only way to use scalable type (applying the term very loosely) in your documents. They were really nothing more than vector-based drawings of characters that you could scale up and down in size. They look okay in CAD drawings, for example, or in plotter output, but they were, and are, quite unattractive as text fonts in laser printed documents. If you have vector fonts installed in your system, and do not plan on using them with a plotter for instance, consider removing them. Vector fonts are named Roman, Modern, and Script.

PostScript

To use PostScript fonts with Windows, you must have Adobe Type Manager installed. Windows itself provides no interface for installing or un-installing Post-Script fonts, and so does not display them in any of its dialog boxes or folders.

PostScript fonts are comprised of two files: a PFB file and a PFM file. The PFB file is the printer outline file and contains all of the PostScript outline data — the lines, curves, points, and hinting instructions that your Windows applications, in conjunction with Adobe Type Manager, need to correctly display and print the font. The PFM contains the metrics — things like kerning pairs and spacing values. Each PFM file corresponds to a PFB file, so when you install fonts in Adobe Type Manager under Windows, you select the PFM file, which points to its PFB file. You will occasionally see *AFM* files, which contain all the information that PFM files contain but in text format. You can open these files with any text editor or word processor, whereas PFM files are encoded binary files (and have much smaller file sizes as a result). AFM files were required by many DOS applications, but Adobe Type Manager does not need them at all. I have provided them on the companion CD, but only for those of you who might need them for DOS applications such as SoftMaker's WordPerfect add-on type manager, or for those of you who just enjoy poking around inside metrics files (like me).

The default directory for PFB files is *\Psfonts*. The default directory for PFM files is *\Psfonts\Pfm*. These are Adobe Type Manager's defaults, and you can change them from the ATM control panel.

INSTALLING AND WORKING WITH FONTS ON YOUR PC

Depending on the Windows platform and the font formats you're working with, there are different installation instructions.

To install TrueType fonts in Windows 3.1:

1. Open the Windows Control Panel and double-click the Fonts icon.

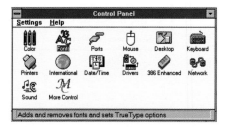

2. Click the "Add..." button.

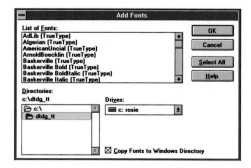

3. Select the drive from the "Drives:" menu, and the directory from the "Directories:" list where the TTF font files reside.

NOTE   This could be a directory on your hard disk, a network drive, or a CD-ROM drive. If the fonts are located on a remote drive, I suggest copying them to your local drive. Select "Copy Fonts to Windows Directory" to do this. Otherwise, if you install a font from a remote drive and use it in a document, that drive must be present and accessible whenever you use the font. For example, if the font was on a CD and you misplaced the CD or lent it to a friend, you'd be out of luck. If on the other hand you want to add fonts from a network drive without using disk space on your computer, then don't select the "Copy Fonts to Windows Directory" option.

It may take Windows a few moments to figure out what fonts are available, or several moments depending on how many TTF files are in the directory. While it is churning through them, it displays the message, "Retrieving font names." An entire CD full of fonts could take Windows over a minute to retrieve them all. When it is through retrieving, it displays all of the typefaces it found in the "List of Fonts" box.

4. Select the fonts you want to install from the list, and click "OK."

It's not necessary for TTF files to be copied to the the System directory in Windows 3.1. You can store them in other directories and add them. Just don't select the "Copy fonts to Windows Directory" option.

5. Click "OK" to install all the fonts you selected from the list.

6. Click "Close."

NOTE   To make sure the fonts you just installed appear in your applications' font menus, you may need to re-select your printer in Printer Setup from the application's File menu. The majority of applications do not require this, but some older applications do.

REMOVING OR DELETING TRUETYPE FONTS IN WINDOWS 3.1

Windows 3.1 lets you un-install TrueType or bitmap fonts in one of two ways: you can remove the font from the list of installed fonts, but keep its disk file around in case you want to reinstall it later, or you can un-install it and delete its disk file. To un-install a TrueType font, open the Control Panel and double-click the Fonts icon. In the Fonts dialog box, choose the font or fonts you want to remove from the list, and click "Remove." Windows displays a dialog box asking whether you're sure you want to do what you just clearly told it you wanted to do. If you want to erase the file from your disk in addition to un-installing it, click the "Delete Font File From Disk" option.

Remove Font
Are you sure you want to remove the Arial (TrueType) font?
☐ **D**elete Font File From Disk
[**Y**es] [Yes to A**ll**] [**N**o] [Cancel]

To Install TrueType Fonts in Windows 95:

Installing TrueType fonts in Windows 95 is much the same as installing them in Windows 3.1. In fact, the Windows 3.1 method is still around, although you now also install fonts graphically by simply dragging them into the Fonts folder.

1. From the Start menu, choose Settings-Control Panel.

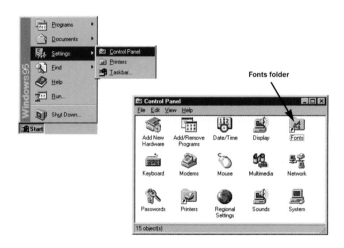

Fonts folder

2. Double-click the Fonts folder icon to open it.

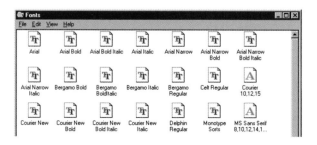

At this point you can continue with the Windows 3.1 method in Step 3 below, or simply copy TrueType fonts into the Fonts folder to install them. For example, you could open a CD-ROM drive, locate any TrueType fonts on it, and copy them into the Fonts folder.

3. Choose "Install New Font..." from the File menu.

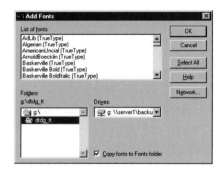

Windows 95 Add Fonts dialog box

This dialog box is exactly the same as Windows 3.1, but with a groovier new look. Also, directories are now called *folders*.

4. Select the drive from the "Drives" menu, and the directory from the "Folders" list where the TTF font files reside.

This could be a directory (oops, I mean folder) on your hard disk, a network drive, or a CD-ROM drive. If the fonts are located on a remote drive, I suggest copying them to your local drive. Select "Copy Fonts to Windows Directory" to do this. Otherwise, if you install a font from a remote drive and use it in a document, that drive must be present and accessible whenever you use the font. For example, if the font was on a CD and you misplaced the CD or lent it to a friend, you'd be out of luck. If on the other hand you want to add fonts from a network drive without using disk space on your computer, select "Copy Fonts to Windows Directory."

It may take Windows a few moments to figure out what fonts are available, or several moments depending on how many TTF files are in the folder. While it is churning through them, it displays the message, "Retrieving font names." An entire CD full of fonts could take Windows over a minute to retrieve them all, or longer. When it is through, it displays all of the typefaces it found in the "List of Fonts" box.

5. Select the fonts you want to install from the list and click "OK."

It's not necessary for TTF files to be copied to the the Fonts folder in Windows 95. You can store them in other directories and add them. Just don't select the "Copy fonts to Fonts folder" option.

6. Click "OK" to install all the fonts you selected from the list.

7. Click "Close."

If you're installing multiple fonts, remember not to double-click the name of a single font in the list, as this will install it, close the dialog box, and return you to the Fonts folder. You'll then have to open the Add Fonts dialog box again, wait for it to retrieve all the font names, and so on. Double-clicking is such a habit that I make this annoying mistake all the time.

DELETING TRUETYPE AND BITMAP FONTS IN WINDOWS 95

To delete a TrueType or bitmap font in Windows 95, simply select it from the Fonts folder and press the Del key on your keyboard. Windows displays the following warning message and places the font files in the Recycle Bin where you can later empty it to delete them.

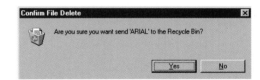

In my mind, Windows 3.1 had a better concept of *removing* fonts, a process that gave you the option to delete the disk file if you so wished; if you didn't, it simply removed the font out of the list of available fonts, and you could later reinstall it. Because of this new Windows 95 interface concept, I recommend creating a folder named "Fonts (disabled)" into which you can move fonts you no longer want installed without actually deleting them or dumping them into the Recycle Bin.

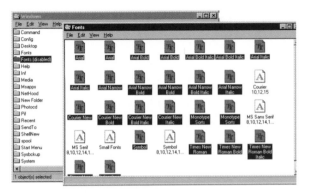

Create a folder named "Fonts (disabled)" in your Windows folder, and
store fonts in it until you want to install them

PREVIEWING TRUETYPE FONTS IN WINDOWS 95

To preview a sample of a TrueType or bitmap font in Windows 95, open the Fonts folder and double-click the font you want to see. Windows 95 displays a rudimentary sample of the typeface. You can also print out the sample by clicking the Print button. Programs such as Ares FontMinder provide much more sophisticated previewing capabilities. See the section at the end of this chapter for more information about using FontMinder to manage and preview fonts in Windows.

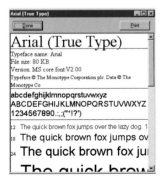

To install PostScript Fonts in Windows 3.1 or Windows 95 with ATM:

1. Open the ATM control panel.

   For Windows 95 users, I suggest keeping a copy, or alias, of the ATM control panel in the Windows Control Panels folder for easy access.

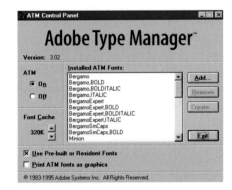

2. Click the "Add…" button.

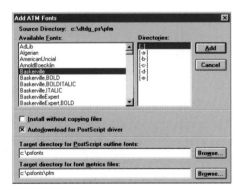

3. From the Directories list, select the directory where the PFM files reside.

   For example, `C:\PSFONTS\PFM`.

4. Select the typefaces you want to install from the Available Fonts list, and click Add.

   To select a range of fonts, hold down the Shift key while dragging the cursor over the fonts. To select multiple individual fonts, hold down the Ctrl key and click the fonts you want to add.
   You return to the ATM control panel, and the fonts are added to the list of installed fonts.

5. Click Exit to return to Windows.

   Now when you start an application, the fonts appear in your Font menu.

Installing and Un-installing Fonts while Applications are Open

Installing or un-installing fonts while applications are open is usually not a problem. The Windows operating system is sufficiently integrated with applications to notify them that if a new font is installed, it should be immediately added to the application's Font menu. For example, say you're working on a WordExpress document (a Windows word processor, the shareware version is included on the companion CD) and you decide you need the font Franklin Gothic. Rather than exiting WordExpress, installing the font, and restarting Word-Express, you can switch to the Program Manager (Windows 3.1) or the Desktop (Windows 95), open the Control Panel or Adobe Type Manager, add the new

font, and pop back to WordExpress. The font menu then contains the font you just added, and you can now select and use it in your document. The same goes for removing a font, although this is often more problematic since Windows does not always tell open applications when fonts have been removed. The solution is to re-select the printer driver by choosing the Printer Setup command from the application's File menu. Otherwise, follow the obvious: don't un-install fonts while applications are open.

MANAGING FONT FILES IN WINDOWS

Everyone likes typefaces and the design flexibility that a large type collection brings. It's great to have lots of type on hand, but font files require system resources, and installing too many at once can degrade system performance, that is, slow down the startup times of your Windows applications. There is a temptation to install every typeface you might ever need — and I've known a few people who have installed so many fonts that it takes a few seconds for them to scroll from the top of their font menus to the bottom — but when you consider that you rarely use more than a handful of fonts in any given document, you need to reevaluate this temptation. The goal of this section is to provide you with information to maximize performance and run with a lean system.

MAKE SURE ATM HAS ENOUGH MEMORY

The Font Cache setting in the ATM Control Panel determines the amount of RAM reserved for Adobe Type Manager to display and print PostScript fonts. Generally speaking, the more fonts you have installed, the higher this value needs to be. If it is too low, ATM won't be able to efficiently rasterize fonts and display them on your screen in true WYSIWYG fashion. If it's too high, you're wasting RAM that could be put to better use by your applications.

How do you know if it's too low?

Your documents will scroll considerably slower than normal, and your fonts might not display correctly on your screen. In Windows, a device font may be substituted instead, however the fonts will probably print correctly. If this happens, open the ATM control panel and increase the size of the font cache. Adobe recommends setting 50K aside for each outline font you use frequently, but this could turn out to be an incredibly large number. My rule of thumb is, if you need to increase this setting above 512K to avoid font display problems, you have installed far too many fonts, and really should be using a type manager such as Ares FontMinder. Of course, if you have gobs of free RAM available, go ahead and reserve 50K per outline. But think about it. If you frequently use four weights of a single typeface — for example, Times, Times Italic, Times Bold, and Times Bold Italic — that's 200K right there.

I like to install as few fonts as possible, installing others on the fly as I need them, and then un-installing them when I don't. Of course, this isn't for the lazy, but the benefits are increased system performance, and more RAM for your applications. Depending on the project, I rarely have more than 15 or 20 fonts installed at any given time. See the section "Managing Fonts with Ares FontMinder" later in this chapter for tips on maximizing your font system.

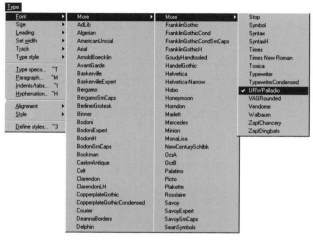

Installing too many fonts can make locating them difficult, and can slow application startup times.

1. Install a font manager and use it religiously.

I highly recommend FontMinder from Ares Software (you already guessed that). FontMinder is a Windows application and driver that you install using the setup program provided by Ares. FontMinder combines all of your font management tasks (installing, un-installing, downloading, previewing, and sampling) into one application. Another Windows-based font manager is FontHandler from QualiType. Both programs provide more or less the same functionality, but I've been using FontMinder for a long time, have never experienced problems with it, and I prefer its interface over FontHandler's. Both of these programs manage Post-Script and TrueType fonts simultaneously.

2. Install only those fonts you need and use regularly.

This applies both to those who use a font manager, and those who don't, but a font manager makes it considerably easier to install fonts as you need them, and un-install them when you don't. For example, if you used the typeface Arnold Boecklin in a document that you won't be opening and editing regularly — and don't foresee using Arnold Boecklin in any other documents any time soon — then don't keep Arnold Boecklin installed in your system. It's just going to clutter your font menus, making it more difficult to choose typefaces you do use regularly, and, depending on your system, it may even slow things down.

The goal is to keep the list of active fonts (those that appear in your applications' font menus) as lean as possible. For me this means having only those fonts I need for a particular document installed (but then, I'm a super-minimalist when it comes to these kinds of things). Without a font manager, this takes considerably more work to accomplish. You would need to access at least two different control panels if you are using True-Type and PostScript fonts, and you wouldn't be able to load and unload fonts as a group. Using a program such as FontMinder, for example, you can manage all of your fonts from a single window, as well as install/un-install fonts with a mouse click or two.

Without a font manager such as FontMinder, True-Type fonts are generally stored in the \System directory (Windows 3.1), or in the Fonts folder located in your Windows folder (Windows 95). These are the default locations. Programs like FontMinder make it easy to store TrueType and PostScript fonts wherever you like, including placing them in different directories or folders, or on network or CD-ROM drives, without having to remember where they all reside.

In Windows 3.1, you can store as many TrueType fonts as you like in the \Windows\System directory, and use the Fonts control panel to install or remove them. But in Windows 95, any TrueType fonts you place in the Fonts folder are automatically installed, and to un-install them you either have to move them out of the Fonts folder entirely (the files can't just hang around in there like in Windows 3.1), or delete them. You probably don't want to delete or erase them, so for fonts you use occasionally, i.e., the majority of your typeface collection, create a folder named "Fonts (disabled)" in your Windows folder. If you view your Windows folder in list view (as I do), the "Fonts (disabled)" folder will appear immediately after the "Fonts" folder. So whenever you need to install additional TrueType fonts, all you need to do is open the "Fonts (disabled)" folder and drag the selected TrueType files to your Fonts folder.

3. Remove any device, bitmap, or vector fonts that you do not use.

If the plotter fonts Roman, Modern, and Script are installed in your system, and you don't have a plotter, consider removing them. Open the Windows Control Panel, double-click the Fonts icon, and follow the steps earlier in this chapter for deleting fonts.

4. Use your font manager to create groups of fonts you can easily install at once.

FontMinder lets you create and edit *font packs*, collections of typefaces you can apply a name to and install as a single unit. For example, for this book project I created and maintained a font pack containing all of the fonts needed to produce the book (barring the

Typeface Classifications chapters, for which I created multiple font packs). It doesn't matter whether the fonts in that pack are located in a single directory, multiple directories, or even spread out over multiple disks, by installing the font pack, I install all the fonts in that pack. Considering the number of typefaces I regularly work with, I figure that this feature alone has saved me hundreds of hours of time looking for and installing individual fonts.

If you're using PostScript fonts, I suggest creating a single font pack for the PostScript base fonts (the Courier, Helvetica, and Times families, plus Zapf Dingbats and the Symbol font). If you're using a PostScript laser printer that contains these resident fonts plus Avant Garde, Bookman, New Century Schoolbook, Palatino, and Zapf Chancery, then you might want to create a separate font pack for them as well. Name the pack "PS Base Fonts" (or something along those lines). I use Bergamo, Franklin Gothic, Syntax, and Sean's Symbols all the time, so I've created a font pack named "Main" for them.

Font packs can be created for individual projects, or by any other categorization method you like—for example, alphabetically (a font pack for typefaces whose names begin with A through D, another for E through J, etc.), by classification (font packs for text fonts, display fonts, etc.), by vendor (Adobe, SoftMaker, etc.), or more specifically ("Lame shareware fonts I never use"), or whatever. And of course, font packs can overlap without any performance penalty. You could, for instance, install a font pack named "Adobe Fonts" that contain all of the fonts you've purchased from Adobe, as well as a font pack named "Newsletter fonts" that might contain some of those same Adobe fonts. The fonts won't be installed twice, because the font packs are really just pointers to the actual font files.

5. Create a directory structure.

I like to keep all my fonts in a directory at the root level of my hard drive. Within this directory you might want to group your fonts by category (for example, text fonts, display fonts, sans serif fonts, and so on) by creating a separate sub-directory for each; by vendor (e.g., \Fonts\Adobe or \Fonts\Sean); or do as I do and simply store them in a single directory. Actually I create two directories: one for all of my TrueType fonts (\Ttfonts), and another for my PostScript fonts (\Psfonts). Since PostScript fonts are comprised of a PFB and a PFM file, I create a sub-directory named \Psfonts\Pfm to store the metrics files (although it is not a requirement that you store these files in a separate sub-directory). This is the default directory structure, by the way, that Adobe Type Manager expects. But within my Psfonts and Ttfonts directories, I don't bother creating directo-ries for sub-categories. Doing so only makes the task of finding and installing fonts more troublesome. Also, updating my libraries in FontMinder is simpler because I know where all of my font files reside.

MANAGING FONTS WITH ARES FONTMINDER

A font management utility is a must-have for any Windows system performing desktop publishing, and of the many available, I've chosen FontMinder from Ares Software. Another product, FontHandler from QualiType Software (313.822.2921), has competitive features and has received positive reviews. At the time of this writing, however, a Windows 95 version of FontHandler was not yet available. By the time you read this, however, one probably will be, so you might want to consider it as an option for your font manage-ment needs. Both products are available for around $50.

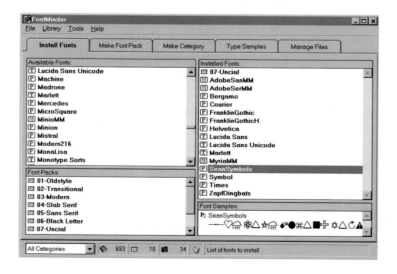

Ares FontMinder 3.0 main window in *library mode*.

Available Fonts: This is a master library of all PostScript and TrueType fonts available on your system. The fonts can span multiple directories and drives, including network and CD-ROM drives. You can let FontMinder build this library automatically, or you can manually specify which directories and drives to search for fonts.

Font Packs: Font Packs are collections of typefaces you can apply a name to and install as a single unit, as if they were individual typefaces. You can create, name, and organize font packs in any manner you like.

Installed Fonts: These are the fonts installed in Windows and available to your applications. You install fonts simply by dragging them from the Available Fonts list, or by dragging font packs from the Font Packs list, into the Installed Fonts list. This list box changes depending on which tab you've selected from the top of the window.

Font Samples: Displays a line showing of the selected font. Simply drag a font—or even an entire font pack—into this section and a sample of it will be displayed. Once a font is in this window, you can double-click it to see a more detailed sample.

Installing FontMinder

The installation process is easy, consisting of a single setup program that installs all files, then checks your disk for all available font files, automatically creating a master font library.

Since FontMinder is an application you will no doubt use on a regular basis, I suggest putting in your Start menu (Windows 95) for easy access.

Using FontMinder

The FontMinder main window is organized into four list boxes. The window itself, as well as the list boxes within the window are resizable (simply move the mouse over the dividers between sections to change their size). Three of the four list boxes, Available Fonts, Font Packs, and Font Samples, will always be displayed. The fourth list box changes depending on which tab you click at the top of the window. When you start FontMinder, it automatically opens to the first tab, Install Fonts.

Font families in FontMinder are identified by the type of icon displayed next to their name. A red *P* is used to indicate PostScript Type 1 fonts; a blue *T* for TrueType; a gold *M* for Multiple Master fonts. The package icon is used to identify font packs, which may themselves contain any combination of TrueType, PostScript Type 1 or Multiple Master fonts. They may even contain other font packs.

When you click one of these icons (not the font name, but the actual icon) FontMinder displays the individual fonts that make up the family in what is called a *tree*. Each one of the icons I mentioned above folds out to display other icons. Some fonts are a family

of one, but clicking its icon will still fold out to show that one family member. Family trees can quickly clutter up a list box. To prune them, click the right mouse button, and choose "Close All Trees" from the pop-up menu. When selecting fonts or font packs, click the font name instead of the icon if you don't want the tree to fold out.

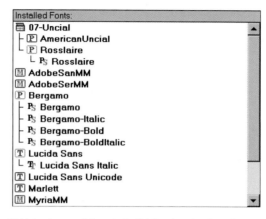

Clicking an icon reveals its contents. Click it again to close it, or click the right mouse button and choose "Close All Trees" to collapse all open icons.

Installing fonts with FontMinder

FontMinder makes installing fonts exceedingly simple. All you need to do is select those fonts you want to install from the Available Fonts list (or a font pack from the Font Packs list) on the left and drag them to the Installed Fonts list on the right (make sure the Install Fonts tab is selected first). When you're satisfied with your selection, press F5, or choose Install Fonts from the File menu. FontMinder displays a dialog box for modifying your Windows font configuration.

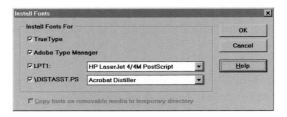

The Install Fonts dialog box modifies all the appropriate Windows INI files
and configuration items when you click OK.

By default, all of these items are checked, and
you should leave them so. The TrueType option
updates the Windows TrueType font configuration.
The Adobe Type Manager option updates ATM.INI
to reflect any PostScript font changes. If you have a
PostScript printer, these are also listed, and will be
updated automatically.

Un-installing fonts is as easy as installing them.
Select those fonts you want to un-install from the
Installed Fonts list and press the Delete key, or drag
them to the trash can icon on the status bar (Font-
Minder's status bar, that is, not Windows'). Then press
F5, or choose Install Fonts from the File menu just as
you did to install them. This method does not delete
the font files; it simply un-installs them.

Deleting font files with FontMinder

To delete font files, or remove them from the list of
available fonts, select them from the Available Fonts list
and press the Delete key, or drag them to the trash can
icon on FontMinder's status bar. FontMinder asks
whether you want to delete the disk files as well. Click
Yes, No, or Cancel. If you click Yes, the physical file
(or files in the case of PostScript fonts) is deleted from
your hard disk. If you click No, the font is removed
from your master library, but the disk files remain
intact. The font will be added to the library again the
next time you choose Update Master Library from the
Library menu.

Just about anything you can do from a menu command in FontMinder, you can also do by clicking the
right mouse button. For example, to add a font to the
list of installed fonts, select it from the Available Fonts
list, click the right mouse button, and choose Add to
Installed Fonts list from the pop-up menu. The pop-up
menu is context sensitive. In other words, it knows
what tasks to display based on the item you clicked and
which list box it happens to be in. If you were to click a
font in the Installed Fonts list, the pop-up menu would
display a different set of commands than it would if you
clicked a font in the Available Fonts list, or the Font
Samples list. I use the right mouse button for doing just
about everything in FontMinder.

Displaying font samples

To display a sample of any font in FontMinder, all you have to do is double-click it. It doesn't matter whether the font is installed or not. Click an icon to open its tree, then double-click one of its members. A brief sample of it is added to the Font Samples list box. To see a more detailed sample, double-click the font from the Font Samples list. This opens another window where you can change the size of the sample text, or even type in different text to sample.

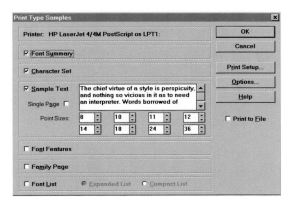

The Font Summary option prints a one-page sample of the font, including samples in a variety of sizes, and the complete character set. The Character Set option prints a chart of the font's character set, complete with ANSI code numbers for each character. This is quite useful for expert set fonts, symbols, borders, and dingbats. The Sample Text option prints the sample text you specify in each of the various point sizes. To reduce the number of point sizes in the print-out, set some of the point sizes to zero.

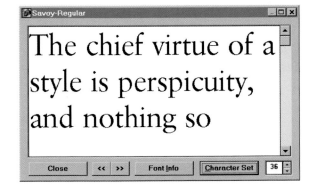

You can type your own sample text and change its point size. Click the Character Set button to see display an ASCII chart with corresponding codes. Click the Font Info button to useful display information about the font such as the directory where it is installed, copyright data, number of kern pairs, etc.

Printing font samples

One of FontMinder's most popular features is its ability to print font samples, or "specimen pages." I use this feature to print samples of every font installed on my system. I keep them all in a three-ring binder for easy reference whenever I need to examine or compare fonts. To choose fonts for print samples, first select the Type Samples tab, then drag fonts from the Available Fonts or Font Packs list into the list on the right. Choose Print Samples from the File menu, or use the right mouse button.

FontMinder 3.0 is compatible with Windows 3.1 and Windows 95 (earlier versions weren't), so you can run it with either version, or both in a dual boot system, with no problems. It manages both PostScript and TrueType fonts at the same time. You can call Ares Software at 800.783.2737 for more information.

Organizing font files with FontMinder

In addition to installing and un-installing fonts in Windows, you can also use FontMinder to move font files from one directory or drive to another. You can organize your fonts (both PostScript and TrueType) into as many different directories as you wish. For PostScript fonts, the only requirement is that PFM files must reside in the same directory, or in an immediate sub-directory, of the corresponding PFB file directory.

For organizing fonts into new directories, the simplest method is to use FontMinder's *Manage Files* feature. First press the Manage Files tab, select the fonts you want to move to a different directory or drive from the Available Fonts list on the left, then drag them to the Manage Files list on the right. Now choose Manage Font Files–Move from the File menu, or click the right mouse button and choose Move Font Files from the pop-up menu. You'll be prompted for the names of the directories to move the fonts into. If the directory names you enter do not already exist, FontMinder will create them for you. FontMinder then moves the font files to the new locations and updates the library in one pass. Doesn't get much easier than that.

It's a good idea not to store any TrueType fonts in the Windows Fonts folder. This directory gets some special (and sometimes undesirable) handling by Windows 95. For example, if you select this directory in

Explorer, every TrueType font in the directory gets installed, whether you wanted them to be installed or not. The only fonts in my Windows Fonts folder are the FON bitmap fonts (MS Sans, MS Serif, Small Fonts). I keep my TrueType fonts in different directories.

Use FontMinder's "Move" feature to move fonts out of the Windows 95 Fonts directory to a different location. It will take care of all the details, even if any of the fonts are currently installed.

There's a real simple way to move fonts. Switch to FontMinder's "Directory Mode," select the source directory, select all the fonts listed (Ctrl-RightMouse), drag them to the "Manage Fonts" tab and select "Move Files." FontMinder will move the files to the new directory (creating the directory if it does not exist) and update the library at the same time. The fonts can even be installed when they are moved.

Cross
Platform
Issues

Cross Platform Issues

IT SURE WOULD BE NICE TO LIVE IN A WORLD WITH ONLY one computer platform, one operating system, and one font format. We'd never have to worry about the inevitable incompatibilities that arise when formats meet, when we shoehorn all those apples and oranges into the same box. But such is not the case, and many of us do have to work to make these different technologies and formats get along. In the preceding chapters, I dealt primarily with one or the other: Macintosh or Windows, PostScript or TrueType. This chapter is about the intersections. I begin with tips on using PostScript and TrueType at the same time on the same system, and then move on to the topic of font conversion—the process of translating fonts from one platform or format to another—before discussing other technologies and issues common to Macintosh and Windows. At first glance, you may wonder why a discussion of Adobe Type Reunion, for example—a Mac-only technology—appears here, but using this utility has some significant ramifications if you plan on sharing Mac documents with Windows-based PCs.

USING POSTSCRIPT AND TRUETYPE FONTS TOGETHER

It is perfectly acceptable to use PostScript and TrueType fonts at the same time. Both Microsoft Windows and the Macintosh operating systems—as well as any applications and font managers—are capable of handling either format, or both, seamlessly (provided you don't install fonts of the same name in both formats). In fact, on the Macintosh it is impossible to distinguish TrueType fonts from PostScript fonts by looking at them in font menus. And by all outward appearances, the system treats them the same. This is more or less the case in Microsoft Windows too, except that many Windows applications

differentiate between the two formats by placing a *PS* or *TT* icon before a font's name in menus.

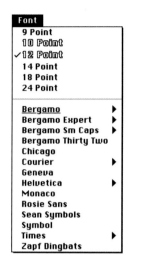

PostScript and TrueType fonts are treated identically on the Macintosh (left). In fact, they are indistinguishable in font menus. Most Windows applications, however, differentiate font formats in menus by placing icons before the font names (right).

So PostScript and TrueType get along just fine together, but with one disclaimer: make sure you don't have the same font, or different fonts with the same name, installed in both formats. Neither the Macintosh or Windows systems prevents you from doing this, but you will *inevitably run into printing and display problems if you do*. For example, if you install the typeface family Franklin Gothic in PostScript format, do not also install the TrueType version of Franklin Gothic. But you can install Franklin Gothic in PostScript and Arial in TrueType, which are different fonts with different names. No problemo. The typefaces on the companion CD are provided in both formats, but I recommend picking one format or the other, i.e., there is no compelling reason to mix the formats.

Regarding printing, the two formats are also compatible on all printers (with the assumption that you're using ATM with your PostScript fonts for printing on non-PostScript printers). But there are other things to consider. PostScript printers print TrueType fonts just fine but are somewhat slower than native PostScript fonts. Also, when using a PostScript printer, you will not be able to print TrueType fonts that have the same name as resident or downloaded PostScript fonts. The only realistic scenario I can think of where this might happen is if your printer is connected to a network, and someone else on the network has downloaded a Post-Script font to the printer that happens to have the same name as one of your TrueType fonts.

For printing to a PostScript printer, I recommend using TrueType fonts only if they are not available in PostScript format. PostScript fonts always get prece-dence on PostScript printers. If you use a TrueType version of Times, for example, to compose text on screen, but get different spacing and line breaks when you print, this is probably because your printer is using the resident version of the font Times, which is more than likely different from the TrueType version.

CONVERTING FONTS

Of all the technical issues surrounding digital type and font management, converting fonts from one platform and format to another is perhaps the most frustrating and troublesome. For this reason, whenever anyone asks me how to convert a font, I first ask "Can you obtain a copy of the font from the manufacturer or developer in the platform or format you need it in?" If so, this is always the best solution. Adobe, for instance, provides its entire type library in both Macin-tosh and PC formats. It does not, however, release its typefaces in TrueType format (and why should it as the developer of PostScript?).

The most common scenario I have seen of a legiti-mate need to convert a font is when a shareware or freeware typeface has been downloaded from an elec-tronic bulletin board, online service, or FTP site and is only available for one platform or another. You're a Windows user, for example, and you need to convert a Mac PostScript Type 1 font you downloaded from America Online.

There are two types of conversions: format conversion (for example, PostScript-to-TrueType), and platform conversion (for example, Macintosh TrueType to Windows TrueType). I'll discuss format conversions first.

PostScript-to-TrueType & TrueType-to-PostScript Conversions

The most important question to ask when attempting conversion from PostScript to TrueType or vice-versa is, Why? This type of conversion is the least desirable because it is essentially of the "apples-to-oranges" vari-ety. Neither format translates with 1:1 accuracy to the other, so *there is always going to be a loss of quality.* Since all Macintosh and Windows computers are capable of using TrueType fonts, there is no practical reason to convert them to PostScript Type 1. Simply install and use them as TrueType fonts. Some people, however, want to con-vert from PostScript Type 1 to TrueType because they don't have the Adobe Type Manager software required to effectively use PostScript fonts. This conversion does not make a whole lot of sense, however. Converting PostScript fonts to TrueType requires software programs that are considerably more expensive than the Adobe Type Manager software. If you don't have a copy of ATM, go out and get one. ATM is cheap (about $40, and bundled free with many applications), and makes using PostScript fonts simple and easy.

FONT CONVERSION POLICIES

Typeface license agreements vary from one manufacturer to another, so it's important to read and understand the policy prior to converting fonts from one platform or format to another. I'm only bringing this up because it may or may not be legal for you to convert fonts. Since I can't list the policy of each type vendor, I'll outline Adobe's and compare it to SoftMaker's.

Adobe's license agreement allows you to use their typefaces on one output device. As long as the fonts are output on a single device, they can be used by more than one person on any number of computers attached to that single output device. If the fonts are used on more than one output device — such as a laser printer and a film recorder, or two laser printers — then a multi-printer license is required from Adobe. In other words, you can't legally print to both devices using the same font files.

Contrast this with SoftMaker's policy (read the typeface license agreement on the companion CD) that lets you install and use fonts on only one computer at a time, but lets you print to as many output devices as you like. With SoftMaker fonts, you could probably convert the font to a different format or platform as long as you no longer have the original around.

To convert PostScript to TrueType and vice-versa, you need to own one of the following programs:

▶ Macromedia Fontographer

▶ Ares FontMonger

Both programs are available for Windows and Macintosh computers. Fontographer, with a street price of around $330, has more editing and conversion features than FontMonger (available for around $100), and produces somewhat higher quality conversions. But you pay for it. Both programs are capable of opening a font from one format, converting it, and generating it in the other.

The bottom line is that, even though there are tools available that make it possible, there is no compelling reason to convert from TrueType to PostScript, and even less to convert from PostScript to TrueType.

Macintosh-to-Windows & Windows-to-Macintosh Conversion

It is possible to convert fonts of the same format (PostScript or TrueType) to different platforms (Macintosh or Windows) without any loss in quality. There are several commercial, shareware, and freeware utilities to help you do this.

A typical scenario for when you might need to convert a font from one platform to another is if you downloaded a font from a bulletin board or FTP site that was intended for a platform other than what you are using. You're a Windows user, for example, and you downloaded from a CompuServe forum an interesting symbol font, which happened to be available for the Macintosh only. First check the site where you obtained the font to make sure a version is not already

available for your platform. If the font was purchased from a commercial developer such as Adobe, you should first inquire about obtaining the font in the correct platform. This, of course, is the easiest method, and the least likely to violate copyright agreements. If a version of the font is not available on the other platform, then follow the steps in the subsections below.

TrueType fonts are the simplest and least troublesome to convert between platforms, so I'll cover them first.

Converting TrueType fonts from Macintosh to Windows and Vice-Versa

The first question I need to ask is, Do you have access to a Macintosh? If you do, I recommend performing all of your conversions on the Mac, regardless of the intended platform. The Mac is better equipped at handling files of foreign formats than is the PC. The Mac, since System 7.5, can also read and write to DOS formatted diskettes without the need for special 3rd party software.

There are several Macintosh programs for converting TrueType fonts to and from Windows, but two stand out: FontHopper from Ares Software, a commercial utility that quickly and easily converts both PostScript Type 1 and TrueType fonts between Macintosh and Windows platforms (street price about $45), and TTConverter, a shareware program developed by Chris Reed (shareware fee $10). Whereas FontHopper lets you convert PostScript fonts as well, TTConverter only convert TrueType fonts. But it does so quickly and seamlessly.

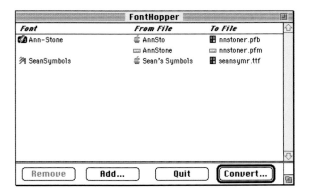

Ares FontHopper easily converts fonts between the Macintosh and PC.

FontHopper is pretty simple. Click the Add button to select those TrueType or PostScript fonts you want to convert from one platform to the other. FontHopper automatically determines the format and platform of both the source and destination. You can specify several files to be converted at once in batch mode. Once files are added to the list, you can rename the converted font by double-clicking the name FontHopper gives it by default in the To File field. When you are ready to convert the fonts, click the Convert button, and FontHopper does the rest.

TTConverter is a "drag and drop" utility on the Macintosh side, meaning that if you want to convert a Macintosh TrueType font to a Windows TrueType font, all you have to do is drag the Mac font to the TTConverter icon and drop it. This starts TTConverter and performs the conversion. Drag and drop functionality is not available, however, when converting a Windows TTF file to the Mac. To convert a Windows TrueType font (.TTF file), first start TTConverter by double-clicking its icon. Choose the "Convert" command from the File menu, use the dialog box to select the TTF file you want to convert, and click Open.

TTConverter then asks you for a filename for the converted font. When you click the Save button, the font is converted and generated with the name you gave it. It doesn't get much simpler than that.

After you have converted TrueType fonts on the Macintosh to the Windows format, insert a PC diskette into the Mac's floppy drive and copy the converted fonts to it. You can then install the font in Windows just like you normally would.

If you don't have access to a Mac, it is practically impossible to convert Mac TrueType fonts to Windows. Technically it's probably not that big a deal — I'm guessing — but to the best of my knowledge there are no Windows-based utilities available for converting Mac TrueType fonts. None. And I've looked.

Converting PostScript fonts from Macintosh to Windows and Vice-Versa

As with TrueType fonts, when converting PostScript fonts the first question is, "Do you have access to a Mac?" If you do, the process is substantially easier than if you don't. There are several Mac utilities that can effortlessly convert PostScript fonts back and forth between platforms. I recommend Ares FontHopper. Then all you need to do is copy the PFB and PFM files from the Mac to a PC disk, and install them under Windows.

You can easily convert PostScript fonts between platforms using other commercial programs such as Macromedia Fontographer or Ares FontMonger, which are available for both Windows and Macintosh. These two products also let you convert between platform *and* format.

If you don't have access to a Mac, converting Mac PostScript Type 1 fonts to Windows becomes a bit more complicated. First of all, Mac PostScript fonts contain *resource forks*, which prevent you from simply file-copying them to a PC. The PC has no way to process resource forks, so you would just end up with a bunch of zero byte files if you tried to copy Mac printer files, for example, to a DOS-formatted diskette. So, to convert Mac PostScript Type 1 fonts to Windows, you must first get them there.

First you have to compress the files — in fact it is the compression process that allows the PC to access the Mac resource fork — copy them to a PC, and un-compress or extract them so that you can then convert them. There are several utilities you need to perform these steps so read carefully.

Before transferring the Mac fonts to the PC, first make sure the Mac fonts have been compressed using popular archive software such as Stuffit or Compact Pro. Files compressed with the former (which is as popular on the Macintosh as *Pkzip* is on the PC), have the extension .SIT. Most electronic BBSs and FTP sites that have Mac fonts will have them in a compressed format, and more than likely will be compressed using Stuffit. Compressed files do not store data in resource forks, so you can copy them to a PC disk just like any other DOS file.

After copying or downloading the compressed file containing the Mac PostScript fonts to your PC, you will need a utility such as *Unsit* a DOS shareware program that lets you un-compress Mac Stuffit archives on your PC, or *Extract*, a shareware program that lets you open and un-compress files created with Compact Pro. Unsit and Extract are available from several online services and bulletin boards.

Okay, so you've copied the archive file to your PC. Now you need to un-compress it. If you're using Unsit, from a DOS prompt, type:

```
UNSIT xb macfont.sit
```

"xb" is the option you need to specify for extracting the Mac data. It seems kind of redundant to have to specify this option. I mean, what else would you be extracting? But, well, you do. "macfont.sit" is the name of the Macintosh Stuffit archive containing the Mac printer font, and preferably the AFM, or metric file, as well, which you will need to create the PFM file required by Adobe Type Manager for Windows.

Unsit will prompt you to enter a DOS filename for the font you are about to convert. Enter one. It should be something that relates to the original font in some way, but since we're talking PC here, it is limited to eight characters. Give it the extension PFB. It will then ask you whether it should have a Mac Binary Header or not. Say No.

You have now extracted the font. The next step is to actually convert it. To do this, you need a program called *Wrefont*, a Windows program that converts Mac printer files into bonafide PFB files, and AFM files into PFM files. *Wrefont* is available as an upgrade to *Refont*. You can obtain Refont from several online services, BBSs, and FTP sites. Then contact the author to obtain the Wrefont upgrade.

Do you really need Wrefont? Yes. The base version of Refont (which is a small DOS program) converts Mac printer fonts to PFB files just fine, but it does not create the PFM file needed by Adobe Type Manager. PFM files contain character metric information such as spacing and kerning pairs, and without them, the PFB file is of little use. Many Macintosh Type 1 fonts available from electronic bulletin boards contain an AFM file which Wrefont can convert to a PFM file.

Hopefully the Stuffit archive containing the Mac printer file also contained an AFM file. After converting the printer file to a PFB file, you will need to use Wrefont to convert the AFM file (if one is present) to a PFM file. PFM files contain all the information of an AFM file, but in a binary format, which means they are considerably smaller in file size, but also can't be modified or previewed using text editors or word processors. If an AFM file is not available, Wrefont can still create a PFM file from the PFB file. This allows you to install and use the font with Adobe Type Manager, but the font will not contain any kerning pairs.

After creating the PFB and PFM files using Wrefont, you can install and use the font as you normally would. Whew!

Now the reverse. To convert PC PostScript fonts to the Macintosh, the best low-cost solution is Ares FontHopper. To use FontHopper, first copy or download the PFB *and* PFM files to your Macintosh, place them in the same folder, and run FontHopper to convert them to Mac files. If you are converting an entire family (regular, italic, bold, and bold italic variations), FontHopper is intelligent enough to create a single family-ized suitcase. So when you install the font, you will be able to press Command-I, for example, to italicize it with true italics.

NOTE Although FontHopper creates a suitcase file containing bitmaps, it cannot create *accurate* bitmaps when it converts a PC file. In other words, the bitmaps it creates do not resemble the font at all. So it fudges this problem by creating bitmaps at a size you'll probably not use very often, if at all—13 points—and relies on Adobe Type Manager to scale the type at other sizes. That is, ATM will accurately draw the font on the screen at 9, 10, 12, 14 points, etc., but not at 13 points. Although the font will print correctly at 13 points, it just won't look right on screen. If you need accurate

bitmaps, the only commercial program that creates them is Macromedia Fontographer.

Rename fonts you convert from one format to another

If you are using a font conversion program such as Ares' FontHopper on the Macintosh, or the shareware program FontMonster for Windows, to convert a Post-Script font to TrueType, you should consider changing the font's name when you convert it. Say you own a copy of Avant Garde in PostScript format, and for whatever reason, you need to convert it to TrueType. The conversion program you use will let you change the font's name, so I suggest appending 'TT' (e.g., AvantGardeTT-Oblique) to it, or something that will make it unique and distinct from the original PostScript version. This way you avoid the naming conflicts that can occur when you print if you have a font in different formats but with the same name, or a resident font like Avant Garde on a PostScript printer.

FONT SUBSTITUTION

We talked a bit about converting fonts—something you might want to do if you need the same font in different formats or on different computer platforms—another option is font substitution. Font substitution is the process whereby your system or application software substitutes for missing fonts. Say you open a document that contains a font you do not have installed. The text won't be invisible, of course—something will always be substituted for it. The system or application will pick a font to use for the missing font. Some programs such as PageMaker let you choose which font you want to substitute, and even let you match it as closely as possible to existing fonts.

This is the principle behind the *Panose Matching* feature built into PageMaker. Other applications such as Microsoft Word will simply pick a font for you. This is application-level font substitution. Font substitution is also handled at the system level by Microsoft Windows, and on the Macintosh if you are using SuperATM.

Panose Matching

Adobe PageMaker uses the Panose font matching technology to substitute missing fonts (or rather, can use Panose; it also relies on ATM, of course, to handle font substitution). Fonts contain certain categorizing data: information such as whether the font is a sans serif or serif font, what types of serifs it has (Oldstyle, Modern, Slab, etc.), how heavy or light it is, whether it is narrow or thin, large x-height or small x-height, and so on. All of this information is built into the font itself by the font's manufacturer. If you were to open a PageMaker document that used a font not installed in your system, Panose would check your installed fonts to see if there were any close fits. The substitution does not occur automatically. A dialog box is displayed when you first open the document that shows the suggested Panose substitutions for any missing fonts. You don't have to accept the substitutions Panose suggests.

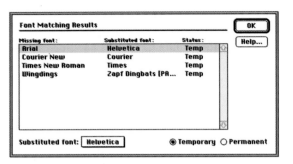

In this example, the Panose system has been set up to substitute the PostScript fonts for the TrueType fonts Arial, Times New Roman, Courier New and Wingdings.

I never accept the Panose substitutions. No matter how close they are, they're still different from what the document's creator used. So I tell Panose to substitute all missing fonts with Zapf Dingbats. By doing so, the missing fonts very clearly stand out in a document (ever try reading Dingbats?), and I am then able to easily find them and make the changes manually, or in most cases, try to install the original font and open the document again. I'm not saying this method is for everyone, or suitable for all circumstances. If you're opening a ReadMe file, for instance, what does it matter whether Times is substituted for Times New Roman…or Palatino? It doesn't. But for publishing work, you probably won't want your fonts substituted. Better to find the original typefaces and install them, re-open the document, and let the Panose system warn you if there are other missing fonts.

```
┌─────────────────────────────────────────────────┐
│ Font Matching Preferences        ┌──────────┐    │
│ ─────────────────────            │    OK    │    │
│ ◆ ATM™ font matching             └──────────┘    │
│ ◆ PANOSE™ font substitution      ┌──────────┐    │
│                                  │  Cancel  │    │
│ Substitution tolerance: 50       └──────────┘    │
│ ⇦[        ▐         ]⇨           ┌──────────┐    │
│ Exact    Normal    Loose         │ Spellings... │ │
│                                  └──────────┘    │
│ Default font: │ Zapf Dingbats │  ┌──────────┐    │
│                                  │Exceptions...│  │
│ ⊠ Show matching results          └──────────┘    │
│ ┌─Information──────────────────  ┌──────────┐    │
│ │Missing fonts will be matched using ATM™. │Help...│ │
│ │If that is unsuccessful, PANOSE™ font substitution will be attempted. │
│ │If no match is found within the specified tolerance, the Default │
│ │font will be used. │                            │
│ └──────────────────────────────                  │
└─────────────────────────────────────────────────┘
```

I set my default substitution font to Zapf Dingbats. That way, when fonts are substituted, I'll be able to easily identify text that was formatted with the missing font.

SuperATM

SuperATM is an enhanced version of Adobe Type Manager for PostScript fonts that provides all the functionality of ATM, but adds automatic, on-the-fly font substitution as well. What this means is that if someone gives you a document created with fonts you don't have installed in your system, rather than trying to locate and install the correct fonts, SuperATM will substitute them using outline data from a special font database it installs in your Fonts folder (sorry Windows users, but Super-ATM is only available on the Macintosh). Of course, the match isn't perfect but is close enough for rough drafts, and it does ensure that spacing and line breaks will be the same as if the missing font or fonts were actually installed and present. Without SuperATM, most programs would substitute the font Courier for any missing fonts.

The substitutions SuperATM makes are temporary. In other words, if you later installed the missing font or fonts, and re-opened the document, the type would

not remain substituted with SuperATM creations. Panose, on the other hand, gives you the option of substituting fonts permanently or temporarily using existing installed fonts. It can't create fonts on the fly like SuperATM.

You might be surprised how close the SuperATM substitutions are, especially if the fonts being substituted are genuine Adobe fonts. Display and script fonts may not substitute very well, but most serif and sans serif text faces are substituted with fonts that simulate the appearance of the original. SuperATM makes no attempt to substitute symbol or dingbat fonts, however.

Overall, SuperATM is a good solution for printing rough drafts, but you wouldn't want to print final drafts with it. It's sort of like taking your sister to the prom. Sure, she wears a dress and looks like a real date from a distance, but you know (and everyone who knows you knows) it's not the same thing. But hey, it could be worse — it could be your mother.

SuperATM retails for $99 but is generally available on the street for under $70. The Panose font matching system is built-in to Adobe PageMaker.

PRINTER RESIDENT FONTS

Whenever you print a document, the application you are printing from in conjunction with the operating system (and ATM if you're using PostScript fonts) must send information to your printer about the typefaces to be printed as well as any graphics on the page. Graphics are treated as individual entities. The software says to the printer "At such-and-such location on the page, print this graphic object thingie." Of course, that's a simplification. There are actually many types of thingies with various properties, characteristics, and technical specifications. If your printer and system software treated text in this manner—with each letter, numeral, punctuation mark, and so on—it would take forever to print even the simplest page of text. Instead, the software first examines a document, finds out which typefaces are being used in it, and sends that information to the printer before it actually attempts to print the document. This way, it doesn't treat each character as an individual graphic object.

The software says to the printer, "Here are instructions for printing the outlines of this font named Whattsit. I'm sending this information to you once, so pay attention, because pretty soon I'll tell you to print a bunch of Es and Ts and As and Bs and so on at various locations on the page, and I don't want to have to keep telling you over and over how to draw an E or a T or whatever. Ready? Okay." So the software sends the font outline information to the printer, and the printer stores it in memory, temporarily of course, using this information to print the various Es and Ts and As and Bs and so on, until it is done printing the document, at which point it forgets everything the software told it. That's one scenario.

But wouldn't it be nice if the printer never forgot that font outline information? Then the software would never have to bother telling it how to print those Es and Ts and As and Bs; it would just say "Here are a bunch of letters. You know how to print them, so do it." Well, the printer doesn't have to go through this process every time you print a page. That first scenario is for non-resident fonts. For printer resident fonts, it's a much simpler scenario.

For PostScript laser printers as well as some non-PostScript laser printers such as the Hewlett-Packard LaserJet 4 (which is also available as a PostScript printer), your system software and applications don't waste time telling the printer how to print certain

fonts—the font outline data is stored in permanent, read-only memory (or ROM) on a chip inside the printer. Of course, it's not all fonts, but just a select few. All PostScript printers have the following base PostScript fonts stored in ROM:

Courier
Courier Bold
Courier Bold Oblique
Courier Oblique
Helvetica
Helvetica Bold
Helvetica Bold Oblique
Helvetica Oblique
Symbol
Times Roman
Times Bold
Times Bold Italic
Times Italic
Zapf Dingbats

Most PostScript printers contain an additional 21 typefaces in ROM:

Avant Garde Book
Avant Garde Demi
Avant Garde Demi Oblique
Avant Garde Book Oblique
Bookman Light
Bookman Light Italic
Bookman Demi
Bookman Demi Italic
Helvetica Narrow
Helvetica Narrow Bold
Helvetica Narrow Oblique
Helvetica Narrow Bold Oblique

New Century Schoolbook Roman
New Century Schoolbook Italic
New Century Schoolbook Bold
New Century Schoolbook Bold Italic
Palatino Roman
Palatino Italic
Palatino Bold
Palatino Bold Italic
Zapf Chancery Medium Italic

These combined with the base fonts, create the PostScript 35. Whenever you see ads for printers with the PostScript 35, that's what they're talking about. These typefaces are also called *resident fonts* because they reside permanently in the printer's memory. If you use one of these fonts in a document, your software does not have to tell your printer how to print it, and consequently your documents will print much faster than if you used non-resident fonts. Unless of course you download them, which brings us to our next topic.

DOWNLOADING FONTS

Most PostScript printers, like computers, have a certain amount of RAM (Random Access Memory). In fact, laser printers are very much like computers in that they have central processors, or CPUs, read-only memory (ROM), RAM, and some even have hard disk drives. As discussed in the previous section, PostScript printers store certain fonts in ROM called resident fonts. When you print a document that uses a non-resident font, the software has to temporarily copy the font outline data into the printer's RAM before it can print the document. This is an automatic process handled by your system software in conjunction with your printer. The software checks to see what fonts are in a document,

then it checks the printer or printer driver to see what fonts are resident, and then it must *download,* or copy into memory, the remainder. This automatic downloading process can often take as much time as it takes to print the rest of the document.

But rather than relying on the software to automatically download fonts to your printer's memory, you can manually download fonts to a PostScript printer. For example, say you use the typeface Bembo in all of your corporate documents, memos, faxes, and so on. Bembo is not resident in any PostScript printers I am aware of, so each time you print using Bembo, your software downloads Bembo to your printer's memory, and then flushes it from the printer's memory at the end of the print job. But if you manually download a font, it remains in the printer's memory until you turn off or reset the printer. Manually downloading fonts requires some special software, and can take a few minutes of time, but if you're printing the same non-resident font often, it is time well spent.

The benefit of downloading fonts is that any documents containing the downloaded fonts will print much faster than if your software has to automatically download. The drawback is that most standard PostScript printers don't have much free RAM available for storing manually downloaded fonts. The printer needs that memory for other things besides storing font data, so be careful not to fill it up or you may receive print errors and be unable to print certain documents until you restart your printer. My rule of thumb is to leave at least 640k of free RAM in my printer.

Don't forget that you can also add RAM to your printer. If you frequently print with a large number of non-resident fonts, you should consider this option. RAM is cheap. Time usually isn't. Most printers accept the same SIMMs used by your computer, which is quite easy to find at computer retailers and mail order firms. You can install up to 32 mb of RAM, for instance, in an HP LaserJet 4 printer.

Another less recommended option is to add a hard disk drive to your printer. Not all PostScript printers support this option, and fonts stored on printer hard drives print considerably slower than fonts stored in printer RAM. So I prefer to add as much RAM to my printers as possible.

There are several utilities for downloading fonts. If you bought a PostScript printer, chances are such a utility was provided on the driver installation and setup disks that came with the printer.

Downloading fonts from a Mac

On the Macintosh, the most popular utility is named, appropriately, the *Downloader,* and is developed and distributed by Adobe Systems. Apple distributes the Laserwriter Utility, and Hewlett-Packard the HP LaserJet Utility, both of which are designed primarily for downloading fonts.

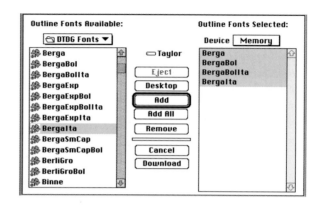

Applications such as Adobe's Downloader (above) and Hewlett-Packard's HP LaserJet Utility (below) let you download Type 1 fonts to your PostScript printer.

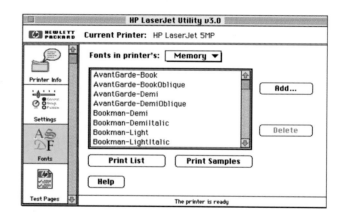

You download the printer fonts — not the bitmap suitcase files — to your printer. Using Adobe's Downloader, for example, you choose the Download Font command from the File menu. From the directory list on the left, you choose the folder where the printer fonts you want to download reside, and you add them to the list on the right by clicking the Download button. The fonts you select remain in the printer's memory until you restart the printer.

You should note the amount of free memory available in your printer before downloading fonts. All downloading utilities provide this information.

Downloading fonts from Windows

In Windows, you can download fonts to a PostScript printer using the download utility bundled with the driver software that came with your printer. There are also two shareware products worth noting—*Psdown* and *Winps.* These two programs are exceptionally easy to use, and available from most computer bulletin boards and online services (check the Desktop Publishing forum on CompuServe). Windows font managers such as Ares FontMinder also provide a facility for easily downloading fonts to PostScript printers.

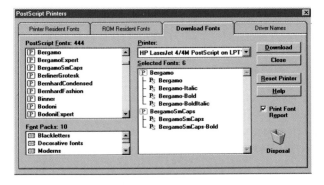

Downloading fonts to your PostScript printer is a snap with FontMinder. First make sure your PostScript printer is selected from the "Printer:" list, then choose those PostScript fonts you want to download from the list box on the left (you can even select entire font packs) and drag them to the "Selected Fonts:" list. Click the Download button when you're ready to begin.

When you download a PostScript font on the PC, you download the PFB file.

Downloading fonts to a printer used by both Macs and PCs

If your PostScript printer is a network or shared printer in a mixed environment (read: Macs and PCs), manually downloading fonts from one platform that will be used by another can be problematic. The issue here is character encoding (discussed at length in Chapter 5). If you download a font to a shared printer from a Windows workstation, and are using that same font on your Mac, you may run into problems when you attempt to print from the Mac. You will be able to print the regular character set (upper and lowercase letters of the alphabet, numbers, and standard punctuation), but extended characters will not print correctly. That is, you will not be able to print foreign characters, typographer's quotes, em and en dashes, bullets, ligatures, and so on. Only the standard keyboard characters.

The reverse of this is true also: If you download a font from a Mac workstation to a shared printer, Windows users will only be able to print the standard character set of that font. If you are working with a shared printer, you really should warn users of other platforms if you download a font.

Adobe Type Reunion

Adobe Type Reunion is a Macintosh system extension that organizes your font menus by sorting and displaying fonts by family name (e.g., "Times"), providing a submenu for the various styles and weights (e.g., Bold, Italic, Bold Italic, and so on). The Windows operating system groups fonts automatically, although it does not provide submenus for font variations. Adobe Type Reunion is not available for Windows.

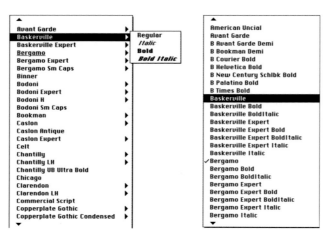

Adobe Type Reunion (left) simplifies and organizes your font menus by
grouping fonts from the same family into distinct submenus.

Without Type Reunion, the font menus in your
Macintosh applications would list a single item for each
style and weight of a particular typeface. For example,
the typeface family Times would appear as "Times,"
"I Times Italic," "B Times Bold," and "BI Times Bold
Italic." Since fonts are listed alphabetically on the Font
menu, depending on the number of fonts installed,
navigating your font menus and choosing fonts could
become quite a chore.

FAMILY-IZED FONTS

A typeface family can contain several variations of
its fonts. For example, the typeface family Times contains bold, italic, and bold italic variations. When a
typeface is *family-ized,* it means you can select bold
or italic versions of a font from the Font menu (*I Times
Bold* or *I Times Italic* or if you have Adobe Type
Reunion, *Italic* from the Times submenu), or you can
choose the Bold and Italic formatting commands

(Command-B/Ctrl-B or Command-I/Ctrl-I) and
achieve the same result. With a typeface that does have
true variations, such as Times or Bembo, using the
formatting command applies the correct variation if
the font has been properly family-ized by the manufacturer. Fonts from reputable vendors such as Adobe,
Monotype, and SoftMaker have been family-ized.

With a typeface that is not family-ized, if you apply
the formatting commands, your application may
oblique, or tilt, the font but it will not be a true variation. For example, the typeface Vendome on the companion CD has a regular and a bold weight, but no
variations for italic or bold italic. Your applications still
let you apply the italic command to this typeface, but it
isn't a *true* italic. Subsequently, it won't look very good
when you print it, if your printer does in fact print it.
(Some applications oblique a font on screen, but if a
true italic is not available for it, the regular weight
prints instead.)

Check your typeface families

Before knowing if you can use both methods of applying bold or italic variations to your font, you have to
know two things. First, does the typeface family actually contain bold, italic, and bold italic variations? Not
all fonts do. Many are made up of one or two weights
but not a set of four. To determine which weights and
variations are available for a font, open its suitcase file
and verify the font names.

The Bergamo suitcase, on the left, contains all four variations — regular, italic, bold, and bold-italic. Vendome, however, only contains the regular and bold variations. If you italicized text formatted with Vendome, it would result in an obliqued typeface, not a true italic.

Second, just because all four weights of a typeface are available still doesn't mean it's family-ized. How can you tell if a typeface has been family-ized? First check the font menu (or the suitcase file) to see if italic, bold, or bold italic variations of it are present. Do you see a font named So-and-so Regular, So-and-so Italic, So-and-so Bold, and so on? Next, apply the Italic command to selected text. Does the true italic variation appear, or is the type simply slanted to the right? If the italic variation of the font appears when you choose the Italic command, the font is family-ized; you can use either the menu or the formatting commands with the same result. Serif text fonts are the easiest to verify. Their italics are usually more distinct so you would know if the application were simply obliquing the characters.

True Italics True Lies

The text on top is set in true italics. The text below has simply been obliqued.

And a third issue. The confusion doesn't end here. There's more. We just talked about obliquing text versus true italics. Well, there are also true obliques and false obliques. Most, but not all, sans serif faces do not have italic variations, but rather oblique variations. And everything I mentioned earlier applies to these typefaces as well. However, it is more difficult to determine whether a sans serif family has been properly family-ized, because the amount of obliquing a program might apply to a non-family-ized face could be very similar to the actual oblique typeface.

It may be nearly impossible to tell a true obliqued font from one that an application has obliqued algorithmically. Generally, if it looks good, stick with it.

You're free to use either the Font menu or formatting commands to apply bold and italic font variations; 1) once you've determined if bold and italic variations of a typeface exist, and 2) you know that the typeface has been properly family-ized by the manufacturer. (Incidentally, it's possible to family-ize a typeface yourself using tools provided with Macromedia's Fontographer.)

If it all seems confusing, we can blame a bit of it on poor design of the operating systems. Both Macintosh and Windows systems let you bold or italicize text by choosing Bold or Italics commands, or by clicking Bold or Italics buttons in dialog boxes, regardless whether bold or italic variations of a font actually exist. In my opinion, if bold or italic variations of a typeface are not available or not installed, choosing a Bold command or clicking an Italic button should not change the appearance of the text in any way, or better yet, Bold or Italic commands should be greyed if they're not available. Some Windows products work this way, such as Microsoft Write which only displays formatting commands for variations that actually exist. It's ironic, but all the more sophisticated word processing and page

FAMILY FEUD AFFAIRS

In Windows 3.1 and 95, all font handling, selection, and font menus are based on font families (for example, Courier is a font family). Except for Adobe Illustrator, I can't think of any Windows applications where you will ever see the actual face name of an individual font (for example, Courier-Bold). In Windows, selecting fonts is really the process of selecting a family and then specifying a style such as regular, italic, bold, or bold-italic.

Because pre-Windows 95 font families are limited to four members, knowing what face one is actually selecting can be quite confusing with large Adobe font families such as Minion and Garamond. With these extended Adobe families, the regular family bold member is really the demi-bold face while the bold family regular member is true bold. This family concept in Windows can also lead to unpleasant problems when selecting members from a font style dialog box when a corresponding face does not exist. This is quite easy to do in PageMaker, which makes no attempt to verify the existence of a family member but simply allows Windows to artificially create it when it does not exist. A good example would be selecting Minion Bold in PageMaker and setting its style to Bold. There is no such face but Windows will gladly further bolden Minion Bold.

The reason Windows 3.1 only allows four members per family is the fault of Apple (they can't grab all the credit for the good stuff, y'know). Windows was originally designed to accomodate up to 900 non-italic family members, and 900 italic family members. The original design spec for the Mac System 7 OS was going to expand the limit of four members per family. At the last minute, however, Apple decided to retain the four-member family in System 7 for compatability with System 6. When Apple did this, Microsoft opted to retain a four-member family for compatability reasons with Apple (go figure).

(continued on page 62 sidebar)

(continued from page 61 sidebar)

Windows 95 is fully compatible with extended families of more than four members. Using a font property editor such as that in FontMinder 3.0, you can setup a single family with 10 or 20 family members all using the same family name. All the members will show up accurately in the Windows font selection common dialog. It works just fine, but presents some really unpleasant compatability problems with applications that have no idea what's going on (for example, older 16-bit applications that don't use the common dialog Font Selector or its equivalent). Also, extended font families can only be created for TrueType fonts because the current Adobe Type Manager is only capable of handling four members per family.

layout programs let you apply non-existing formats to text. The Word Pad application that ships with Windows 95 handles this in an interesting way: it lets you select style variations that are not part of a typeface, or that aren't installed, but it tells you that such variations are imitated for the display, and that the closest matching style will be used for printing. Hmmm. Wouldn't it just be easier if the applications simply didn't let you choose non-existing variations?

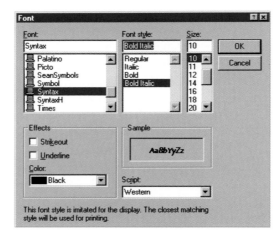

Word Pad lets you apply non-existing style variations to a font. In this example, the Bold Italic font style was applied to the typeface Syntax. Since Syntax does not have a Bold Italic variation, Word Pad notifies you at the bottom of the dialog box that this style will be imitated for screen display, and that the closest matching style will be used for printing.

If you plan on sharing Macintosh documents with Windows users — such as PageMaker files, which are easily transferred and editable by both platforms — use the Bold or Italic formatting commands to format text on the Mac rather than selecting the italic or bold fonts. Otherwise you will actually run into font substitution problems. I know, it makes little sense. Even though the variations exist, Windows forces you to use the

regular variation of a font and bold or italicize it using program commands. But this is because Windows automatically substitutes the bold or italic fonts (if they are available). In other words, Windows does not give you the choice to select the italic variation of a typeface from the Font menu, and it doesn't want you to do so on the Macintosh either.

TrueType fonts and Adobe Type Reunion

TrueType fonts are almost never available with Adobe Type Reunion-style submenus for italics, bold, and bold italics, even though these variations exist. So for most TrueType fonts, including those on the companion CD, you must format them using formatting commands. In other words, you won't be able to select the typeface So-and-so Italic from the Font menu, but you will be able to select So-and-so and then apply the Italic command. Everything else still applies.

Arial MT	
Bergamo	▶
Chicago	
Courier	▶
Geneva	
Helvetica	▶
Monaco	
Palatino	▶
Sean Symbols	
Symbol	
Times	▶
Wingdings	
Zapf Dingbats	

The typeface Arial is a TrueType font, and does not use Adobe Type Reunion-style submenus for bold, italic, and bold italic, even though these variations exist. If you're using TrueType and Post-Script fonts simultaneously, be aware of this.

MULTIPLE MASTER TYPEFACES

Multiple Masters are PostScript Type 1 fonts on steroids. The technology, developed by Adobe Systems (although a few other manufacturers have released multiple master typefaces) and available on the

Macintosh and Windows, lets you specify a degree of boldness or italics.

With non-multiple master typefaces, you can format a font as bold or italics, and if it is an extended typeface family such as Futura, other variations such as light, heavy, extra-bold, etc. are available. But what if you want the font to be somewhere in between? Say, "almost heavy," or "really light," or "super bold." With standard typefaces, you're stuck with the weights provided by the designer. But with multiple master fonts, you can specify the degree of boldness you want on a sliding scale, from a dynamic range.

Imagine that each typeface has a range from zero to 10 (the numbers are actually different than this, but just to give you an idea), with zero being very, very light, and 10 being very, very bold. A normal text weight might have a value of around 4 or so. You could choose a standard bold weight just like you would a non-multiple master typeface (e.g., by choosing the Bold command from the format menu), but you could also create your own weight of say, 5.2. You could create this new weight either on-the-fly in multiple master-savvy applications, such as PageMaker, that provide multiple master formatting options in their dialog boxes, or you could create variations using the Font Creator program (Macintosh) that ships with Adobe Type Manager. For Windows users, this is built in to the Adobe Type Manager control panel (Windows). However you do it, any variations you create, called *instances,* are available to all your applications and appear in all the font menus.

Certain instances have been pre-defined by the font manufacturer or designer, much as a standard font might have bold, heavy, and light weights. These are called *primary instances,* and cannot be deleted or changed. But you're free to experiment with your own instances. So for example, if Adobe uses the weight 5.2 for a specific font, this number is unavailable to you for your own instance of the specific font but you'd have the numbers around it like 5.1 and 5.3.

So far, I have only mentioned creating variations of weight, that is, from light to bold. In most multiple master fonts, weight is one of the variables, called a *design axis,* that you can change. But multiple master fonts usually have more than one design axis. Width is another common axis, allowing you to specify a range from very condensed to extra-extended, for example. Some multiple master fonts even let you specify the type of serif on a sliding scale, from sans serif to slab serif, and all points in between. The design axes you can control depend on the typeface and the typeface designer. Most let you control weight and width, and a few let you control a third axis as well. ■

MULTIMASTER FONTS FROM ADOBE

Adobe's Myriad has two axes—one for weight (light to black) and another for width (condensed to extended).

MMMMM MMMMM

Penumbra has the unique ability to gradually change from a sans serif face to a serif face.

CHAPTER 5

Working with
Characters

Working with Characters

250-pt. Bergamo

THE TERM **CHARACTER** REFERS TO THE BASIC component of a font—a letter of the alphabet, a number, a symbol, or a punctuation mark. It is a single unit that appears when you press a key, or a combination of keys, from your keyboard. This chapter focuses on these basic components. How to find them. How to type them. How to know which ones are the same from computer to computer, from font to font, and which ones are different. Using more key combinations than those available on a typewriter keyboard opens a whole new world to you.

When you sit down and type at your computer, you understand that when you press the S key on your keyboard, the letter *s* appears on your screen. Or that when you hold down the Shift key and type it, the letter *S* appears. Pretty basic stuff. Whatever is printed on the keyboard key is what you expect to appear on your screen when you press it. This is as natural to you as breathing. Your computer keyboard hasn't changed much from the typewriter model upon which it's based. It still has about 47 keys for typing letters of the alphabet, numbers, symbols, and punctuation. The Shift key doubles this amount, letting you create about 94 different characters. These 94 characters (95 if you include the Space Bar) are *more or less* the same from typeface to typeface, from computer to computer, and from operating system to operating system. And if all you ever typed were these basic characters, there would never be a problem. But there are many characters beyond those you can see on your keyboard, and the problem is, they're not always the same from font to font, and never the same from operating system to operating system. The Macintosh operating system and Microsoft Windows, for example—the operating systems we're discussing in this book—have different rules for specifying which characters go where. These rules are called *character encoding schemes*, and determine the combination of keys you need to press to access certain characters whose likenesses do not appear on the keyboard keys themselves.

The term "character encoding scheme" sounds kind of evil (and well, maybe it is), but the concept is fairly simple. You and I (and most of the people we know, presumably) think in terms of visualization and symbolic representation—things like words and letters and symbols and pictures are meaningful to us. But this is not the case with today's computer operating systems. Computers deal with everything on a numeric level. Even fonts and letters and things you and I think of symbolically are interpreted by our computers as numbers. The letters S-e-a-n, for example, are known to the Macintosh or Windows operating systems as 83, 101, 97 and 110, respectively. In fact, anything you type from your keyboard has a corresponding number, and this number determines what is displayed on your screen. This is what is meant by character encoding: each character is represented by a number.

The Mac and Windows operating systems are designed in such a way that they can identify and represent 256 different characters (this number is being increased with new technologies such as Quick-Draw GX). The character positions zero through 31 are reserved, for the most part, for the operating systems themselves. Character positions 32 through 126 are the characters we see on our keyboards (including the Space Bar), and are the same from operating system to operating system. But characters 127 through 255 are different. In the PC world of DOS and Windows, these characters are referred to as *extended* characters, and represent letters and diacritics found in European alphabets (Áá, Ûû, Øø, etc.), analphabetic symbols such as em and en dashes, typographer's quotation marks, registration, trademark and copyright symbols, currency symbols, and additional punctuation.

ASCII, SHMASCII, WHAT DOES IT MEAN?

If you've hung about in the computer world for any length of time, you've no doubt heard talk of *ASCII codes, 7-bit ASCII, 8-bit ASCII,* or what have you. It's no big mystery. ASCII is an acronym for American Standard Code for Information Interchange, the standard by which letters of the English and Amurkin alphabets are assigned numbers, ensuring that the letter A, for example, is the letter A no matter whether it's on a Macintosh or an IBM PC or a HAL 9000. The characters at positions zero through 127 (i.e., the standard keyboard characters) are sometimes referred to as *7-bit* ASCII characters. This is geek-speak for 128 characters: 7-bit equals 2 to the seventh power, which equals 128. I mentioned earlier that computers store everything, even letters of the alphabet, as numbers. To be more precise, these numbers are binary numbers, meaning they are expressed using only the digits 1 and 0. The uppercase letter A for example is located at character position 65. But this is the decimal way of expressing it. To your computer, in binary, it is known as 1000001. Notice that there are 7 digits. The largest number that can be represented with seven digits in binary format is 127, or 1111111, and since programmers always count from zero, not from 1, you get 128 character positions total. The characters 128 through 255 (i.e., the extended characters) are also referred to as *8-bit* ASCII (2 to the eighth power equals 256). So a character such as the copyright symbol (©) has a decimal value of 169, a number that requires 8 binary digits to represent it: 10101001. Does your brain hurt yet? Don't worry, none of this will be on the test, and of course, none

of this means much if anything to a Mac user who simply has to type Option-G to create a © symbol, but the Windows user might want to know why she has to type Alt-0169 to create the durned thing.

Most of these extended characters are assigned different numbers by the Macintosh and Windows operating systems. An em dash (—) for example, is 209 on the Mac, but 151 in Windows. The characters *å, é, î, ø, ü* and *ÿ* are brought to you by the numbers 140, 142, 148, 191, 159 and 216 on the Macintosh, but 229, 233, 238, 248, 252 and 255 in Windows. Are you taking notes? Don't. It's not important to remember these numbers. Dustin Hoffman's *Rainman* character might be able to remember which characters go with which numbers, but the rest of us use charts. Definitely use charts.

Macintosh Character Chart

Characters available in both Macintosh and Windows.

Characters not available in Windows. If you plan on sharing your documents with Windows users, do not include these characters in your Macintosh documents.

Characters available in Windows, but not all Macintosh applications permit access to them. Many Macintosh applications simply will not let you type these characters.

Undefined characters.

Macintosh Character Chart grid. Each cell lists a keystroke combination, a character, and its numeric code (0–255). Selected entries:

- Space Bar (32), 0 (48), Sh-2 @ (64), Sh-P P (80), ` (96), P p (112), Op-U Sh-A Ä (128), Op-I E ê (144), Op-T † (160), Op-5 ∞ (176), Sh-Op-/ ¿ (192), Op-Hyphen – (208), Sh-Op-7 ‡ (224), Sh-Op-K ♣ (240)
- Control-A Đ (1), Sh-1 ! (33), 1 (49), Sh-A A (65), Sh-Q Q (81), Q q (97), Sh-Op-A Å (113), Op-U E ë (129), Sh-Op-8 ° (145), Sh-Op-Equal ± (161), Op-1 ¡ (177), Sh-Op-Hyph — (193), Sh-Op-9 · (209), Sh-Op-L Ò (225)
- Control-B ð (2), Sh-' " (34), 2 (50), Sh-B B (66), Sh-R R (82), B b (98), r (114), Sh-Op-C Ç (130), Op-E I í (146), Op-4 ¢ (162), Op-Comma ≤ (178), Op-L ¬ (194), Op-[" (210), Sh-Op-0 , (226), Sh-Op-; Ú (242)
- Control-C Ł (3), Sh-3 # (35), 3 (51), Sh-C C (67), Sh-S S (83), C c (99), s (115), Op-E Sh-E É (131), Op-` I ì (147), Op-3 £ (163), Op-Period ≥ (179), Op-V √ (195), Sh-Op-[" (211), Sh-Op-W „ (227), Op-I Sh-U Û (243)
- Control-D ł (4), Sh-4 $ (36), 4 (52), Sh-D D (68), Sh-T T (84), D d (100), t (116), Op-N Sh-N Ñ (132), Op-I I î (148), Op-6 § (164), Op-Y ¥ (180), Op-F ƒ (196), Op-] ' (212), Sh-Op-R ‰ (228), Op-` Sh-U Ù (244)
- Control-E Š (5), Control-U ½ (21), Sh-5 % (37), 5 (53), Sh-E E (69), Sh-U U (85), E e (101), u (117), Op-U Sh-O Ö (133), Op-U I ï (149), Op-8 • (165), Op-M µ (181), Sh-Op-] ≈ (197), Sh-Op-M ' (213), Sh-Op-B Â (229), 1 (245)
- Control-F š (6), Control-V ¼ (22), Sh-7 & (38), 6 (54), Sh-F F (70), Sh-V V (86), F f (102), v (118), Op-U Sh-U Ü (134), Op-N N ñ (150), Op-7 ¶ (166), Op-D ∂ (182), Op-J Δ (198), Op-Slash ÷ (214), Op-I Sh-E Ê (230), Sh-Op-I ^ (246)
- Control-G Ý (7), Control-W 1 (23), 7 (55), Sh-G G (71), Sh-W W (87), G g (103), w (119), Op-E A á (135), Op-E O ó (151), Op-S ß (167), Op-W Σ (183), Op-\ « (199), Sh-Op-V ◊ (215), Sh-Op-Y Á (231), ~ (247)
- Control-H ý (8), Control-X ¾ (24), Sh-9 ((40), 8 (56), Sh-H H (72), Sh-X X (88), H h (104), x (120), Op-` A à (136), Op-` O ò (152), Op-R ® (168), Sh-Op-P ∏ (184), Sh-Op-\ » (200), Op-U Y ÿ (216), Op-U Sh-E Ë (232), Sh-Op-Comma – (248)
- Control-Y 3 (25), Sh-0) (41), 9 (57), Sh-I I (73), Sh-Y Y (89), I i (105), Y y (121), Op-I A â (137), Op-I O ô (153), Op-G © (169), Op-P π (185), Op-; … (201), Op-U Sh-Y Ÿ (217), Op-` Sh-E È (233), Sh-Op-Period ˘ (249)
- Control-Z 2 (26), Sh-8 ★ (42), Sh-; : (58), Sh-J J (74), Sh-Z Z (90), J j (106), z (122), Op-U A ä (138), Op-U O ö (154), TM (170), Op-B ∫ (186), Op-Space (non-breaking space) (202), Sh-Op-1 / (218), Sh-Op-S Í (234), Op-H (250)
- Control-K Þ (11), Control-[¦ (27), Sh-Equal + (43), ; (59), Sh-K K (75), [(91), K k (107), { (123), Op-N A ã (139), Op-N O õ (155), Sh-Op-E ´ (171), Op-9 ª (187), Op-` Sh-A À (203), Sh-Op-2 ¤ (219), Sh-Op-D Î (235), Op-K ° (251)
- Control-L þ (12), Control-\ – (28), Comma , (44), Sh-Comma < (60), Sh-L L (76), \ (92), L l (108), | (124), Op-A å (140), Op-E U ú (156), Sh-Op-U ¨ (172), Op-0 º (188), Op-N Sh-A Ã (204), Sh-Op-3 ‹ (220), Sh-Op-F Ï (236), Sh-Op-Z ˍ (252)
- Control-] × (29), Hyphen - (45), Equal = (61), Sh-M M (77),] (93), M m (109), } (125), Op-C ç (141), Op-` U ù (157), Op-Equal ≠ (173), Op-Z Ω (189), Op-N Sh-O Õ (205), Sh-Op-4 › (221), Op-` Sh-I Ì (237), Sh-Op-G ˝ (253)
- Control-N Ž (14), Period . (46), Sh-Period > (62), Sh-N N (78), Sh-6 ^ (94), N n (110), Sh-` ~ (126), Op-E E é (142), Op-I U û (158), Sh-Op-' Æ (174), Op-' æ (190), Sh-Op-Q Œ (206), Sh-Op-5 fi (222), Sh-Op-H Ó (238), Sh-Op-X ˇ (254)
- Control-O ž (15), Slash / (47), Sh-Slash ? (63), Sh-O O (79), Sh-Hyphen _ (95), O o (111), Op-` E è (143), Op-U U ü (159), Sh-Op-O Ø (175), Op-Q ø (191), Sh-Op-6 œ (207), Sh-Op-T Ô (255)

Windows Character Chart

0	16	Space Bar 32	0 48	Sh-2 @ 64	Sh-P P 80	` 96	P p 112	• 128	• 144	Alt-0160 (non-breaking space) 160	Alt-0176 ° 176	Alt-0192 À 192	Alt-0208 Ð 208	Alt-0224 à 224	Alt-0240 ð 240
1	17	Sh-1 ! 33	1 49	Sh-A A 65	Sh-Q Q 81	A a 97	Q q 113	• 129	Alt-0145 ' 145	Alt-0161 ¡ 161	Alt-0177 ± 177	Alt-0193 Á 193	Alt-0209 Ñ 209	Alt-0225 á 225	Alt-0241 ñ 241
2	18	Sh-' " 34	2 50	Sh-B B 66	Sh-R R 82	B b 98	R r 114	Alt-0130 , 130	Alt-0146 ' 146	Alt-0162 ¢ 162	Alt-0178 ² 178	Alt-0194 Â 194	Alt-0210 Ò 210	Alt-0226 â 226	Alt-0242 ò 242
3	19	Sh-3 # 35	3 51	Sh-C C 67	Sh-S S 83	C c 99	S s 115	Alt-0131 ƒ 131	Alt-0147 " 147	Alt-0163 £ 163	Alt-0179 ³ 179	Alt-0195 Ã 195	Alt-0211 Ó 211	Alt-0227 ã 227	Alt-0243 ó 243
4	20	Sh-4 $ 36	4 52	Sh-D D 68	Sh-T T 84	D d 100	T t 116	Alt-0132 „ 132	Alt-0148 " 148	Alt-0164 ¤ 164	Alt-0180 ´ 180	Alt-0196 Ä 196	Alt-0212 Ô 212	Alt-0228 ä 228	Alt-0244 ô 244
5	21	Sh-5 % 37	5 53	Sh-E E 69	Sh-U U 85	E e 101	U u 117	Alt-0133 … 133	Alt-0149 • 149	Alt-0165 ¥ 165	Alt-0181 µ 181	Alt-0197 Å 197	Alt-0213 Õ 213	Alt-0229 å 229	Alt-0245 õ 245
6	22	Sh-7 & 38	6 54	Sh-F F 70	Sh-V V 86	F f 102	V v 118	Alt-0134 † 134	Alt-0150 – 150	Alt-0166 ¦ 166	Alt-0182 ¶ 182	Alt-0198 Æ 198	Alt-0214 Ö 214	Alt-0230 æ 230	Alt-0246 ö 246
7	23	' 39	7 55	Sh-G G 71	Sh-W W 87	G g 103	W w 119	Alt-0135 ‡ 135	Alt-0151 — 151	Alt-0167 § 167	Alt-0183 · 183	Alt-0199 Ç 199	Alt-0215 × 215	Alt-0231 ç 231	Alt-0247 ÷ 247
8	24	Sh-9 (40	8 56	Sh-H H 72	Sh-X X 88	H h 104	X x 120	Alt-0136 ˆ 136	Alt-0152 ˜ 152	Alt-0168 ¨ 168	Alt-0184 ¸ 184	Alt-0200 È 200	Alt-0216 Ø 216	Alt-0232 è 232	Alt-0248 ø 248
9	25	Sh-0) 41	9 57	Sh-I I 73	Sh-Y Y 89	I i 105	Y y 121	Alt-0137 ‰ 137	Alt-0153 ™ 153	Alt-0169 © 169	Alt-0185 ¹ 185	Alt-0201 É 201	Alt-0217 Ù 217	Alt-0233 é 233	Alt-0249 ù 249
10	26	Sh-8 ★ 42	Sh-; : 58	Sh-J J 74	Sh-Z Z 90	J j 106	Z z 122	Alt-0138 Š 138	Alt-0154 š 154	Alt-0170 ª 170	Alt-0186 º 186	Alt-0202 Ê 202	Alt-0218 Ú 218	Alt-0234 ê 234	Alt-0250 ú 250
11	27	Sh-Equal + 43	; 59	Sh-K K 75	[91	K k 107	Sh-[{ 123	Alt-0139 ‹ 139	Alt-0155 › 155	Alt-0171 « 171	Alt-0187 » 187	Alt-0203 Ë 203	Alt-0219 Û 219	Alt-0235 ë 235	Alt-0251 û 251
12	28	Comma , 44	Sh-Comma < 60	Sh-L L 76	\ 92	L l 108	Sh-\	124	Alt-0140 Œ 140	Alt-0156 œ 156	Alt-0172 ¬ 172	Alt-0188 ¼ 188	Alt-0204 Ì 204	Alt-0220 Ü 220	Alt-0236 ì 236	Alt-0252 ü 252
13	29	Hyphen - 45	Equal = 61	Sh-M M 77	] 93	M m 109	Sh-] } 125	• 141	• 157	Alt-0173 – 173	Alt-0189 ½ 189	Alt-0205 Í 205	Alt-0221 Ý 221	Alt-0237 í 237	Alt-0253 ý 253
14	30	Period . 46	Sh-Period > 62	Sh-N N 78	Sh-6 ^ 94	N n 110	Sh-` ~ 126	• 142	• 158	Alt-0174 ® 174	Alt-0190 ¾ 190	Alt-0206 Î 206	Alt-0222 Þ 222	Alt-0238 î 238	Alt-0254 þ 254
15	31	Slash / 47	Sh-Slash ? 63	Sh-O O 79	Sh-Hyphen _ 95	O o 111	• 127	• 143	Alt-0159 Ÿ 159	Alt-0175 ¯ 175	Alt-0191 ¿ 191	Alt-0207 Ï 207	Alt-0223 ß 223	Alt-0239 ï 239	Alt-0255 ÿ 255

Characters available in both Windows and Macintosh.

Characters generally not available to Macintosh users.

Avoid typing these characters. Depending on the application, they may appear as bullets, or simply as blank characters.

Undefined characters.

The fact that the Mac and Windows operating systems use different numbers to represent different characters is not a problem in itself. Even though the em dash is 209 on the Mac and 151 in Windows, the translation is easy enough: when a Mac program opens a Windows document (or vice versa) it knows that whenever it sees a character encoded with the number 151 to translate it to 209. So everything's fine, right?

Wrong.

If we were talking about the same 256 characters, and just had to worry about them being arranged in different order, there would be no problem; it would just be a matter of translation. But it's not the same 256 characters. See, there are actually more than 256 characters in most fonts, but only 256 can be recognized by your computer. The situation is not unlike a game of musical chairs with 285 people, for example, but only 256 chairs. Not everyone is going to have a seat when the music stops. There are certain characters that Macintosh gave seats but Windows left standing, that is, Windows has not assigned them numbers within the range 128 to 255. Likewise, there are certain characters available in Windows that the Mac can not readily access.

That said, the encoding scheme used by the Mac is superior to that used by Windows for three primary reasons: fi, fl and /. These are characters that didn't get seats in Windows when the music stopped, but which anyone at all interested in fine typography will tell you they should have. These are the ligatures fi, fl, and the fraction bar (see Chapter 6 for information on using these characters, and how to access them from expert sets if you're a Windows user). There are other characters available on the Mac but not in Windows, but their use is not as common, and so aren't likely to be missed. Of course, there are some characters available

to Windows that the Mac cannot access, but these characters are really only pertinent to speakers of Old English, Icelandic, Faroese, and a few Slavic languages. Fractions, also, are more plentiful in the Windows encoding scheme. But even for these characters, the Mac does offers limited access to them in some fonts: the SoftMaker typefaces on the companion CD, for example, place these uncommon characters in positions zero through 32. While this makes access to them tricky—and downright impossible in some applications—they are nonetheless present.

TYPING EXTENDED CHARACTERS IN WINDOWS

Like we talked about earlier, extended characters are those characters that don't appear on your keyboard keys. In Microsoft Windows, you access extended characters by holding down the Alt key, and typing 0 (zero) from the numeric keypad followed by the character's number (see the character charts at the end of this chapter). An em dash is represented by the number 151 in Windows, so to create one, you hold down the Alt key while typing the numbers 0151 from the numeric keypad (don't use the regular number keys—your computer will just beep at you if you do).

In Microsoft Windows, all extended characters are accessed the same way: by holding down the Alt key and typing 0 plus the character's number on the numeric keypad. When you release the Alt key, the character appears. Boom, it's as simple as that. Again, don't memorize; refer to the Windows character chart to determine the Alt+0 code for the character you want to create.

NOTE Microsoft Word for Windows also requires that Num Lock be on before typing extended characters using the Alt key combinations. It is, as far as I know, the only Windows program requiring you to do this. Don't know why this is, but it is.

If you don't have a character chart or this book handy (and you should always have this book handy), and you haven't memorized all of the Alt key combinations, use the Character Map accessory that comes with Windows. This handy utility displays all the characters available in a font, tells you the Alt+0 codes for each one, as well as lets you copy characters to the Clipboard so you can paste them into a document without having to type the necessary key combinations.

From the Windows 95 Start menu, select Programs, select Accessories, and then choose Character Map. (Gotta love those nested menus!)

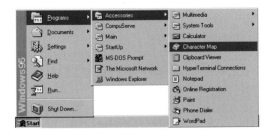

To find a character's Alt+0 code, locate the character and then click it. The key combination required to create the character is displayed in the lower-right corner of the dialog box.

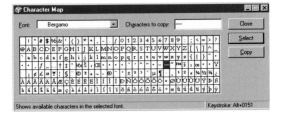

To copy a character to the Clipboard, simply double-click it. When you do so, the character is added to the "Characters to copy" box. You can add as many characters to this box as you like. Now return to your application and choose Paste. The characters are pasted at the cursor location.

Characters whose Alt-key combinations you should commit to memory

You probably won't memorize all of the Alt key combinations required to create extended characters, but there are a few you should, namely the dashes, typographer's quotation marks, ellipsis, and bullet characters.

CHARACTER	KEY COMBINATION
— (en dash)	Alt-0150
— (em dash)	Alt-0151
'	Alt-0145
'	Alt-0146
"	Alt-0147
"	Alt-0148
• (bullet)	Alt-0149
… (ellipsis)	Alt-0133

Some programs such as Adobe PageMaker for Windows assign their own keystrokes to these characters, although the Alt key combinations still work. For example, to create an en dash, you could type Ctrl-Equal, or Ctrl-Shift-Equal to create an em dash, Ctrl-Shift-8 to create a bullet. But these key combinations only work while you're in PageMaker. They are macros, really, that substitute the Alt-key combination for its own.

Concerning the bullet character, the Character Map accessory shows several bullet characters, all identical, besides the one at position Alt-0149. DO NOT USE THESE BULLETS if you intend to open the document at some point on a Mac. In fact, these characters may even cause problems in other Windows applications. For this reason, I recommend that you always type Alt-0149 to create a bullet. So disregard the bullets shown at positions 127 through 129, 141 through 144, and 157 and 158 (if your font does indeed show them; not all will, but most fonts from Adobe, Monotype, and SoftMaker do). I call these little beasties the "Langoliers" (thank you, Stephen King), and they will only cause you headaches if you use them, especially if your documents will be edited on multiple platforms.

TYPING EXTENDED CHARACTERS ON THE MACINTOSH

You access extended characters on the Macintosh using four alternative key combinations:

NOTE In some applications, you use Control keys to type certain characters but there are limitations that I discuss later in this chapter.

1. *Option+key.* For example, if you hold down the Option key and press A, the letter 'å' appears (this is a common vowel in Swedish, Norwegian, and Danish). Throughout the text, the Option key is abbreviated as Op.

2. *Shift+Option+key.* For example, if you hold down Shift and Option, and press A, the letter 'Å' appears. This is, as might be expected, the uppercase of 'å'. The Shift key is abbreviated as Sh.

3. *Option+key, release, key.* For example, if you want to type the letter 'ó', press the Option and E keys,

release them (that is, don't continue to hold them down), and then immediately type O. Most but not all of the accented letters are created in this manner. It's fairly straightforward but only certain keys are available for the first and second keystrokes. The first keystroke combination determines the type of accent (combined with Option, the keys E, I, N, U or ` are available), and the second keystroke completes the character (only the keys A, E, I, O, U, Y, and N are available).

4. *Option+key, release, Shift+key.* To create the uppercase 'Ó', press Option-E, release, then type Shift-O. The same keys are available here as for the third combination above (E, I, N, U or ` for the first keystroke combination; A, E, I, O, U, Y, and N for the second keystroke).

For these third and fourth extended character combinations, the types of accents and the available characters it applies to are as follows:

ACCENT	FIRST KEYSTROKE	SECOND KEYSTROKE (AVAILABLE LETTERS)	FREESTANDING ACCENT*
grave	Op-E	Áá Éé Íí Óó Úú	Sh-Op-E
circumflex	Op-I	Ââ Êê Îî Ôô Ûû	` key
tilde**	Op-N	Ãã Ññ Õõ	Sh-Op-N
umlaut †	Op-U	Ää Ëë Ïï Öö Üü Ÿÿ	Sh-Op-U
acute	Op-`	Àà Èè Ìì Òò Ùù	` key

*The accent itself without a letter associated with it.

**This tilde is not the same as the character you create when you type Shift-`. Also known as the ASCII tilde, this character is larger than the tilde, and is positioned higher above the baseline.

† Also known as a diæresis.

These combinations do not mix with other characters. For example, you could not create a g-tilde by typing Option-N followed by G, which is really too bad, because this letter is fairly common in Quechuan (why, I was just saying in Quechuan the other day…). Your only alternative to forming accented letters is to build your own font, or apply some radical negative kerning in programs such as PageMaker or QuarkXPress (which I discuss below).

Use the Key Caps desk accessory that comes with the Mac operating system to see where extended characters are located and to graphically determine the keystrokes required to type them. This utility displays all the characters available in a font, and lets you copy characters to the Clipboard so you can paste them into a document without having to type the necessary key combinations.

Choose "Key Caps" from the Apple menu (this is where it is normally, although not necessarily, located).

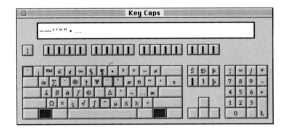

To copy characters from the list of characters you typed to the Clipboard, simply select them with the mouse and choose Copy from the Edit menu. Now switch back to your application and choose Paste. The characters are pasted at the cursor location.

Key Caps is okay, but I prefer to use a shareware program called "ASCII Chart" (available on the companion CD) which displays all the characters available in a font at once on a single screen (unlike Key Caps which only lets you view one keyboard full o' characters at a time). Click on a character to see the keystroke required to create it, or choose Copy from the Edit menu and ASCII Chart will copy it to the Clipboard. Pressing the ⌘ key displays the currently selected character at a large size.

Holding down the Shift, Option, Shift-Option, or Control keys changes the keyboard that Key Caps displays. Type a character to add it to the list of characters, or click the key you want to type with the mouse.

ASCII Chart desk accessary gives you quick access to every character in a font.

ASCII Chart and Key Caps are especially useful when working with symbol or dingbat fonts such as Zapf Dingbats, Symbol, Picto, and Sean's Symbols (the latter two are available on the companion CD). Use them to determine which characters are assigned to which keys.

Characters whose keystrokes you should commit to memory

You probably won't memorize all of the key combinations required to create extended characters, but there are a few you should, namely the dashes, typographer's quotation marks, ellipsis, and bullet characters.

CHARACTER	KEY COMBINATION
— (en dash)	Op-Hyphen
— (em dash)	Sh-Op-Hyphen
'	Op-]
'	Sh-Op-]
"	Op-[
"	Sh-Op-[
• (bullet)	Op-8
… (ellipsis)	Op-;

KEY COMBINATIONS FOR EXTENDED CHARACTERS

The remaining key combinations for Macintosh and Windows are listed here for reference. Any asterisk beside a Macintosh key combination means they are accessed with the Control key, the details of which are discussed at the end of these tables.

Inches, Ticks, and Quotation Marks

The ' and " characters found on a normal keyboard are often used as quotation marks. And while this may be unavoidable when conversing online, for example, where you are limited to the standard keyboard characters, you should always use the true, or typographer's, quotation marks in printed matter. So what are those ' and " characters? Many people use them as foot and inch marks, but even these characters have better substitutes. Using them requires the Symbol font that is available on most Macintosh and Windows systems. To use genuine foot and inch marks, first select the Symbol font, then enter the following:

CHARACTER	MAC KEYSTROKES	WINDOWS KEY CODES
′ (feet)	Op-4	Alt-0162
″ (inches)	Op-Comma	Alt-0178

8'10″
8'10"

Compare the *primes* created using the Symbol font (above) to the tick marks (below)

Accents and Accented Characters

CHARACTER	MAC KEYSTROKES	WINDOWS KEY CODES
acute		
´	Sh-Op-E	Alt-0180
Á	Sh-Op-Y	Alt-0193
á	Op-E A	Alt-0225
É	Op-E Sh-E	Alt-0201
é	Op-E E	Alt-0233
Í	Sh-Op-S	Alt-0205
í	Op-E I	Alt-0237
Ó	Sh-Op-H	Alt-0211
ó	Op-E O	Alt-0243
Ú	Sh-Op-;	Alt-0218
ú	Op-E U	Alt-0250
Ý	Control-G*	Alt-0221
ý	Control-H*	Alt-0253
breve		
˘	Sh-Op-Period	Not Available
caron		
ˇ	Sh-Op-T	Not Available
Š	Control-E*	Alt-0138
š	Control-F*	Alt-0154
Ž	Control-N*	Not Available
ž	Control-O*	Not Available

CHARACTER	MAC KEYSTROKES	WINDOWS KEY CODES
cedilla		
¸	Sh-Op-Z	Alt-0184
Ç	Sh-Op-C	Alt-0199
ç	Op-C	Alt-0231
circumflex		
^	Sh-Op-I	Alt-0136
Â	Sh-Op-M	Alt-0194
â	Op-I A	Alt-0226
Ê	Op-I Sh-E	Alt-0202
ê	Op-I E	Alt-0234
Î	Sh-Op-D	Alt-0206
î	Op-I I	Alt-0238
Ô	Sh-Op-J	Alt-0212
ô	Op-I O	Alt-0244
Û	Op-I Sh-U	Alt-0219
û	Op-I U	Alt-0251
diaeresis/umlaut		
¨	Sh-Op-U	Alt-0168
Ä	Op-U Sh-A	Alt-0196
ä	Op-U A	Alt-0228
Ë	Op-U Sh-E	Alt-0203
ë	Op-U E	Alt-0235
Ï	Sh-Op-F	Alt-0207
ï	Op-U I	Alt-0239
Ö	Op-U Sh-O	Alt-0214
ö	Op-U O	Alt-0246
Ü	Op-U Sh-U	Alt-0220
ü	Op-U U	Alt-0252
ÿ	Op-U Y	Alt-0255
Ÿ	Op-U Sh-Y	Alt-0159
double acute/Hungarian umlaut		
˝	Sh-Op-G	Not Available

CHARACTER	MAC KEYSTROKES	WINDOWS KEY CODES
grave		
`	`	` (grave by itself)
À	Op-` Sh-A	Alt-0192
à	Op-` A	Alt-0224
È	Op-` Sh-E	Alt-0200
è	Op-` E	Alt-0232
Ì	Op-` Sh-I	Alt-0204
ì	Op-` I	Alt-0236
Ò	Sh-Op-L	Alt-0210
ò	Op-` O	Alt-0242
Ù	Op-` Sh-U	Alt-0217
ù	Op-` U	Alt-0249
macron		
¯	Sh-Op-Comma	Alt-0175
ogonek		
˛	Sh-Op-X	Not Available
overdot		
·	Op-H	Not Available
ring/kroužek		
°	Op-K	Not Available
Å	Sh-Op-A	Alt-0197
å	Op-A	Alt-0229
tilde		
˜	Sh-Op-N	Alt-0152
Ã	Op-N Sh-A	Alt-0195
ã	Op-N A	Alt-0227
Ñ	Op-N Sh-N	Alt-0209
ñ	Op-N N	Alt-0241
Õ	Op-N Sh-O	Alt-0213
õ	Op-N O	Alt-0245

Other Alphabetic Characters

Ø (O slash)	Sh-Op-O	Alt-0216
ø (o slash)	Op-O	Alt-0248

The ø and Ø characters are common vowels in Norwegian and Danish. Remember the "møøse" from the credits to *Monty Python's Holy Grail?*

Æ (Æsc)	Sh-Op-'	Alt-0198
æ (æsc)	Op-'	Alt-0230

Pronounced *ash*, these characters are actually ligatures in Norwegian, Danish, and Old English, representing a vowel sound like the *a* in *bad*. While quite common in Latin and Latinized Greek, in English, however, the æ is usually represented by just *e* (encyclopedia instead of encyclopædia, ethereal instead of æthereal)—except in proper names (Cæsar), in literal Roman or Greek words and phrases (aqua vitæ, ætatis suæ), and in scientific or technical terms (æcium), especially plurals (nebulæ, supernovæ). If you really want to impress your friends, not to mention the typothetæ, consider using it in words such as sundæ (as in ice cream), Fannie Mæ (as in home mortgage loans), and reggæ (as in hæ mon).

Œ (Œthel)	Sh-Op-Q	Alt-0140
œ (œthel)	Op-Q	Alt-0156

Also known as *ethel*, these ligatures are common in French words such as "hors d'œuvre," but like the æsc character, their use is not very common in English—except by lit majors (Œdipus Rex), psychology majors (œdipal complex), and vinicultural majors (œnophilia).

CHARACTER	MAC KEYSTROKES	WINDOWS KEY CODES
Þ (Thorn)	Control-K*	Alt-0222
þ (thorn)	Control-L*	Alt-0254

These letters were common in Old English, and are still part of the Icelandic alphabet. Pronounced as the *th* in words such as *thin* and *bath*.

CHARACTER	MAC KEYSTROKES	WINDOWS KEY CODES
Ð (Eth)	Control-A*	Alt-0208
ð (eth)	Control-B*	Alt-0240

These letters were used in Old English writing to represent both the voiced and unvoiced *th*, and in modern Icelandic and in phonetic alphabets to represent the voiced *th*. Pronounced in such words as *then* and *bathe*.

CHARACTER	MAC KEYSTROKES	WINDOWS KEY CODES
Ł (L slash)	Control-C*	Not Available
ł (l slash)	Control-D*	Not Available

This is a common letter in the Polish alphabet, pronounced like a combination between an L and a W, as in the name "Jarasław" (YAH roh swav).

*These characters are not available in all fonts for the Macintosh. And even in those fonts that do contain these characters, not all Macintosh applications permit access to them. See the next section for more detail.

Control Keys on the Macintosh

The key combinations in the charts above that contain the ★ symbol denote characters that appear below ASCII position 32. The Control key (not to be confused with ⌘ or Option keys) lets you type characters in those mysterious positions below position 32. Position 32 is the space character created when you press the Space Bar, and is generally regarded as the first "real" character in a font. In Windows, no characters are located below this position; the Windows operating system forbids it. Though the Mac is not quite so stingy about it, not all font vendors put characters in these positions. Adobe fonts, for instance, do not have characters below position 32 (the slots are empty instead).

Making matters more difficult is the fact that even if the typeface you are using does contain characters at these positions (such as most SoftMaker fonts), many applications do not let you access them. Applications such as HyperCard, for example, refuse to let you access characters with a Control key origin. SimpleText, and Microsoft Word, on the other hand, will let you type *most* of them, and PageMaker will let you type a few of them. This applies to importing documents that might contain these characters as well. The only way to know for sure whether your application lets you type these characters is to try it. Simply hold down the Control key and type one of the characters listed in the charts. Your program will either display the character, beep and do nothing, or do something you might not have expected, such as insert a blank line or backspace over the character immediately preceding the cursor. This is because Control-C, for example, is frequently used by many applications as the equivalent to the Enter or Return key; likewise, Control-H is often equivalent to pressing the Delete key.

One way to avoid these problems is to use a font editor such as Macromedia's Fontographer, or Ares FontMonger to map these characters to locations above ASCII position 32. Both of these programs are available in Windows and Macintosh versions. Fontographer is considerably more powerful than FontMonger, but with a street price of $350, it is also considerably more expensive (FontMonger can be found for under $100).

REARRANGING CHARACTERS WITH FONTMONGER

For the sake of example, say you are laying out an article about the Anglo-Saxon story of Beowulf and Grendel. These stories were originally written in Old English, a language that makes frequent use of the thorn and eth characters. Since these characters are created by typing Control-A, B, K, and L, they aren't accessible in all Mac programs. So we're going to re-map them to different keys using Ares Software Corporation's FontMonger program. (If you're a Windows user, these characters are already easily accessible to you, in which case there is no logical reason for rearranging them. But since FontMonger for the Mac is virtually identical to the Windows version, the following procedure applies if you want to re-map any characters. Just change the example.)

1. Start FontMonger

2. Open the font you want to re-map

Choose Open from the File menu, select the folder or directory where the PostScript outline files or True-Type files are located, and open one. The font appears in a new untitled window resembling a keyboard. Click the modifier keys — Option (⌥), Control (⌃), Shift (⇧), or Caps Lock (⇪) — to display the characters assigned to those keystrokes.

NOTE   Even if you intend to use TrueType fonts, it is better to open and edit the PostScript version if one is available (and all the fonts on the companion CD are available in both formats). Font quality is slightly better if you open a PostScript font and convert it to True-Type, rather than open a TrueType font and save it as

TrueType. What…sense no this to you makes? Well, programs such as FontMonger and Fontographer are basically *PostScript editors*, that is, the PostScript language is their native tongue. So even if you open a TrueType font, these programs will first convert it to PostScript. This means that if you want to save it as TrueType, you will have converted the font twice: once on the way in, and again on the way out. If you open the PostScript font, however, when you save it as TrueType, it is only being converted once. The fewer conversions, the less reduction in quality.

3. Select the character you want to assign to a different key and choose Copy from the Edit menu.

In this example, we want to copy the eth and thorn characters to different keyboard locations, so start with the uppercase eth: first click the ⌃ keycap to display those characters with Control key origins, then click the 'Ð' keycap and choose Copy from the Edit menu.

4. Select the character you want to replace and choose Paste from the Edit menu.

I rarely use the guillemet characters, so I'm going to put the 'Đ' character where the '‹' character normally resides: at Shift-Option-3. To do this, press Shift-Option-3, which selects that character, and then choose Paste from the Edit menu. The character that previously occupied that position is gone, deleted, poof.

5. Repeat Steps 3 and 4 for as many characters as you want to rearrange.

I put the lowercase eth (ð) at Option-3, so I could easily remember that Shift-Option-3 was the uppercase eth. Following this pattern, I copied the lowercase

thorn (þ) to Option-4, and the uppercase thorn (Þ) to Shift-Option-4.

6. Rename the font so as not to overwrite the original.

This is an important step. While nothing will stop you from directly changing the original font, doing so is generally not a good idea. To rename the font, choose Set Font Information from the Options menu, and enter a different name in the Family Name field. In this example, since I am creating a font to use for setting text in Old English, I renamed my font to "BergamoOE."

7. Build a new font.

This is the step that actually creates the PostScript or TrueType files you will later install and use. Choose Build Font from the File menu and enter a name for the font. This will be the name of the suitcase file, not the PostScript outline file or the TrueType file itself (the name you entered in the Set Font Information dialog box determines that). Next select the format— PostScript Type 1 or TrueType—and save the font. If you're a Windows user, you of course don't have to worry about things like "suitcase" files, but you will want to save your font with a unique filename.

8. Save the FontMonger file.

This step saves your changes in a FontMonger database so you won't have to open the original font, change its family info, and so on, if you later decide you want to make additional edits or rearrange other characters, for example.

9. Repeat Steps 1 through 8 for each member of the typeface family.

For example, you need to do this if you want to create bold, italic, and bold-italic weights of your edited font: open the bold weight of the original font, rearrange the characters, change the family name, build and save; do the same thing with the italic, and so on.

10. Install the new fonts in your system.

If you're a Mac user, you might first want to combine the different suitcase files (the normal, bold, italic, and bold-italic suitcases) into a single suitcase file. Although this is not necessary, it makes font file management easier if you are using programs like Master-Juggler or Suitcase. To do this, select the bold, italic, and bold-italic suitcases, and drag them onto the normal suitcase.

Now that the thorns and eths are in place, I can set my Old English text:

> Ða cōm of mōre   under misthleoþum
> Grendel gongan   Godes yrre bær;
> mynte se mānscaða   manna cynnes
> sumne besyrwan   in seþe lām hēan.
>
> …Ne wæs þæt forma sið.
>
> Translation:
>
> Then came from the moor, under cover of darkness
> Grendel, moving. God's wrath he bore.
> The evil-doer intended, to the race of man,
> Some trap in the great hall.
>
> …Nor was that the first time.

Notice the macron vowels, that is, the vowels with the line above them. The macron is part of a normal Mac font, but to use it requires some radical negative kerning, a process you simply can't do in some word processing programs such as Microsoft Word—although programs such as QuarkXPress and Page-Maker make this a snap. So I altered my base font using FontMonger and created the macron vowels ā ē ī ō ū and ȳ.

After starting FontMonger, open the font you want to create macron characters for, and then:

1. Copy the letter you want to create a macron for to a different character position.

In this example, start with the lowercase letter 'a'. Press the A key on your keyboard to select the character, then choose Copy from the Edit menu. Select the character position you want for the new character, and choose Paste from the Edit menu. This will replace any character currently occupying that position. For this reason, you may want to create a new font (just choose New from the File menu) and copy the characters to the same positions they occupy in the original font. For example, open your base font, copy the lowercase 'a', create a new font and paste the 'a' to the 'a' character in the new font. You'll probably then want to name this new font "Times Macron," or something along those lines to distinguish it from the original (in this case "Times").

2. Go to the macron character (Sh-Op-comma) and double-click it to open its window.

3. Select the pen tool.

4. Choose Select All from the Edit menu, and then choose Copy to copy the outline of the macron character to the Clipboard.

    Be sure to copy just the outlines of the macron, not the entire character position as you did in Step 1; the pen tool must first be selected before you can do this.

5. Go to the key where you copied the letter 'a' in Step 1 and double-click it.

6. Select the pen tool, and choose Paste. The macron is inserted in the window along with the outline of the letter 'a'.

7. Position the macron relative to the letter.

    When you paste the macron, its vertical position should already be correct (for lowercase characters), but you need to optically center it horizontally. The easiest way to do this is to use the left and right cursor keys immediately after pasting it, that is, while it's still selected.

8. Follow the steps in the previous example to build, save, and install the font. ■

*Ligatures and
Expert Set
Characters*

Ligatures and Expert Set Characters

130-pt. Bergamo

130-pt. Bergamo Expert

LIGATURES ARE CHARACTERS MADE UP OF TWO OR MORE characters, usually the lowercase letter *f* in conjunction with other characters that might ordinarily collide with the *f's* overhang. The most common ligatures are made using the characters *fi* and *fl*.

flyfish **flyfish** flyfish
flyfish **flyfish** flyfish

The top row contains regular alphabetic characters. The bottom row contains fi and fl ligatures. This is often an improvement with many typefaces, but a waste of time with others, such as most sans serif typefaces.

As you can see from these examples, some fonts, especially Oldstyle designs, look considerably better when ligatures are used. Consider using ligatures with these fonts: Bembo (on the companion CD as *Bergamo*) Caslon, Garamond, Baskerville, Bodoni, and Clarendon. Some fonts where ligatures are available but not necessarily required are Sabon (on the companion CD as *Savoy*), URW Palladio, and most of the sans serifs such as Helvetica, Arial, and Futura (*Function*). With these sans serif typefaces, the ligatures appear the same as the standard characters, so there is no benefit to using them. Gill Sans (below), however, is one of the few sans serif typefaces where you might want to consider using ligatures. Avoid using ligatures with Courier, Letter Gothic, or any other fixed-width font.

flyfish
flyfish

On the Macintosh, the two ligatures *fi* and *fl* are part of the normal character set, and are available in most fonts by pressing Shift-Option-5 and Shift-Option-6. In Windows, however, they are contained in *expert font sets* because the Windows encoding scheme does not let you access ligatures directly, really an unexplainable oversight on the part of whoever designed this aspect of the Windows operating system. Even though the ligatures are present in the font, you would have to open the font with a program such as Fontographer or FontMonger, copy the ligatures into character positions that Windows recognizes (consequently replacing characters that already exist in those positions), and regenerate the font (I discuss how to do this at the end of Chapter 5).

Should I always use ligatures whenever possible?

No. Ligatures are generally only effective at text sizes, that is, at point sizes in the range of 8 to 14 points. And you should avoid using ligatures at all in letterspaced type (text whose spacing has been expanded or condensed). This is because the space between the characters that comprise a ligature will always be the same, so if you increase or decrease the amount of space between other characters, the ligatures will stand out. In the following example, the text on top was typed without using ligatures. But notice the difference when the text is letterspaced. The ligatures are completely inappropriate. (And so is the letterspacing, which has been exaggerated here for the purposes of illustration. Egads, don't space text like this!)

The fish flop effusively on the soft office floor, unafflicted by our affinity for offtrack betting.

The fish flop effusively on the soft office floor, unafflicted by our affinity for offtrack betting.

Ligatures should not be used with letterspaced type.

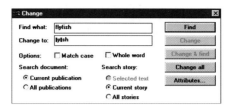

Many applications let you enter ligatures in dialog boxes, but don't properly display them. Be careful to enter the correct character.

Ligatures make for fine typography, and are truly the mark of a sophisticated user (and if you have a name like Griffith or Hoeffler, for example, they're simply too inviting not to use). But there are some drawbacks to using them: Most word processors and page layout programs do not have spelling checkers sophisticated enough to identify ligatures, and will always flag words containing them as misspelled.

If you're using the *fi* and *fl* ligatures available in standard, that is, non-expert, typefaces on the Mac, searching and replacing text can also be a bit more of a chore. This is because the dialog boxes these programs display often use built-in system fonts that make entering ligatures difficult: the system font itself does not contain ligatures, so it represents them as rectangles. It will search and replace the correct characters, but the dialog box display is confusing nonetheless — you're never sure if you've entered the correct character to search or replace. Some programs such as Nisus Writer for the Macintosh overcome this limitation and display the correct characters in dialog boxes.

The expert set typefaces provided on the companion CD contain several additional ligatures not available in the regular, non-expert typefaces. The expert fonts contain the *fi* and *fl* ligatures as well, and if you're a Windows user, this is the best way to access these characters.

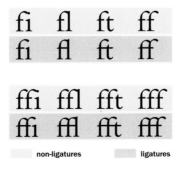

non-ligatures   ligatures

'F'-ligatures are the most common

The following ligatures are available in the expert set fonts provided on the companion CD. Other characters are available as well (for example, fractions, inferior and superior numerals, and foreign currency symbols) in addition to the ligatures shown here and are discussed in the section, "Using Expert Set Typefaces."

LIGATURE	SOFTMAKER EXPERT	ADOBE EXPERT
fi	Semicolon	Sh-W
fl	Sh-comma	Sh-X
ff	Sh-semicolon	Sh-V
ft	=	n/a*
ffi	Sh-/	SH-Y
ffl	Sh-2	Sh-Z
fft	Sh-A	n/a*
fff	Sh-period	n/a*

* These ligatures are generally not available in Adobe Expert Sets.

I don't know why or when you might need to use the ligature fff—in fact, I can not think of a single word in English that has three consecutive *f*s…Pfff perhaps? But it's there, just in case. If you or anyone you know ever comes upon such a word (no made-up ones now), please contact me via e-mail to let me know and I'll send you a free typeface or something.

Non-English Ligatures

There are other ligatures that are not made up of the letter *f*, and whose use is generally restricted to non-English languages: German, French, Dutch, and Norwegian, for example. These ligatures differ from f-ligatures in that they represent two characters that are always pronounced as one, such as the ß (*eszett*, or

double s) in German, the œ and Œ (*ethel*) in French, and the Norwegian and Danish æ and Æ (*æsc*)

These characters are part of most normal fonts (you don't need expert fonts to access them), and can be created using the following key combinations:

LIGATURE	MACINTOSH	WINDOWS
ß	Op-S	Alt-0223
œ	Op-Q	Alt-0156
Œ	Sh-Op-Q	Alt-0140
æ	Op-'	Alt-0230
Æ	Sh-Op-'	Alt-0198

The expert set typefaces contain a few more non-English ligatures, such as the Dutch ij, or the ŋ (eng) ligature commonly used in linguistics and lexicography (or the Sami language, although a true uppercase ŋ is not available).

LIGATURE	SOFTMAKER EXPERT	ADOBE EXPERT
ij	Sh-`	n/a
ŋ	]	n/a
ŋ	\	n/a

AMPERSANDS

You probably didn't realize it, but even the ampersand (&) is a ligature of sorts. It has been highly stylized in various typefaces, but it is a contraction of the Latin word for *and*: et. This is generally more recognizable when the ampersand is italicized. In the typeface Bembo, the italicized ampersand clearly resembles the contraction of an uppercase 'E' and a lowercase 't'.

Some common ampersands

The first ampersand belongs to the typeface Caslon. Pretty basic stuff. The other ampersands are from the italics of Baskerville, Garamond, Bergamo, and URW Palladio. I almost always use italicized ampersands rather than regular ones, in both ordinary text and display sizes. The italic versions are simply classier; adding them to regular text is like wearing an imaginative tie with a conservative suit.

Casady & Greene
Casady *&* Greene

To use italic ampersands within normal text, simply type the ampersand character (Shift-7), select it, and italicize it from your application's Font menu or dialog box.

USING EXPERT SET TYPEFACES

Expert sets are typefaces that contain additional characters — ligatures, fractions, inferior and superior numerals, and some international currency symbols — not normally available in the standard typefaces. An expert set typeface is a subset of a standard typeface, thus each expert set typeface *belongs* to a corresponding standard typeface. In other words, you probably wouldn't use an expert set font by itself (unless you were just setting fractions in a document). Garamond Expert, for example, is really only useful if you are using Garamond. This is because the expert sets do not contain the normal keyboard or alphabetic characters, so if you typed your name in an expert set font, it wouldn't look anything like your name ("Sean Cavanaugh" looks like "$_1$ma$\frac{1}{3}$ ^{1}a$\frac{1}{6}$a$\frac{1}{3}$a$\frac{4}{5}$or") when typed in an expert set font).

They are called "expert sets" because such characters were traditionally used only in fine typography, or for very specific typesetting needs, by professional typesetters (book designers and printers for example). And for the majority of the documents you create, you probably will have no need for them.

So who needs 'em then?

Well, some people just love using f-ligatures — and the expert sets contain several of them — but the expert sets also contain several fraction characters. So if you will be setting text with numbers requiring fractions, you may find the expert sets quite useful. For example, if you are setting stock quotes, the fractions and numerals contained in expert sets are more appropriate and easier to set than using the keyboard numerals found in standard fonts. Compare the following:

Stock	**Close**	**Chg**
SquidCo	37 1/2	-7/8
SquidCo	37½	-⅞

Compare the expert fractions in the second row to the standard numerals in the first.

The first line was set by typing numerals from a standard font, and making fractions by typing a number, followed by a slash, followed by the second number. There are several drawbacks to this method: you must enter a space before the fraction, or it will be unclear as to what number you are actually representing (is 371/2, for example, thirty-seven and one-half, or three-hundred seventy-one divided by two?). It also doesn't look very good.

The second line was created using fractions from an expert set font. The fraction can be preceded by a space, or not... either way is acceptable because the fraction is clearly distinct from the number.

The following fractions are available in expert set fonts. Note that the expert set fonts provided on the companion CD use a different character encoding scheme than that used by Adobe. For the most part, the same characters are available (the SoftMaker expert fonts contain a few more characters), but the two encoding schemes assign them to different keys on your keyboard. Typing the M key, for example, while using a SoftMaker expert font will create the fraction one-half (½). To create the same character in a font that uses Adobe Expert Encoding, you would type Shift-H.

FRACTION	SOFTMAKER EXPERT	ADOBE EXPERT
¾	Q	Sh-I
⅚	W	n/a
⅕	R	n/a
⅗	T	n/a
⅜	Y	Sh-K
⅔	O	Sh-O
¼	P	Sh-G
⅖	S	n/a
1⁄1	L	n/a
⅝	Z	Sh-L
⅛	X	Sh-J
⅙	V	n/a
⅓	N	n/a
½	M	Sh-H
⅞	Sh-[	n/a

You can create other fractions from expert sets using inferior and superior numerals separated by a fraction bar. For example, say you wanted to create a fraction for three-sixteenths. Using one of the SoftMaker expert set fonts on the companion CD, you would type Shift-E to create a superior three, then Shift-backslash to create the solidus, followed by Shift-S and Shift-X to create the inferior sixteen:

3⁄16

The following superior and inferior numerals are available in the expert set fonts provided on the companion CD:

SUPERIOR NUMERAL (NUMERATOR)	SOFTMAKER EXPERT
0	Sh-B
1	Sh-C
2	Sh-D
3	Sh-E
4	Sh-F
5	Sh-G
6	Sh-H
7	Sh-I
8	Sh-J
9	Sh-K

INFERIOR NUMERAL (DENOMINATOR)	SOFTMAKER EXPERT
0	Sh-R
1	Sh-S
2	Sh-T
3	Sh-U
4	Sh-V
5	Sh-W
6	Sh-X
7	Sh-Y
8	Sh-Z
9	[

Inferior and superior numerals are available in Adobe Expert fonts in the same locations as standard keyboard numerals, but you must type Option–number to create an inferior numeral, and Shift–Option–number to create a superior number. The fraction bar in an Adobe Expert font is created by typing the standard slash character.

The slash, or *virgule*, character located on your keyboard is really intended for use as a separator and is commonly used for entering dates, addresses, and phone numbers. The fraction bar, or *solidus*, is available in expert set fonts by typing Shift–Backslash. It is also available in most Macintosh fonts by typing Shift–Option-1 (sorry Windows users…the fraction bar is not part of the Windows character set, so you will have to use the expert set fonts to create this character).

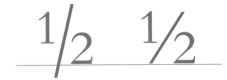

Compare the slash character on the left to the fraction bar on the right. The fraction bar is not quite as long as the slash, and its angle is considerably less steep (the fraction bar is just under 60 degrees, while the slash is just under 80 degrees).

Creating fractions without expert sets

Even if you don't have expert set fonts, you can still create attractive fractions by noodling with font size and superscript values. If you're a Mac user, you will need a font with a fraction bar. Most have them, and are available by pressing Shift–Option-1. Unfortunately the fraction bar is not part of the Windows character set, so Windows users will have to try this procedure using the slash character.

1. Type the integer part of the number, and note the point size. In this example, the integer is 24 points. I'm using a large point size for illustration purposes, but this works for smaller point sizes too.

7

2. Type the numerator (the top number of the fraction), followed by the fraction bar (Shift-Option-1), followed by the denominator.

73⁄8

3. Select the numerator and reduce its point size by a factor of 50%. In this example, the point size is 24, so change the size of the numerator to 12 points if you are using Microsoft Word (Windows or Mac). If you are using a program such as WordExpress for Windows (available on the companion CD), or PageMaker, there is no need to change the point size, a feature I discuss below.

7₃⁄8

4. With the numerator still selected, superscript it by 33% of the original point size. One-third of 24 is 8 points, so if you are using Microsoft Word 5.1 for the Macintosh, open the Character dialog box, click Superscript, and set the "By" amount to 8 pt. If you are using Word 6.0 for Windows, open the Font dialog box, but do not choose the Superscript option—instead, click the Character Spacing tab, choose "Raised" from the Position menu, and set

the "By" amount to 8 points. The concept here is the same as the Mac version.

7³⁄8

5. Now select the denominator, and reduce its size by 50%: in this example, 12 points. Voilà.

7³⁄₈

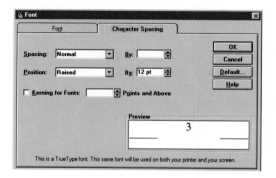

Word 6.0 for Windows Font dialog box with values for raising the numerator.

Programs such as PageMaker (the Mac and Windows versions are virtually identical) and WordExpress for Windows handle the whole superscript/subscript thing much more elegantly than does Microsoft Word. I'll explain PageMaker's method first:

To create nice looking fractions in PageMaker, format the numerator part of the fraction by setting the position to "Superscript" in the Type Specifications dialog box, and then clicking the "Options…" button and changing the "Super/subscript size" to 50%. Page-Maker sets the superscript position to 33.3% by default, so there is no need to change this value. To format the denominator, set its position to "Subscript" and change the "Subscript position" value to 0%.

Type options

Small caps size:	70	% of point size
Super/subscript size:	50	% of point size
Superscript position:	33.3	% of point size
Subscript position:	0	% of point size
Baseline shift:	0	points ● Up ○ Down

OK
Cancel

PageMaker's Type Option dialog box is where you set
the parameters for creating fractions.

WordExpress handles super- and subscripting in much the same fashion as PageMaker, but rather than changing the superscript position to 33%, you should change it to 20%. The two programs apparently measure from different positions when determining the placement of superscript characters. You still set the subscript position to 0%, however.

WordExpress character dialog box with values
entered for superscript position

The benefit to the PageMaker and WordExpress way of doing things is that you never have to change the numerator's or denominator's point size — you are only changing percentage values — so you can select the entire number (integer and fraction) and change its point size in one shot. The numerator and denominator will be re-sized automatically. In other words, the whole fraction could be set to 24 points, for example, yet the numerator and denominator would be half as large as the surrounding text. If you changed the point size of all your text to 12 points, the fraction would be changed to 6 points without you having to do so manually. Using the Microsoft Word method, however, you would have to twiddle the point size as well as the superscript values whenever you changed the size of the surrounding text.

Try-out versions of PageMaker, WordExpress, and Nisus Writer are available on the companion CD. ■

CHAPTER 7

The Rules of Digital Typography

The Rules of Digital Typography

I HATE THE WORD "RULES." IT CONVEYS A DEGREE OF authoritarianism that really annoys me. Perhaps "guidelines" would be a better word, but there are some things in typography that you really ought not-a do, and some other things you really oughta do; "guidelines" doesn't quite capture the essence here. So I'll call these things rules. Grudgingly and hesitatingly.

The goal of these "rules" is to create good-looking documents that bespeak the professionalism and attention to detail that went into creating them. Does that make it sound as if these things are a reflection on you? Well guess what? They are! Perhaps it isn't fair to judge ideas (and the presenter of those ideas) by the presentation, but life isn't fair and this is just one of those things we have to accept.

Fortunately, following these rules doesn't take much more time than ignoring them. And there are many benefits:

1. Your documents will look great

2. People will think you really know a lot about computers and software

3. People will admire your artistic talents

There's also at least one drawback I feel I must warn you about:

▶ People will ask you for help creating their own documents. (Assuming you don't have the time, what with your busy schedule and all, just tell them to buy a copy of this book. You'll thank me later.)

The rules of setting type fall into two basic categories: (1) those you should follow at all times, and (2) those you should follow if you have enough time. This decision is dependent on the software you are using, and its level of sophistication and control over text. Category One rules can be followed on just about any Macintosh or Windows word processing or Desktop Publishing package. I'll discuss them first.

1 *Insert only a single space after all punctuation.*

If you grew up prior to the advent of desktop publishing, chances are you were taught to put two spaces after periods, question marks, exclamation marks, and colons. The rationale was that it is easier for the eye to distinguish sentences in this fashion; when using monospaced fonts (read: typewriter fonts), there might be some validity to this. But this only applied to documents created with a typewriter. Since the advent of the printing press in the 15th century, typesetters have never inserted two spaces after punctuation. As far as I can tell, the practice of inserting two spaces between sentences originated with high school typing teachers. It sure didn't originate in the world of typography. I've heard the technique referred to as the "French method," and despite their admiration for Jerry Lewis, I doubt even the French would adopt such a method. When preparing text for printing, regardless of the font, use only one space after all punctuation. There are no exceptions to this.

Well, except one. While not necessary, it is acceptable and often more readable when composing e-mail (text that will be read online and not printed) to insert two spaces after periods, question and exclamation marks, and colons. See Chapter 8 for an introduction to e-mail typography.

Last summer, a Mr. Norris was drinking in a bar in
San Francisco. It was Sunday night and he'd had six
or seven. Turning to the guy on the next stool, he
said, "What are you up to."

Last summer, a Mr. Norris was drinking in a bar in
San Francisco. It was Sunday night and he'd had six
or seven. Turning to the guy on the next stool, he
said, "What are you up to."

Studies have shown that two spaces is approximately one too many.

2 *Use proper em and en dashes where appropriate.*

Also a throwback to the days of typewriters, two
hyphens--like these--were used to make a dash
because true dash characters are not available on a typewriter. But this is a major no-no in typesetting and
desktop publishing, where *em dashes* — like these —
should be used instead. An em is a unit of measure
equal to the point size you are using. For example,
using 10-point type, an em dash would be approximately 10 points (≈ 0.14 inches) wide, but this is dependent on the individual typeface. Actually, this is
probably the widest it would be. Many typefaces have
em dashes that are slightly narrower than a full em, but
still considerably wider than a hyphen.

Fiction--if it all aspires to be art--appeals to temperament.

Fiction—if it all aspires to be art—appeals to temperament.

Em dashes always look better than two hyphens.

Hyphens are used to hyphenate words and separate
phone numbers. They should never be used as dashes.
A dash, more specifically, an em dash, is a form of
punctuation used to offset clauses in a sentence.

An *en dash* is typically half the length of an em dash
(sometimes slightly wider than half, depending on the
typeface) but still longer than a hyphen. En dashes are
primarily used to denote duration, as in 8:00–5:00, or
August 12–14, or Aardvark–Adelaide. Some people use
them to separate phone numbers, but I think they are
too large and look awkward for this. Compare the en
dash in the first example to the hyphens in the second:

505–466–0649
505-466-0649

The hyphens appear much more natural. We are
used to seeing phone numbers represented in this fashion. Some people avoid the hyphen vs. en dash question altogether by using periods or spaces to separate
phone numbers:

505.466.0649
505 466 0649

The period is preferable to the space, but this is
purely a matter of personal taste. Phone numbers
separated by spaces are quite common in Europe,
less so in the U.S.

When creating em and en dashes, you can add
space before and after the dash — or not. I prefer to
add either a small amount of space (usually via the
application's kerning commands), or no space at all.
Page layout programs such as Adobe PageMaker
and QuarkXPress let you adjust space between
characters at a micro level (i.e., kerning), as do

illustration programs such as Illustrator and FreeHand, but many word processors are limited in this regard and only allow you to add space via the Space Bar. The normal space created with the Space Bar seems a bit too wide for my tastes, but you may find it acceptable. Generally speaking, the wider the column of text, the more space you can insert before and after dashes (up to a full space). In a typical word processed document such as a memo or letter, for example, where your column width might be as great as 5 or 6 inches, inserting a normal space before and after a dash looks just fine. But in a document with narrower columns, say a newsletter with three columns of text, this much space will stand out, and your dashes will resemble diving boards. In this case, I would suggest adding no space at all, and simply use the program's kerning commands (if available) to tweak the space as necessary.

In PageMaker, press the Cmd key in conjunction with the Left and Right Arrow keys to decrease and increase kerning (the amount of space between characters) respectively. Hold down the Shift and Cmd keys if you want to increase or decrease kerning in smaller units. In QuarkXPress, press Cmd-Shift in conjunction with the Left and Right Bracket keys to kern text. Hold down the Cmd, Shift, and Option keys if you want to kern in smaller units. In PageMaker, a value of about 0.1 should suffice; in QuarkXPress, consider a value of about 20 before and after a dash.

If you do add a full space by pressing the Space Bar, it is important to add it before and after the dash. Sometimes people will add a space after a dash to break a line. Then, if they edit the text or change the layout, the dash — with a space after it but no space before — will appear rather awkward looking.

To create an em dash in most Mac applications, press Shift-Option-hyphen. To create an en dash, press Option-hyphen.

To create an em dash in most Windows applications, press Alt-0151. To create an en dash, press Alt-0150.

Some expert font sets contain a three-quarter em dash, but in reality, most em dashes are about this wide anyway. That is, most em dashes are not one em in width, and depend on the individual typeface. The three-quarter em dash can be substituted for the em dash — the two are interchangeable, in fact — but is too wide to be used when you would normally use an en dash.

It is also acceptable to use an en dash instead of an em dash to set off clauses in text. I don't like the practice, but it's not incorrect to do so. If you do substitute en dashes, consider adding space before and after them.

3 *Use true quotation marks and apostrophes.*

Quotation marks and apostrophes you enter directly from your keyboard by typing ' and " (Shift+') are not really quotation marks, but rather hash marks (or tick marks). It's okay to use them to represent feet and inches (e.g., "I have a 9'6" Walden surfboard."), but using them as quotation marks sends the message "I don't really care how this stuff looks." Like double spacing between sentences and using hyphens as dashes, using tick marks instead of curly quotes (also called typographer's quotation marks) is the calling card of a DTP amateur.

"This is a beautiful creek," he said. "It reminds me of Evangeline's hearing aid."

"This is a beautiful creek," he said. "It reminds me of Evangeline's hearing aid."

True quotes and apostrophes should be used in place of tick marks whenever possible.

Fortunately, most DTP applications and word processors made within the past few years give you the option of automatically substituting curly quotes when you type the ' and " characters. This feature is referred to as *Smart Quotes.* I use it in all my applications that offer it as an option (Word, PageMaker, and Quark-XPress). Typing the ' and " characters is much easier than typing Alt-0147 or Cmd-Shift-Bracket, for example.

Punctuation Inside vs. Outside Quotation Marks

There is some debate amongst the various style guides as to whether to place punctuation inside or outside quotation marks…and whether to use single or double quotes. The American standard is to place all punctuation (commas, periods, question marks, etc.) inside the quotation marks. The British standard is to place them on the outside. The Brits generally use single quotes in place of double quotes too, but this can pose some minor unsightliness if the text you are quoting ends with a contraction. For example:

'Jack thought we shouldn't'.

See how that 't' is just kind of stranded out there? The problem is further compounded by placing punc-

tuation on the outside. The American method offers an improvement:

"Jack thought we shouldn't."

It's not a show-stopper as problems go, but the American system is a bit more clear. Sometimes I balk at placing punctuation inside the quotation marks. Especially if the punctuation is not part of the material being quoted. Consider:

Was it you who stated so emphatically "Macs are better than PCs. Period?"

Obviously that question mark was not part of the quote—or was it?—but if we strictly adhere to the rule of placing punctuation within quotation marks, we do so at the expense of clarity (which, in my book anyway, is sort of a license to break rules). In this case, I would consider:

Was it you who stated so emphatically "Macs are better than PCs. Period."?

Again, on purely aesthetic grounds, I prefer the American standard. It poses fewer problems on average, but from a typographical standpoint, the rule here is: be consistent. If you like using single quotation marks in place of double quotation marks, make sure you don't switch to double quotation marks in the middle of the document.

Use a closed single quotation mark for apostrophes, such as *can't, Sean's,* or *'tis.* It's amazing the number of signs, brochures, direct mail pieces, advertisements and other "professional" documents that don't follow this rule, using instead the typewriter tick marks.

You create quotation marks with the following keystrokes:

CHARACTER	MAC	WINDOWS
'	Op-]	Alt-0145
'	Sh-Op-]	Alt-0146
"	Op-[	Alt-0147
"	Sh-Op-[	Alt-0148

So what are those ' and " characters?

It is okay to use these characters to represent feet and inches (1' = 12") or minutes and seconds of arc (60' = 360" = 1° of arc) but better substitutes are available. Using them requires the Symbol font, which is available on most Macintosh and Windows systems. First select the Symbol font, and then enter the following:

CHARACTER	MAC	WINDOWS
′ (feet, minutes)	Op-4	Alt-0162
″ (inches, seconds)	Op-Comma	Alt-0178

Compare:

1' = 12"   1′ = 12″

These marks are also known as *primes*. When using them (especially the standard upright ones which are available in any font), consider adding a bit of space between the number and the prime with your application's kerning commands. If such commands are not an option (as is the case in many word processors), you'll have to leave them unspaced. I wouldn't recommend adding a whole space by pressing the Space Bar, as this will be too much. The primes available in the Symbol font don't need extra spacing in most cases.

4 *Use a smaller point size for all-uppercase text.*

When entering all-uppercase letters such as titles, acronyms, initials, and other capitalized text passages—WYSIWYG, BMWRA, USA, or any string of text made up of two or more capital letters—use a point size that is slightly smaller than the surrounding text. Otherwise, your capitals will SCREAM at the reader. In this paragraph, the text is 10-point, so I set the uppercase text to 8.5 points. Of course it depends on the typeface, but generally a reduction of 1–1.5 points is sufficient for text 11 points and smaller. A 2-pt or greater reduction may be necessary for text larger than 12 points.

To see how well your CAPITALIZED text looks when you reduce its size, print it and turn the page upside down. It should blend in. If not, consider reducing the size a little more.

The BMW Riders Association (BMWRA) is an organization dedicated to owners of BMW motorcylces.

The BMW Riders Association (BMWRA) is an organization dedicated to owners of BMW motorcylces.

Can you see which capital letters blend better with the surrounding text?

Many programs have a formatting option called *Small Caps,* which creates a capital letter that is about 70–80% the size of the surrounding text. Unless you can adjust the setting (and in applications such as

PageMaker and QuarkXPress you can), I think this is a tad too small. Just like you don't want to draw attention to text that is too big, you also don't want to draw attention to text that is too small. An optimal size for small caps is somewhere in the range of 80–90% of the size of the surrounding text.

Another option is to use true small caps, if they are in fact available. Many of the fonts on the companion CD, for example, have matching small caps. But I often use small cap fonts for titles only, and not for capitalized text within normal text. Of course, you can use true small caps in such a fashion, and for fine typography you should. It's easier, however, to type text from the regular font in all uppercase and then select it and reduce its point size, than it is to change to the small cap font, type the text, and then change it back to the regular font. There's also the added benefit of using fewer fonts (the fewer fonts in a document, the quicker it will print).

Compare the following four paragraphs. The first paragraph was set using Garamond 9-point with no size reduction and no additional letter spacing for the text in all caps. The second paragraph is set using Garamond 9-point with Garamond Small Caps 9-point. Both typefaces are set to the same size, but Garamond Small Caps looks a bit too small. The third paragraph is Garamond 9-point, but the capitalized text was reduced to 6.5 points (except for the initial 'T'). This creates an interesting look, but notice how different it is from the true small caps in the 2nd and 4th paragraphs. The capitalized text appears slightly condensed. The final paragraph is set using Garamond 9-point with Garamond Small Caps 9.5-point.

THIS IS A BEAUTIFUL LIBRARY, timed perfectly, lush and American. The hour is midnight and the library is deep and carried like a dreaming child into the darkness of these pages.

THIS IS A BEAUTIFUL LIBRARY, timed perfectly, lush and American. The hour is midnight and the library is deep and carried like a dreaming child into the darkness of these pages.

THIS IS A BEAUTIFUL LIBRARY, timed perfectly, lush and American. The hour is midnight and the library is deep and carried like a dreaming child into the darkness of these pages.

THIS IS A BEAUTIFUL LIBRARY, timed perfectly, lush and American. The hour is midnight and the library is deep and carried like a dreaming child into the darkness of these pages.

Can you tell which paragraphs are set with true small caps?

If you combine a true small caps typeface with the normal typeface within text, you may need to increase the size of the small cap slightly (just a half a point in the above example made quite a noticeable difference.)

5 *Add letterspacing to capitalized text and small caps.*

Letterspacing refers to the amount of space between letters in a word. Normal body text ordinarily needs no additional letterspacing beyond that which is built into the fonts. Capitalized text or small caps appearing within normal text can appear too tight and crowded compared to the surrounding text, and really needs to be loosened up a bit. Programs such as PageMaker, QuarkXPress and Illustrator, for example, refer to this letterspacing as *tracking*, and it should be set to a positive value for capitalized text. In PageMaker and Illustrator, consider setting the tracking to a value of 20 or so. In QuarkXPress, try a value of about 2 or 3 (obviously

Oldstyle figures are only available for some fonts, and are almost never present in standard typefaces. On the companion CD, for example, oldstyle figures are available in all fonts labeled "Small Caps" or containing the name "SC+OsF." This naming convention is more or less common practice with other vendors such as Adobe and Monotype as well. Oldstyle figures are rarely available in TrueType format (although the fonts with oldstyle figures on the companion CD are available in both TrueType and PostScript). This is not the case with QuickDraw GX fonts, however, which contain oldstyle figures as part of the standard font. Of course, to date, QDGX is only available on the Macintosh, where it has so far only experienced modest acceptance at best.

we're talking different measurement systems in these programs, but the results are about the same).

Most word processors don't handle this as elegantly as page layout and illustration programs. Word 5.1 for the Macintosh, for example, lets you *expand* text as opposed to tracking it, but this can be problematic. The tracking features in the programs mentioned above adjust automatically to compensate if you decide to change the point size. Word's expand setting, on the other hand, is a fixed value entered in points, so the amount of space it adds is the same regardless whether your text is 10 points or 100 points. There are exceptions to this: Nisus Writer offers tracking to letterspace text. If your word processor doesn't have a tracking command, you should leave the text as is. Don't add letterspacing by typing the Space Bar between letters. This adds way too much space.

6 *Use oldstyle figures when available and where appropriate.*

Oldstyle figures are also known as non-lining numerals. The term *non-lining* is used because the numerals do not all line up on the baseline as do regular, or *lining*, numerals. In this regard, it might help to think of oldstyle figures as lowercase numbers. Oldstyle figures, like lowercase letters, contain characters that descend below the baseline. Uppercase letters, on the other hand, as well as lining numerals, do not descend below the baseline. The regular numbers available in fonts, just like uppercase alphabetic characters, are aligned to the baseline. Think of these numbers as uppercase numbers.

0123456789   0123456789

0123456789   0123456789

The numerals on the left are the standard lining numerals found in fonts. Notice how each character sits above the baseline. Those on the right are oldstyle, or non-lining, numerals.

ABCDEFG123456789
abcdefg123456789

Non-lining numbers are better substitutes than lining numbers in most text situations, that is, in passages of text where numbers, dates, and dollar amounts, for example, are intermixed, but lining numbers should be used when mixing numbers with all-uppercase text. Use non-lining numbers with small caps, however.

ABCDEFG123456789

I use non-lining numerals to such a degree that I have swapped the normal numbers with those from the small caps and oldstyle figures sets (using Macromedia's Fontographer) for many of the typefaces I use on a regular basis. I then copy the lining figures to the SC+OsF fonts. Doing this in Fontographer is relatively easy, although you will have to adjust kerning as necessary.

the continuity of your text. I once heard someone describe paragraphs containing boldface text as looking like chocolate chip cookies. And that's an apt description. Bold words stand out like little chocolate bits. Bold text is best used in headings, captions, logos or sometimes at the start of a paragraph as a stylistic device. In place of bold, consider using italics for emphasis. Italics blend in more smoothly with surrounding text, yet clearly indicate emphatic stress. Or simply write in such a way that the emphasis is apparent without having to rely on font or style changes (easier *said* than done, he said, with a flick of the Italic command).

Reserve boldface for items that can be set entirely in bold, and avoid mixing with normal, or non-boldface, text.

I used Fontographer to copy the Oldstyle numerals from the Small Caps font to the standard font (as well as to copy the standard numerals to the Small Cap font). After regenerating the font and installing it, the oldstyle numbers are available without first having to choose the Small Cap font.

7 *Use a slightly smaller point size for numbers (when Oldstyle numerals are not available).*

The reason here is the same as that regarding capitalized text. By entering numbers in a slightly smaller point size (85–90%) of the surrounding text, they blend in better and don't jump at the reader.

In 1492 Columbus sailed the ocean blue.
In 1492 Columbus sailed the ocean blue.

8 *Use boldface text sparingly.*

Avoid the temptation to use boldface text to emphasize words within a passage of text. Bold text is like a **magnet** to our eyes, and if used incorrectly, ruins

In memory of **Charley J. Langer**, District Forest Ranger, Challis National Forest, Pilot Captain **Billy Kelly** and Co-Pilot **Arthur A. Crofts**, of the U.S. Army killed in an airplane crash April 5, 1943, near this point while searching for survivors of an Army bomber crew.

In memory of *Charley J. Langer*, District Forest Ranger, Challis National Forest, Pilot Captain *Billy Kelly* and Co-Pilot *Arthur A. Crofts*, of the U.S. Army killed in an airplane crash April 5, 1943, near this point while searching for survivors of an Army bomber crew.

Bold face text within normal text provides too much emphasis.

9 *Avoid using underlined text.*

Even more distracting than boldface text is underlined text, which is a typographic <u>abomination</u> that should be avoided. Back in the days of typewriters, underlining was the accepted, if not only way to add emphasis. Unfortunately, this carried over into the design of operating systems, explaining why we have Underline commands under our Format menus when we never use the feature. When typesetting, underlined text is only used in special situations such as financial or academic publications. It is also common in the design of web pages.

Underlined text was used in this book—gasp!—to distinguish an item selected from a list. Check out the manner in which the decorative fonts are presented in Chapter 11.

In memory of <u>Charley J. Langer</u>, District Forest Ranger, Challis National Forest, Pilot Captain <u>Billy Kelly</u> and Co-Pilot <u>Arthur A. Crofts</u>, of the U.S. Army killed in an airplane crash April 5, 1943, near this point while searching for survivors of an Army bomber crew.

In memory of *Charley J. Langer*, District Forest Ranger, Challis National Forest, Pilot Captain *Billy Kelly* and Co-Pilot *Arthur A. Crofts*, of the U.S. Army killed in an airplane crash April 5, 1943, near this point while searching for survivors of an Army bomber crew.

Underlined text is nearly as unsightly as bold face.

10 *The © (copyright), ® (registered trademark), and ™ (trademark) characters almost always need to be reduced, sometimes by as much as 50%, depending on the font.*

The trademark symbol ™ you create by typing Option-2 on the Mac or Alt-0153 in Windows is already superscripted, and usually sized correctly for the font. In programs such as PageMaker, for instance, I still prefer to type the letters 'T' and 'M' and superscript them. I set the superscript size option to 50%. This creates a trademark slightly smaller than the trademark character.

The copyright symbol © you create by typing Option-G on the Mac or Alt-0169 in Windows is too large. I prefer this character to be approximately 70% the size of the surrounding text. If your body text is 12 points, for example, the copyright symbol should be set to 8.5 points. This varies from font to font, but I try to set the size of the symbol to the x-height. Unlike the trademark symbol, the copyright symbol should not be superscripted, rather it should remain on the baseline.

The registered trademark symbol ® you create by typing Option-R on the Mac or Alt-0174 in Windows is also too large. This character can be placed either on the baseline like the © symbol, or superscripted like the ™ symbol. If you place it on the baseline, reduce its size exactly as you would the copyright symbol, that is, reduce it so that it matches the x-height. If you superscript it, reduce its size to 60% that of the surrounding text.

©1995. All rights reserved. Bass-o-Matic® Microsoft® Windows™

©1995. All rights reserved. Bass-o-Matic® Microsoft® Windows™

11 *Use the true ellipsis character (…) rather than periods.*

The ellipsis is used to denote a rhetorical pause or omission in a quotation. An ellipsis can be made up of periods, but dashes and sometimes even asterisks are used. The latter hasn't seen widespread use since the early part of this century, but the dash is quite commonly used as an elliptical mark indicating interruption…

> Private Johnson started to say, "But—" "But no
> *buts,* Private!" roared the drill instructor.

…or omission…

> Don't blame me when the s— hits the fan.

Elliptical periods, however, are the most common form of the ellipsis. In fact, when I use the term "ellipsis" I am actually referring to elliptical periods. People often create an ellipsis by typing the period three or four times, but you should use the ellipsis character, which is a standard character in most fonts, instead. You create an ellipsis by typing Option-Semicolon on the Mac or Alt-0133 in Windows. The ellipsis character looks better than three consecutive periods because it has slightly more space between each dot.

Compare the faux ellipsis on top to the ellipsis character below:

> Dust...American...Dust
> Dust…American…Dust

If the ellipsis comes at the end of a sentence, many grammarians insist that it should be followed by a period. But this is a grammatical rule, not a typographi-cal one, and it's broken quite often. It's not a rule I follow. If you do opt to add the period, you may need to manually kern it so that it is spaced equally with the other dots in the ellipsis. In many fonts, you won't have to worry about it, but this isn't always the case. In some fonts, the period may appear too close to the ellipsis, in which case it should be kerned…or deleted altogether.

When creating an ellipsis, you should consider adding a small amount of space (via your application's kerning commands) before and after it, or no space at all. The normal space created with the Space Bar is too wide to place before an ellipsis, although it is okay to place a full space after it if it appears at the end of a sentence.

12 *Decrease the size of ballot boxes.*

The ballot box characters available in the Zapf Dingbats font should be set smaller than the surrounding text. Ballot boxes are oh-so popular among desktop publishers, and are created by typing the O, P, Q, and R keys when the Zapf Dingbats font is selected. As a general rule, these characters should be about two points smaller than surrounding text.

In the first example, all text is set to 10-point; in the second, the text is 10-point, but the ballot boxes have been reduced to 8 points.

> ❏ Ballot boxes
> ❐ such as this
> ❏ and this
> ❐ are too large.

> ❏ Ballot boxes
> ❐ such as this
> ❏ and this
> ❐ are just right.

For more information on typeface classification, see chapter **11**.

I tend to think these ballot boxes are a tad overused, however. They serve a definite purpose—that is, as check boxes on forms, reply cards, and of course, ballots—but I see them used quite often in place of bullet characters, and in this role they look kind of cheesy.

13 *Consider using other characters besides • bullets.*

The bullet character • you create by typing Option-8 on the Mac, or Alt-0149 in Windows is rather boring and overused. Consider using more attractive symbols such as the ¶ symbol (Option-7, Alt-0182) available in most fonts, or use symbol fonts such as Sean's Symbols (available on the companion CD) or Zapf Dingbats.

The following characters from Sean's Symbols make interesting bullets:

☛   This character is created by typing Option-E, Shift-U (Mac) or Alt-0218 (Win)

◆   This character is created by pressing the L key

▲   This character is created by typing Option-Shift-' (Mac) or Alt-0198 (Win)

✿   This character is created by typing Option-Shift-R (Mac) or Alt-0137 (Win)

▶   This character is created by pressing the Period key

☺   This character is created by typing Option-E, Shift-I (Mac) or Alt-0204 (Win)

There are many, many other bullet characters available in the Sean's Symbols typeface, the above are simply some of my favorites.

Like ballot boxes, I decreased the size of these bullets 2 points from the surrounding text. This amount varies with the bullet you are using and the text font you have chosen. Generally speaking, a 20–30% size reduction should suffice.

14 *Increase line spacing to improve readability in body text.*

Line spacing, also called "leading," because printers used to insert thin strips of lead between lines of type to add space, is very important not only for readability but also for appearance. When setting text for continuous reading (this does not necessarily apply to headline or display text) words should be set close to each other, about as far apart as the width of the letter i. This is accomplished automatically by your word processing or page layout software (and is discussed in more detail in the section on Word Spacing). Line spacing, measured from baseline to baseline, needs to be significantly greater than this.

As a general rule, the amount of space between lines, expressed as a percentage of point size, should be no less than 120%. For example, if your text is 10-point, you should consider a line spacing setting of at least 12 points. If a typical line contains more than about 12 words, however, a leading value of 120% may not be enough. In other words, leading should be increased proportionally as line length increases.

The leading you choose depends on the typeface, but generally speaking, there are no text faces that look bad with more leading, although decreasing the leading can make just about any font look bad as a text font. As a display font, such as in headlines for example, decreased leading, even negative leading, may be appropriate.

Most Oldstyle designs such as Bembo, Caslon, Garamond, Galliard, and Sabon do not require leading beyond the 120% mentioned above. Transitional designs such as Baskerville and Times Roman require a bit more, and Moderns such as Bodoni and Walbaum require even more still. Again, exact amounts will depend on point size and line length, but keep this general knowledge in mind as you use these typefaces. Quite often people will come to me for advice on a document, telling me that something is not quite right about it, but that they don't know what that something is. In just about every case it comes down to two problems: their line length is too long, and the leading is too little. Decreasing the former and increasing the latter — or a combination of both — improves the appearance and transforms the "not quite right" into the "pretty neat." Font choice and justification options are almost always secondary concerns to leading and line width.

If you are using sans serif typefaces for body text, leading needs to be increased even more, sometimes to as much as 135–140% of point size, e.g., a 10-point sans serif font would probably look best with a leading of between 13 and 14 points.

Unlike body text where a baseline leading of 120% of the point size is suggested, for headlines I generally begin with *solid* leading, and increase or decrease it from there. Solid leading means that the line spacing is equivalent to the point size. If my headline is 24 points, for example, a solid leading would also be 24 points.

Most programs have a leading setting of "Auto," which is usually about 120% of the point size, but I recommend setting the leading to a fixed amount. If I'm using 10 point text, for example, I set the leading

to 12 points even though choosing the "Auto" leading option would do this anyway. Then if I need to change the size of a character or word, the leading won't be automatically adjusted; it will remain at 12 points.

In many places in this book, you will see fonts indicated as "Garamond 10/12," for example, or "Futura 12/15." The first number is the point size, the second is the leading. This is the standard notation. You may sometimes see line length included as well, generally in the form *Fontname* 10/12 x 20. Line length — the third number — is given in picas, not points. In this case, 20 picas. (One pica equals 12 points.)

15 *Sans serif typefaces are often less legible than serif typefaces.*

When setting body text — i.e., text that is meant to be read continuously — serif typefaces are naturally better suited than sans serif typefaces. Serifs are the small finishing strokes on the arms and stems of letters, and serve to form a link between letters. This link is important because when we read, our mind (in most western cultures anyway) is trained to recognize the shapes of words rather than reading letter by letter.

All of the serif text faces are appropriate for continuous reading. Many sans serif typefaces are as well. Consider sans serif fonts such as Gill Sans, Goudy Sans, and Optima for setting text meant for continuous reading. This isn't to say that you shouldn't use other sans serif fonts for body text, but generally speaking, avoid setting long passages of text in geometric sans serif typefaces such as Futura, for example, which is better suited for headlines, captions, and other short passages.

When designing forms such as time sheets, invoices, expense reports and order forms, consider using sans serif typefaces rather than serifs. Sans serifs naturally look better when aligned to vertical and horizontal lines, so common in forms. For best results, use loosely spaced All Caps set at a small size (8 points and below). Typefaces such as Futura and Franklin Gothic are particularly well-suited to designing forms.

16 *You can probably set body text to a point size smaller than you think.*

Type size for body text generally ranges from 9 to 14 points. Keep in mind that text set too small can be difficult to read in large quantities. On the other hand, text set too large often appears trivial, or meant for children, à la Dick and Jane books. If you're new to the world of type and document design, you can probably set text a bit smaller than your initial choice. A point size of 12 is probably the most common size, and on the screen it may even look rather petite, but when you print it, chances are it will appear larger than you thought. I recommend starting with 10-point text, then increase or decrease it a point or half-point as necessary. To my eyes, 12-point type looks absolutely huge, and this is probably the largest point size I would use for setting body text.

If your documents are intended primarily for on-screen display, as opposed to printed output, 12-point text is a good minimum. Of course, this depends on the typeface and whether or not it has legible bitmaps for small point sizes. Typefaces like Geneva on the Macintosh, and MS Sans in Microsoft Windows, are quite attractive and readable at 9 points (okay, maybe not attractive), but a typeface such as Times Roman will be difficult to read on-screen below 10 points.

17 *Decrease line length and increase margins.*

Or, the more white space the better. If text size can be decreased more than you originally thought, margins can be increased. An optimal line length for 10-point text is between 18 and 30 picas, or between 3 and 5 inches (4.25 inches is the column width I choose most frequently when designing single-column word processor documents). So if you're working with 8.5 by 11 inch paper with a portrait orientation, then you are going to have at least 3.5 inches of left and right margin, assuming your text consists of a single column. If it consists of multiple columns, there is also the margin, or *gutter*, between columns to consider.

I recommend offsetting your margins. That is, creating left and right margins of different widths. If your right margin is 1.5 inches, for example, consider a left margin of 2 inches. Keep in mind that this advice is highly generalized. Your specific margin requirements are as varied and interdependent as your choice of type.

18 *Avoid letterspacing lowercase body text.*

By this I mean do not add space between the letters of normal lowercase text. This is a big no-no. Although most programs provide features for expanding text, or increasing the tracking, these formatting options should only be applied to text set in all caps (or small caps and numbers), or display text where looser type spacing may increase legibility. In body text, however, looser spacing always decreases legibility.

In some instances — very narrow columns, less than about 2 inches, for example — it may improve the line breaks, and thus the appearance, to decrease letter spacing somewhat. Be careful though. Tight letterspacing isn't quite as difficult to read as overly loose letterspacing, but if the letters are bunched together or overlap, the net result is the same: ugliness. In the vast majority of cases, there is no reason to change the default letterspacing that your page layout program or word processor uses.

19 *Word spacing should be fairly close.*

Word spacing refers to the amount of space between words in a paragraph. For text meant for extended reading, this amount should be fairly close, about the width of a lowercase letter *i*.

Wynken Blynken & Nod
LONDON • PARIS • TOKYO • HOBOKEN

For the most part, your word processor controls this for you, and most people don't even consider it. In fact most word processors do not let you directly control word spacing, although several let you control letterspacing (the amount of space between letters in a word), or give you indirect control by letting you adjust hyphenation and justification settings — two factors inextricably bound to word spacing. And even though DTP programs handle word spacing for you, and do a fairly decent job of it, they can also be blatant violators.

The reason for close word spacing is not aesthetic, not because it looks better (although it almost always does), but because it is easier to read. We sometimes forget when entering text that we can read much faster than we can type, and so tend not to notice word spacing on screen. Screen resolution, too, is usually much less than printed output, so quite often words that might appear too close together on your monitor will look just fine — or maybe even too far apart — on the printed page.

What is easy to read?

Cognitive science has shown that our eyes process words not one at a time, but rather in chunks, and our brains can apparently sort out the chunks as quickly as our eyes can provide them. Of course, individual mileage may vary, for example, for a child learning to read, a chunk may be one word, whereas for Evelyn Wood a chunk might consist of thirty words. Regardless, the goal is to not slow down the normal left-to-right scanning of the eye, to avoid interrupting the rhythm. There's a limit of course: if the words are

A RIVER RUNS THROUGH IT

Flyfishing and typography have more in common than you might think.

spaced too close, they appear as one giant word, and the chunk-processing mechanism comes to a halt.

So, to aid this rhythm of reading, we need to keep the spaces between words not only fairly thin, but consistent and even; that is, we need to avoid setting paragraphs where the space between words varies from thin to not-so-thin to wide. Word spacing problems really only occur when you've set the alignment of your text to justified. In order for a word processor or page layout program to justify text, it must pull some words apart and push others together. The less it has to do this, the better your text will look, and the easier it will be to read. The primary factors affecting this are column width and hyphenation. In a word processor, where the number of columns is usually 1, you control the width by increasing or decreasing the margins. In an application that lets you set up multiple columns, you control width by three settings: the number of columns, the amount of space between columns, also known as *gutter*, and the outside margins. The narrower the columns, the more you invite the opportunity for word spacing problems. The ideal column width for single-column pages is about 4.25 inches, or roughly 26 picas, but in multi-column text, your columns could be as narrow as 2 inches. Turning on your application's hyphenation feature (or manually hyphenating text) can improve word spacing, but it can also cause other problems, such as the unsightliness of having too many consecutively hyphenated lines.

One way to avoid most word spacing problems is to set the alignment of your paragraphs to left aligned. In left-aligned text, you may run across the occasional odd line break, but odd line breaks are always preferable to inconsistent word spacing. And besides, they are considerably easier to correct. There have been some "studies" over the years indicating the relative read-

ability of justified versus left-aligned text, and supposedly, justified text is easier to read. Assuming you trust the validity of these studies (I don't, particularly), justified text may be somewhat easier to read, but only if the word spacing is perfect; otherwise left-aligned text is preferable. I generally prefer left-aligned text anyway, and you've no doubt noticed that the text for this book is set left-aligned.

First rule of word spacing: If you notice the spacing, there are problems with it.

Hold a *printed* page (you might not notice it on a computer monitor) at arm's length. If you can see any vertical patterns of white space, also known as *rivers,* running through your text from top to bottom, these are problems that need to be fixed.

Not that his name ought to be Bob at all. In respect of his behavior during a certain trying period which I am presently to recount, he ought to be called Sir Philip Sidney: yet, by virtue of his conduct in another very troublesome business which I will relate, he has equal claim to be known as Don Quixote de la Mancha: while, in consideration that he is the voice of his whole race, singing the passions of all his fellows better than any one could sing his own, he is clearly entitled to be named William Shakespeare. For Bob is our mocking-bird. He fell to us out of the top of a certain great pine in a certain small city on the sea-coast of Georgia. In this tree and a host of his lordly fellows which tower over that little city, the mocking-birds abound in unusual numbers. They love the prodigious masses of the leaves, and the generous breezes from the neighboring Gulf Stream, and, most of all, the infinite flood of the sunlight which is so rich and cordial that it will make even a man lift his head towards the sky, as a mocking-bird lifts

Not that his name ought to be Bob at all. In respect of his behavior during a certain trying period which I am presently to recount, he ought to be called Sir Philip Sidney: yet, by virtue of his conduct in another very troublesome business which I will relate, he has equal claim to be known as Don Quixote de la Mancha: while, in consideration that he is the voice of his whole race, singing the passions of all his fellows better than any one could sing his own, he is clearly entitled to be named William Shakespeare. For Bob is our mocking-bird. He fell to us out of the top of a certain great pine in a certain small city on the sea-coast of Georgia. In this tree and a host of his lordly fellows which tower over that little city, the mocking-birds abound in unusual numbers. They love the prodigious masses of the leaves, and the generous breezes from the neighboring Gulf Stream, and, most of all, the infinite flood of the sunlight which is so rich and cordial that it will make even a man lift his head towards the sky, as a mocking-bird lifts his beak, and try to sing something or other.

Compare the paragraphs above. The first paragraph has obvious word spacing problems. The first few lines are okay, but then the gaps between words get larger. By contrast, the spacing of the second paragraph is even and consistent. You notice the space between the lines, but not the space between words.

In most word processors, you can correct the problem by:

▶ Setting your text left-aligned

…or any combination of the following:

▶ Adjust the size of your margins.

Start with values no greater than ⅛th inch, increasing or decreasing the width of one or both margins. If your text must be a certain width, or your margins a specific size, then obviously such adjustments are not an option. But as you decrease or increase the width of your columns, notice its affect on any rivers of white space.

▶ Decrease the size of your text.

The smaller the point size, the more words that can fit on a single line, and thus the more spaces and opportunities your word processor has for line breaks. But there are other factors here you must consider. I mentioned earlier that my optimal line length for single-column text is about four and one-quarter inches, but this is for 10-pt type. If I were using 12-pt type, I could increase this to four and one-half or even five inches; if I were using 9-pt type, however, I would want to decrease this length. The smaller the point size of the text, the shorter your lines should be. Another way of it looking at it is to keep the average number of words per line to about 12.

▶ Turn on your word processor's auto-hyphenation feature.

If your word processor does not have such a feature, then it's time for a new word processor. All leading word processors, such as Microsoft Word, Nisus Writer for the Mac, and WordExpress for Windows (the latter are available on the companion CD) have auto-hyphenation features. Hyphenating words, like decreasing the point size, effectively lets your word processor place more words on a line, and therefore gives it more available options for line breaks. If you are justifying text, there is no reason not to use automatic hyphenation.

▶ Manually hyphenate the text.

Do this either in addition to, or in lieu of auto-hyphenation. Most word processors give you the option of inserting "soft-hyphens," for example, hyphens that will only split a word if it appears at the end of a line. If the line end changes, the word will no longer be hyphenated. Contrast this to a "hard hyphen," or a hyphen that will appear no matter where the word is located. Hard hyphens are created whenever you press the hyphen, or minus, key on your keyboard. Soft hyphens usually involve pressing the command or Ctrl keys in conjunction with the hyphen key.

Page layout programs such as Adobe PageMaker and QuarkXPress offer more sophisticated control over word spacing parameters. In addition to adjusting column width, point size, and hyphenating text, you can also set minimum, maximum, and optimal word and letter spacing parameters.

In Adobe PageMaker, you access these values by opening the Paragraph Specifications dialog box and clicking the "Spacing…" button. Notice the default values for word and letter spacing:

```
┌──────────────────────────────────────────────────┐
│ Spacing attributes                    ┌────────┐   │
│ ──────────────────────────────────────│   OK   │   │
│ Word space:           Letter space:   └────────┘   │
│ Minimum  [75]  %      Minimum  [-5]  % ┌────────┐   │
│                                        │ Cancel │   │
│ Desired  [100] %      Desired  [0]   % └────────┘   │
│                                        ┌────────┐   │
│ Maximum  [150] %      Maximum  [25]  % │ Reset  │   │
│                                        └────────┘   │
│ Pair kerning: ☒ Auto above [4]  points             │
│                                                    │
│ Leading method:       Autoleading:                 │
│ ◉ Proportional        [120] % of point size        │
│ ○ Top of caps                                      │
│ ○ Baseline                                         │
└──────────────────────────────────────────────────┘
```

These settings are approximately those used by most word processors, although most word processors provide no interface for editing these values. Fortunately PageMaker does. And you should edit these values. I think the default values are not quite optimal. The minimum word space setting of 75% is a bit too low, and the maximum of 150% is a bit too high. (These percentage values, by the way, are a percentage of the normal space character built into a font.) Like we discussed earlier, the goal is evenness and consistency, and a variation of 75% from minimum to maximum is not quite even. So bump up the minimum setting, and knock down the maximum. Kathleen Tinkel, a designer and sysop of CompuServe's Desktop Publishing Forum (GO: DTPFOR) suggests a minimum setting of 80% and a maximum of 133%. I've tried these values, and they work quite well for most purposes.

Also, when working with body text (this does not apply to heading or display text, but text meant for extended reading) you should change all of the letter-space values to 0%. (The default minimum value of

−5% might not produce unsightly letterspacing, but a 25% maximum is too high.) Again, letterspacing is the amount of space between letters within a word, and for lowercase body text, increasing this space is generally considered a no-no.

In QuarkXPress, you edit these same values by choosing the "H&Js…" command from the Edit menu.

20 *Choose an alignment option that suits your text.*

Body text is usually aligned in one of two ways: justified or ragged right (also called flush left, depending on how you look at it). Justified text is set from the left margin or left side of a column to the right, with both sides even, or flush. Text that is even on the left and uneven on the right is referred to as ragged. The text in this book, for example, is ragged.

Justified text imparts a formal, rational and business-like tone, whereas ragged text is more casual and personal. Compare the text in a magazine such as Time, for example, to Sunset. The difference in tone is fairly striking.

There is a common bias that since justified text is more business-like that it is also more professional. This just isn't the case. In fact, I prefer ragged text, and would even go so far as to say it's easier to read, but I have no real evidence to support this claim (other than I think it's easier for me to read, which would account for 100% of the studies I've conducted). Justified text is more difficult to set without the inevitable word spacing problems that will arise. And maybe because it's more difficult to do, people just assume that pulling it off is more professional. Well, running a mile as fast as you can is also more difficult to do than strolling it leisurely, but no one will accuse you of looking more professional for puking on your tennies afterwards.

Unless your text has to be justified, consider setting it ragged. You won't have to worry about word-spacing problems. Line breaks will be your primary concern here, and these are much easier to manage.

Other alignment methods—flush right and centered—are not generally used for body text. There are some exceptions; poetry and verse are often set center-aligned, and headlines and captions are often set right-aligned.

21 *Hyphenate text intelligently.*

Most word processing and page layout programs have the ability to hyphenate text automatically. The level of sophistication, however, varies widely from program to program. For example, some programs will automatically hyphenate text wherever it is "legal" to do so, in other words, using a dictionary to determine where hyphens may and may not be inserted. More sophisticated programs apply rules to enhance the aesthetics of hyphenated text, for example, limiting the number of consecutively hyphenated lines, or controlling the minimum space before a word is broken.

The basic rule here is don't let your software make all the decisions. Rely on your eye to determine what looks good and what doesn't. Here are a few guidelines:

When a line is hyphenated, make sure at least two characters are left behind and at least three characters are carried to the next line.

For example, "El-egantly" is acceptable, but "Ele-gant-ly" is not because only two characters are carried to the next line.

22 *Make sure the stub-end of a hyphenated word is not the last word of a paragraph.*

In most cases it is undesirable to end a paragraph with a single word. This is especially undesirable (maddeningly undesirable) if the word is shorter than four characters. The options available for fixing such problems are somewhat limited: 1) You can edit the writing itself to alter the line breaks, or 2) insert a manual line break forcing a word (or words) from the second-to-last line to the last line. A third, and non-recommended, option is to attempt to tighten, or decrease, the letterspacing to affect a change in line endings. This is always a last resort in my opinion, something to be tried when items 1 and 2 simply won't do the trick.

23 *Limit the number of consecutively hyphenated lines to three.*

Sometimes even two consecutively hyphenated lines may be the limit. Three however, is the outside limit. Beyond this, it appears as if diving boards or ladders are present on the right side of your paragraph. This problem is much more noticeable in justified text than in ragged text, and much more common, because of the line break adjustments necessary in justified text.

24 *Avoid beginning three consecutive lines with the same word.*

This problem relates back to grammar school when your primary concern was writing about your summer vacation without starting every sentence with 'I'. But the problem here isn't so much beginning a *sentence* with the same word, as beginning a *line* with the same word. Since software controls line breaks automatically based on a number of variables (margins, point size, and justification/hyphenation settings) it is possible, in fact quite common, to see paragraphs having consecutive lines beginning with the same word. The word "and" seems to fall into this trap with greater frequency than most others. Dunno why. Coincidence? Hard to say.

25 *Avoid hyphenating or breaking proper names and titles.*

Proper names should never be hyphenated, and really shouldn't break at the end of a line either. The best way to prevent this from happening is to get yourself in the habit of typing *non-breaking spaces* between proper names. A non-breaking space will make certain that the words immediately before and after it will always appear on the same line. It's a good idea to type non-breaking spaces between proper names even if they don't appear near line endings. You never know if a subsequent formatting or editing change might alter the flow of the text, causing the words to break.

To create a non-breaking space in most★ Mac applications, press Option-Space Bar. To create a non-breaking space in most★ Windows applications, press Alt-0160. ■

★ Some applications such as QuarkXPress ignore the normal non-breaking space built into fonts, and require that you type Cmd-Space Bar instead.

CHAPTER 8

E-mail
Typography

E-mail Typography

WHAT'S THIS, YOU ASK, A CHAPTER DEVOTED TO E-MAIL typography? Isn't the online world of the Internet, CompuServe, AOL, etc. free from such aesthetic issues as typography and design?

It's true that many of the traditions and standards of typography are moot when it comes to e-mail—it's generally not possible to make font choices, for example, or choose different point sizes, or even to italicize, bold or underline text in cyberspace—but it's still important to design what you write, and there are still design issues to consider when you compose forum messages and electronic mail.

Beatrice Warde once said that fonts are clothing for words. I guess all the words in cyberspace are naked then—or wearing the same futuristic jumpsuits or something like that—because all the attractive (and expensive) fonts you've bought over the years are useless on the net. Although this will no doubt change in the not-too-distant future, the various online services, e-mail readers, and messaging systems almost always restrict you to a single font, and usually a monospaced system font at that, a font you'd never choose in a million years to craft a newsletter or a brochure or even a letter to your folks. And those few online services that do let you make font changes (eWorld, for example) will only display your typographic choices to users on the same system who happen to have installed the same fonts you have. Everyone else sees the plain old unformatted text file.

The clock is ticking…

Much of the culture of the net arose out of concerns for speed. It costs money to be online after all, so communication tends to be brief, spelling tends to be, well, not a priority, grammar not much higher, and acronyms flourish. Rhetorical niceties and segues such as "by the way," "on the other hand," "as far as I'm concerned," are reduced to BTW, OTOH, AFAIC. It used to be that a user would have to read his mail and respond to it online, that is, while he was connected live to an online service, with the clock ticking (and for the service provider as well as the subscriber, nothing is more true than "time is money"). But today most correspondence and forum messaging is conducted off-line: the user logs onto a service, retrieves his mail, then logs off and reads it off-line, composes his responses, then goes online again and sends them.

Off-line readers or no, the acronyms stayed, and unfortunately, so too did the rushed style, the spelling and grammar mistakes, the lack of attention to formatting and visual presentation. The message is "Hey, I'm online. I'm cool, and I don't care about these things." It's not uncommon to see bloated screenfuls of unedited thoughts, yet the author will pepper it with acronyms to save himself, and you the reader, presumably, a few nano-seconds of download time. I happen to spend a good deal of time online, and I see many more lengthy, difficult to read, poorly formatted tomes than I do brief, witty, and quick-to-retrieve messages.

The goal in cyberspace is to be read, to attract as much of an audience as possible. The best way to achieve this is to write well, to be interesting and funny, and to have something to say worth reading. Well, I can't help you with these things, but I can help make your already wonderfully written prose look better. So I'll start with the basics.

1 *Don't write in ALL CAPS unless you want to give the impression of shouting.*

For some reason, newcomers to the net tend to write messages and e-mail in all uppercase letters. No one knows why this is so — after all, these same people don't create documents in their word processors or desktop publishing programs in all caps — but everyone enjoys chiding them for doing it. The surest way to get lots of attention in a public forum is to post a message in all caps. If there are one hundred forum members, for example, at least ten of them will take the time to tell you not to write messages in all caps (of which maybe one of those will also take the time to respond to whatever it was you were actually trying to communicate in the first place); the remaining ninety will dismiss you as a newbie, and won't read your message past the first line. I've heard people describe this public chastisement as the quintessential Jan Brady experience: embarrassment mixed with an acute feeling of rejection. So, only use all uppercase text for strong emphasis, and use it sparingly, i.e., try to avoid typing more than a few consecutive words in all caps.

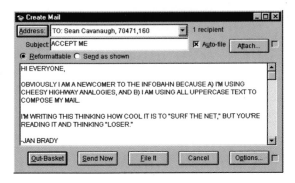

All uppercase text is the cyber equivalent of shouting.

2 *Insert a blank line (carriage return) between all paragraphs.*

For printed text, it is quite readable and attractive to eliminate blank lines between paragraphs, relying instead on indented first lines to distinguish one paragraph from the next (such as the text in this book). But this should be avoided online, where resolution is considerably less, and text is more difficult to read.

3 *Indent the first line of each paragraph with at least two spaces.*

For the same reasons you should add blank lines between paragraphs, you should also indent the first lines: it simply makes it easier to distinguish one paragraph from the next. However, don't use the Tab key for this — tabs are interpreted differently by different networks and off-line readers, and sometimes ignored completely — use the Space bar instead. I recommend using at least two, but generally no more than three spaces to indent paragraphs. This depends on whether the font is monospaced or not. If it's not, an indent of 3–5 spaces may be acceptable. If the font is monospaced (and most are) an indent of 2–3 spaces is sufficient.

4 *Consider adding a double-space between sentences.*

What?!? I know, you're not supposed to double space anymore, and you've just taken the time to unlearn this habit drilled into you by high school typing teachers. Well, the fact is, you shouldn't double space for printed text, but most online messages are displayed on screen using system fonts that quite often look better and are easier to read with two spaces after the period. This is purely a personal choice, not a rule, but all in all, I think two spaces look better online.

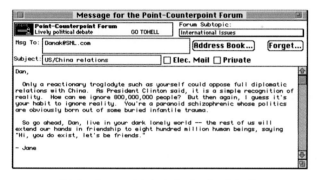

Note how the message looks good and reads well, despite the fact that it is using a monospaced font. Paragraphs are clearly indicated, and sentences are easy to distinguish.

5 *Use asterisks, hyphens or underscores to emphasize text.*

When I want to place special emphasis on a word or phrase, but stopping somewhere short of the strong emphasis typing in all caps provides, I type an asterisk immediately before and after it. If you want especially strong emphasis, use all caps and asterisks. Some people substitute the hyphen or the underscore for the asterisk, and this works pretty well too. I usually reserve the underscores to offset book and magazine titles (just like underlining on a typewriter), and hyphens to place special emphasis on personal pronouns:

```
-I- said that?

I'm interested in -your- opinion.

It's only a problem if someone *else* is doing it.

Well, um, that was the POINT after all.

Rather, that *was* the point.

Kenneth Grahame was the author of _The Wind in
the Willows_.
```

6 *Use angle brackets (>) to indicate that you are quoting someone's message verbatim.*

When responding to an e-mail or forum message, it's common practice to copy and paste the text you are responding to, such as a specific question for example, into your response. This is a particularly good idea if you are responding to a message after a couple of days. The quoted text will refresh the sender's memory and clearly indicate what you are talking about or responding to. Of course, you don't need to quote the entire message, just a key sentence or two. If you find the quote takes up more than about five lines, consider paring it down.

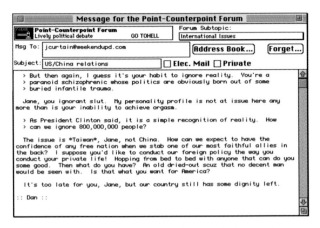

```
┌──────────────────────────────────────────────────────┐
│ ▪      Message for the Point-Counterpoint Forum      ▣│
├──────────────────────────────────────────────────────┤
│ ▐▀▀▙ Point-Counterpoint Forum    ┌─ Forum Subtopic:   │
│ ▐▄▄▟ Lively political debate  GO TOHELL │International Issues │
│ Msg To: │jcurtain@weekendupd.com │  ┌Address Book...┐ ┌Forget...┐│
│ Subject:│US/China relations     │  ☐ Elec. Mail ☐ Private │
├──────────────────────────────────────────────────────┤
│ > But then again, I guess it's your habit to ignore reality.  You're a │▲│
│ > paranoid schizophrenic whose politics are obviously born out of some │
│ > buried infantile trauma.                              │
│                                                          │
│ Jane, you ignorant slut.  My personality profile is not at issue here any │
│ more than is your inability to achieve orgasm.          │
│                                                          │
│ > As President Clinton said, it is a simple recognition of reality.  How │
│ > can we ignore 800,000,000 people?                     │
│                                                          │
│ The issue is *Taiwan*, Jane, not China.  How can we expect to have the │
│ confidence of any free nation when we stab one of our most faithful allies in │
│ the back?  I suppose you'd like to conduct our foreign policy the way you │
│ conduct your private life!  Hopping from bed to bed with anyone that can do you │
│ some good.  Then what do you have?  An old dried-out scuz that no decent man │
│ would be seen with.  Is that what you want for America? │
│                                                          │
│ It's too late for you, Jane, but our country still has some dignity left. │
│                                                          │
│ :: Dan ::                                               │▼│
└──────────────────────────────────────────────────────┘
```

Note how the sender quoted portions from the message he is responding to.

7 *If you are quoting a previous exchange (your previous comments as well as someone's response to it) type two angle brackets (>>) to indicate the oldest quote and a single angle bracket (>) to indicate the response.*

```
┌──────────────────────────────────────────────────────┐
│ ▪      Message for the Point-Counterpoint Forum      ▣│
├──────────────────────────────────────────────────────┤
│ ▐▀▀▙ Point-Counterpoint Forum    ┌─ Forum Subtopic:   │
│ ▐▄▄▟ Lively political debate  GO TOHELL │International Issues │
│ Msg To: │Danak@SNL.com          │  ┌Address Book...┐ ┌Forget...┐│
│ Subject:│US/China relations     │  ☐ Elec. Mail ☐ Private │
├──────────────────────────────────────────────────────┤
│ >> But then again, I guess it's your habit to ignore reality.  You're a │▲│
│ >> paranoid schizophrenic whose politics are obviously born out of some │
│ >> buried infantile trauma.                             │
│                                                          │
│ > Jane, you ignorant slut.  My personality profile is not at issue here │
│ > any more than is your inability to achieve orgasm.    │
│                                                          │
│ Well, well, Dan.  Seems you're good at tossing out insults, but you whimper │
│ and whine like an emasculated puppy when you get them in return.  Anyway, my │
│ so-called "inability to achieve orgasm" was actually the result of your failure │
│ to give me one. <g>                                     │
│                                                          │
│ - Jane                                                  │▼│
└──────────────────────────────────────────────────────┘
```

Here the sender is not only quoting from the sender's message she is responding to, but she is also including part of her previous response, indicated by the double-angle brackets. Using this method, the single-angle bracket will always refer to the last message being quoted.

If you are quoting the previous exchange, plus the comment before that, well, do everyone a favor and don't do this. Quoting from two messages back is more than enough. Quoting from three messages back is needless.

8 *Create bulleted lists using the colon and bracket characters.*

Since no real bullet characters are available in 7-bit ASCII text, you have to get creative with standard keyboard characters. Typing two colons or bracket characters makes for a nice bullet character.

```
We need to be aware of the following:

:: Lions — large and heavily-built social cats of open
   or rocky areas chiefly of sub-Saharan Africa.

:: Tigers — large Asian carnivorous mammals of the cat
   family having a tawny coat transversely striped with
   black.

:: Bears — large, heavy mammals of America and Eurasia
   that have long shaggy hair, rudimentary tails, and feed
   largely on fruit and insects as well as on flesh.

We need to be aware of the following:

[] Lions — large and heavily-built social cats of open
   or rocky areas chiefly of sub-Saharan Africa.

[] Tigers — large Asian carnivorous mammals of the cat
   family having a tawny coat transversely striped with
   black.

[] Bears — large, heavy mammals of America and Eurasia
   that have long shaggy hair, rudimentary tails, and feed
   largely on fruit and insects as well as on flesh.

Oh my!
```

9 *Avoid signing your messages with boilerplate remarks, lengthy quotes, or nifty graphics drawn with ASCII characters.*

It's not uncommon to see entire messages on CompuServe or AOL, for instance, that contain less characters than the sender's signature! In the following example, the sender was kind enough to use acronyms for "Pardon me for jutting in" (PMFJI) and "In my humble opinion" (IMHO), but nevertheless inundated us with his personal epithet and all of his e-mail addresses.

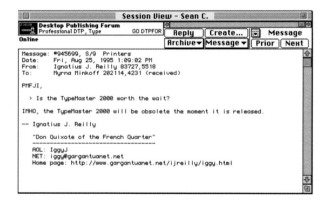

This is just cyber litter. Give a hoot, don't pollute. Simply signing off with your name is plenty. Maybe add a hyphen or two before it, but beyond that you're wasting pixels.

10 *Use emoticons sparingly.*

Commonly referred to as "emoticons," I call these typographic creations *smiloglyphs*. They're created by typing various characters for the eyes, nose and mouth, and if you tilt your head to the left, they resemble faces.

Some of the most common ones are :-) and ;-)

The first one is just smiling, the second one winking and smiling. Cute, huh?

Of course, there are about as many variations on these as there people with e-mail accounts. Thousands of years from now, when archaeologists dig through the remains of our culture, they'll no doubt need clues as to what these symbols mean. So here's a rosetta stone for them: ◄ THIS END UP ◄

Don't get carried away with them, however. If you say something that reads harshly, or has the potential to be misinterpreted as mean-spirited or disparaging, you might consider adding a smiloglyph. You may also consider using the more refined, slightly more abstract <g>, which simply means that you are grinning. Is it a light-hearted grin? A sly grin? A cynical grin? That may be up to your reader to decide.

I rarely, if ever, use smiloglyphs, but depending on the subject and the receiver, I sometimes pepper my remarks quite liberally with <g>s.

11 *Don't go overboard with acronyms.*

The use of acronyms in e-mail originated as a way to save time while people composed their on-line missives, live, connected to a service provider. But it's since become much more than that. The use of acronyms conveys a casual attitude, a sort of schoolyard lingo for the cyber set. But they're easy to overdo. An e-mail message with too many of them looks awkward, as if you're trying too hard to make it look as if you're not trying very hard.

Here are some of the more common acronyms:

BTW	By The Way
IAC	In Any Case
IMO	In My Opinion
IMHO	In My Humble Opinion
OTOH	On The Other Hand
PMFJI	Pardon Me For Jutting In
LOL	Laughing Out Loud
ROFL	Rolling On Floor Laughing
ROFLMAO	Rolling On Floor Laughing My Ass Off

CHAPTER 9

Type as
Graphic
Element

Type as Graphic Element

PROGRAMS LIKE ADOBE ILLUSTRATOR, ADOBE Photoshop, and Macromedia FreeHand open a whole new world to working with type. They take type out of the relatively tidy and controlled world of text processing (desktop publishing and word processing) where the primary metaphor for working with it is lines and paragraphs and pages (type as type), and into the realm of high-resolution raster graphics (Photoshop) and vector graphics (Illustrator, Free-Hand) where anything can happen (type as graphic element). Here type belongs not just to the realm of words, but to images, graphics, logos, signs, video, multimedia displays, and so on.

Photoshop lets you blur, distort, twist, rotate, stretch, emboss, spin, and twirl type. You can colorize, spherize, crystallize, and polarize. Photoshop treats everything, including type, as images. It provides an interface for entering type into the image, but once it's there, the pixels that combine to make a letter 'E' for example, are no di:erent than the pixels of a scanned photograph, or squiggles from a drawing tablet.

Vector-based graphics programs aren't quite as "any-thing goes" as Photoshop, but they're close. Applications such as Illustrator and FreeHand let you convert text into their component lines and curves where you can perform hundreds of different operations on them — stretch, compress, twist, flip, reverse, colorize, add shadows, enhance edges, change line weights and colors, and so on.

In this chapter you will learn some neat tricks for using Photoshop and Illustrator to create type-based images. The examples will hopefully inspire you, and the steps should provide you with the skills to continue learning these very powerful programs.

THE
YOUNG
PERSON'S
PLANETARIUM
OF SAN DIEGO

Function Bold & Bergamo Small Caps
Swirl effect created with KPT Vector Effects

Courier

Here's an example where text that might be considered typographically undesirable (the font used is Courier) suddenly becomes much more than itself when it's part of a graphic image. The text takes on an eery, almost ghostlike quality when presented in this context. Now when was the last time you heard someone describe Courier as ethereal, eery, or ghostlike? In a traditional desktop published document, probably never. But in a graphic, the constraints we usually associate with this "typewriter font" no longer necessarily apply. This graphic was created by Southern California artist Stephanie Clinesmith.

The obverse of this applies to the next image. Here the image itself is rather mundane — a bowling ball and some beach sand — but the text and the text effects make it visually appealing, almost exciting. If there really was such a thing as beach bowling, you might very well hit the Barcalounger™ and watch it. The photo images are from KPT Power Photos, an excellent collection of royalty-free Adobe Photoshop images from HSC Software. Ken Oyer and I went from initial concept to completed file in under an hour using Adobe Photoshop.

Function Condensed Heavy, Stop & Hudson
Image composited using KPT Power Photos

Drop Shadows

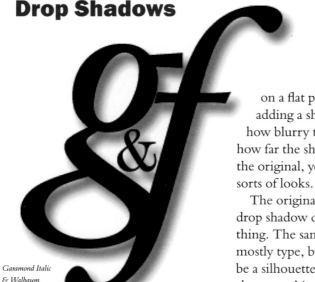

Garamond Italic
& Walbaum

This is probably the most basic and most common text effect you'll use. But don't let its simplicity fool you. Drop shadows add elegance and depth to just about any application, bringing plain old text to life. You can create the illusion of depth

on a flat piece of paper by adding a shadow. By varying how blurry the edges are and how far the shadow is offset from the original, you can produce all sorts of looks.

The original object creating the drop shadow can be almost anything. The samples used here are mostly type, but it could very well be a silhouette of a person or just about anything else.

💡 Drop shadows usually look better when used with bolder or larger type. This is just a guideline and not an absolute rule of course. I have seen some very nice shadows using small or thin type. You just need to experiment.

ground. Photoshop indicates that an area is transparent by displaying it on screen with a checkerboard pattern.

2 CREATE YOUR ORIGINAL OBJECT

In this example we are using large lowercase letters. The letters were created in Adobe Illustrator and then Placed (File-Place) into Photoshop. Because of Photoshop's limited capabilities for entering, formatting, and editing type, I prefer to use Illustrator to compose type and then Place it into Photoshop. But in some cases, Photoshop's type tool works just fine (such as when you are only working with one word, or with text you are certain you will not edit later). After you have Placed your type, deselect it by choosing None from the Select menu.

1 CREATE A NEW DOCUMENT IN PHOTOSHOP

In the New document dialog box, make sure Transparent is selected under Contents. If you are starting with an object in a scan, you must first select it and paste it into a document with a transparent back-

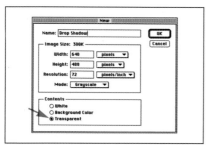

3 RENAME AND DUPLICATE LAYER

In the Layers palette, double-click on the layer name and change it to "Original type." Then in the Layers palette, click and hold the mouse down on the "Original type" layer, drag it to the left-most icon at the bottom of the palette

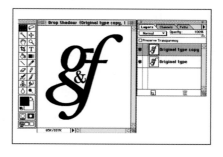

(the one that looks like a page with one corner turned up), and then release it. This creates a duplicate of the layer, named "Original type copy." Now you have two layers that are exactly the same in exactly the same position.

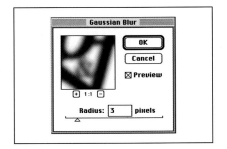

4 RENAME, ARRANGE AND APPLY GAUSSIAN BLUR

Rename "Original type copy" to "Shadow," and rearrange it in the list so it is below "Original type." Simply click and drag the name below the "Original type" layer. With the "Shadow" layer selected, apply a Gaussian Blur. You'll probably want to experiment a bit on the amount of blur, but generally speaking, a radius value below 5 pixels should suffice. I used 3 pixels. Click OK. The screen shows the shadow already offset from its original placement. This is to show what the blur looks like. The actual offset is done in the next step.

5 APPLY OFFSET FILTER

Apply the Filter-Other-Offset filter or use the Move tool to move it visually. When using the Offset filter, my rule of thumb is to use a larger number than what was used in the Gaussian Blur. Since I used 3 for a Gaussian Blur, I used 5 for an offset. Click OK.

6 ADJUST OPACITY ON SHADOW

Make sure the Shadow layer is still selected and adjust the Opacity slider at the top of the Layers palette.

💡 Shadows usually look lighter on the monitor than they print on paper.

MAC USERS: You can use Alien Skin's Drop Shadow filter (available on most online services) which does all of the above.

💡 You can also make a new layer below the Shadow layer and place a photo or a texture to simulate the effect of type casting a shadow onto a surface. When using this technique, remember to select the shadow layer and then choose the Darken option from the Calculation pop-up menu (it is located just to the left of the Opacity slider bar in the Layers palette). This will blend the shadow smoothly into the background image.

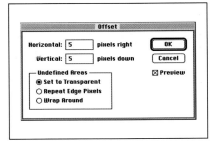

Type on a Path

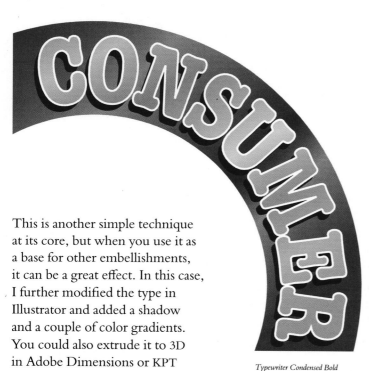

Typewriter Condensed Bold

This is another simple technique at its core, but when you use it as a base for other embellishments, it can be a great effect. In this case, I further modified the type in Illustrator and added a shadow and a couple of color gradients. You could also extrude it to 3D in Adobe Dimensions or KPT Vector Effects.

See the "Type in Flames" procedure at the end of this section to see how I used this technique in conjunction with another to complete a final logo design.

1 DRAW TWO CIRCLES
Draw concentric circles with enough room separating them to place your type. Select both circles and choose Compound Paths-Make from the Object menu.

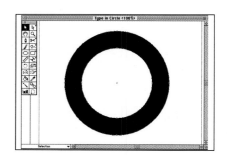

2 DRAW TYPE BASELINE CIRCLE
Draw the circle that will be the baseline for the type. This third circle should be slightly larger than the inner circle. You might want to be in the non-preview mode from here on out.

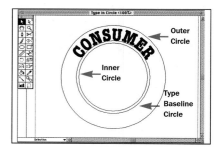

3 SELECT THE PATH TYPE TOOL
Click the cursor at the high noon point on the circle you just drew, and type your text. Then center the text by choosing Alignment-Center from the Type menu. Choose a font and adjust the point size so that it fits comfortably within the concentric circles.

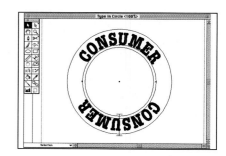

4 COPY, PASTE AND ROTATE TYPE
Select the type on a circle element and copy it to the Clipboard. Paste the copy on top of itself by choosing Paste In Front from the Edit Menu. Now rotate it from the center point 180 degrees by double-clicking the Rotate tool and

entering an angle of 180. Click OK. If needed, select the copied text and type the new text.

Front (make sure the text itself is NOT selected before doing this).

NOTE FOR WINDOWS USERS After the rectangle is drawn, convert it to a guide by choosing Object-Guide-Make. Select the scissors, cut the circles where they intersect with the guides, and then join the endpoints.

5 ADJUST BASELINE OF BOTTOM TEXT
With the Selection tool, double-click the I-beam of the bottom type to reverse the baseline from the outside of the circle to the inside. Adjust the baseline shift in the Character floating palette until it looks right. Start with a negative value approximately two-thirds of the type size and experiment from there.

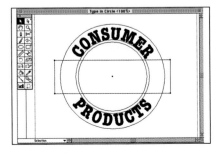

6 RECTANGLE KNOCKOUT
This next step shows how I embellished the design you see in the Fire Type Photoshop sample at the end of this chapter. Draw a rectangle from the circle center, select both the rectangle and the circle, and choose Filter-Pathfinder-Minus

Type with a Neon Glow

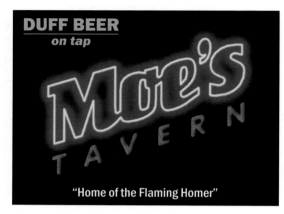

Salut, VAG Rounded Bold & Franklin Gothic

This procedure mimics the appearance of neon signs, but can be modified to simply cast a glow or aura (hey, like wow) around your type.

The first thing to think about when adding a Neon Glow to your type is what kind of background to use. For that typical neon sign look, solid black backgrounds work best. It can be applied to photo or textured backgrounds, but the effect can be diminished somewhat depending on image content.

The sample shown was created in a CMYK file in Photoshop but I was really just using the Black and Yellow channels. The reason is as you blend from one color to another, one color decreases in value as the other increases. To

get a smooth blend from 100% Yellow to 100% Black I needed to start with a background of exactly that—100% of each color. I couldn't use the default Black because it only has 51% of Yellow, so I created a special black with 100% of both Black and Yellow. How to do all this is covered in Step 2.

For the proper effect we need to create a path in Photoshop. We can do this three ways: 1) simply draw it using Photoshop's Pen tool. For simple graphics this is probably the best; 2) turn a selection into a path. After you have made a selection, open the Path palette's submenu and select Make Path. A channel can be made into a selection which then can be made into a path; 3) paste an Illustrator Path directly into Photoshop. This is my favorite. Photoshop's Pen tool is very handy, but less versatile then Illustrator's. After you have created the path in Illustrator, simply copy the path to the Clipboard. Step 3 will cover this technique in detail.

1 CREATE AND MANIPULATE YOUR TEXT IN ILLUSTRATOR

Open Illustrator and draw the graphic. Then copy the graphic to the Clipboard.

2 CREATE A NEW PHOTOSHOP DOCUMENT

Before you select New document, change the background color to 100% Yellow and 100% Black. Now create a new CMYK document and change the Contents option to background color.

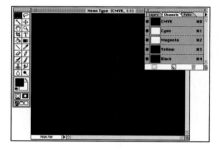

3 PASTE ILLUSTRATOR PATH FROM CLIPBOARD

Select Edit-Paste. In the Paste dialog box select Paste as Paths. This will open a new path in the Paths palette named Work Path. Photoshop automatically shows the Paths palette if it is not already open.

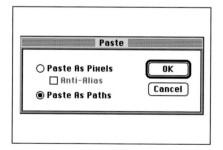

4 STROKE THE PATH TO CREATE THE OUTER GLOW

This step creates the outer glow by stroking the path with the Brush tool. First we must make sure we have all the proper variables set correctly. Click the foreground color icon and make it 100% Yellow

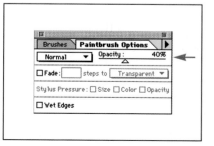

only. Click the Brush tool and select a soft-edged brush about 50 pixels wide. Adjust the Opacity slider bar to 40%. You can find the Opacity slider bar by double clicking a Brush tool. The color, brush size, and opacity all come into play when you apply the stroke. With the Brush tool selected, select the Work Path in the Paths palette and press Enter. You can also apply a stroke to a path by dragging the path name onto the second-from-the-left icon at the bottom of the Paths palette.

5 STROKE THE PATH TO CREATE THE NEON TUBING

Select a Brush size of 5 pixels and change the opacity to 100%. Apply the stroke again as before.

6 STROKE A HIGHLIGHT PATH

The final step (and this is really just icing) is to apply a thin white line slightly offset from the middle of the tubing for highlighting. Make a copy of the original path by dragging the path name onto the second-from-the-right icon at the

bottom of the Paths palette. With the copy highlighted in grey in the Paths palette, choose the arrow tool in the Paths palette and select the entire path. Using the arrow keys on your keyboard, move the path up and to the left by clicking once on the Up and Left Arrows. Now select the Brush tool with a 1- or 2-pixel brush, and change its Opacity slider bar to 100%. Make the foreground color White and apply the stroke again as before.

You can always experiment with other colors and pixel widths. This probably goes without saying, but experimentation is always recommended when trying out effects such as this.

Notice the word "Tavern" in our example. This was part of the original Illustrator type outlines we imported into Photoshop. We then split it into two pieces, with "Moe's" being one path and "Tavern" the other. We applied the neon glow procedure to "Moe's," but to the "Tavern" path we simply filled it with Cyan, added some noise to it using the Filter-Noise-Add Noise command, and then airbrushed some Black around the edges to add dimension.

Bevel Type

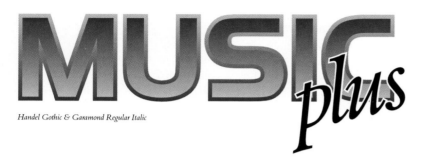

Handel Gothic & Garamond Regular Italic

This technique is very simple, but can add a lot of punch by giving your text more dimension in depth and color. The combination of 3D and color gradients is attention grabbing and professional looking, and is effective for logos, signs, and corporate identity. I think this technique is especially well-suited for consumer and retail-related products and businesses.

☹ This technique relies on filter functions that are only available in Illustrator 5.x. If you are using Illustrator 4.0 for Windows, you will not be able to follow the steps in this technique.

1 MAKE AN ILLUSTRATOR FILE

In the new document, open the Layers palette and add a second layer to the list (under the palette choose New Layer). Name the top layer "Inner Bevel," and the bottom layer "Outer Bevel."

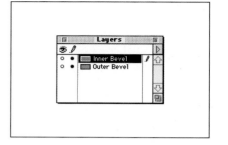

2 CREATE SOME TYPE

Large fat type usually works the best. You'll want to put some extra space (increased tracking) between the letters to accommodate the bevels. Convert the letters to graphic elements by first selecting the type and then choosing the Create Outlines command from the Type menu. Make sure the outlines are on the Inner Bevel layer.

3 APPLY OFFSET PATH FILTER

With the type selected, choose Filter-Objects-Offset Path. The Offset variable determines how thick the bevel will be. Positive numbers go outward from the letter, and negative numbers inward. Start with 2 or 3 points.

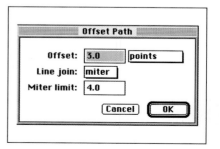

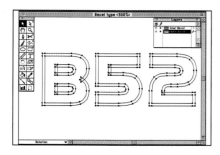

4 MOVE NEW PATH TO OUTER BEVEL LAYER

Make sure the new path is selected. In the Layers palette, click and hold the mouse on the small pencil icon to the right of the Inner Bevel layer name. Drag it down to the Outer Bevel layer.

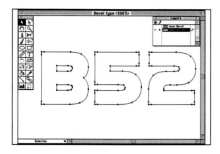

5 APPLY MERGE FILTER

With the new path still selected apply the Merge filter (Filter–Pathfinder–Merge). This will clean up any overlapping paths created by the Merge filter. Now you have two independent paths on two different layers.

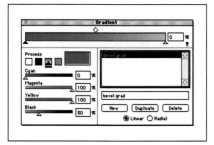

6 CREATE AND APPLY GRADIENT

A simple two-color gradient from a dark color to a light color works fine, but you might want to experiment with multiple-color gradients. A two-color gradient was used for this sample. Apply the same gradient to both sets of paths, and using the Gradient Vector tool, redirect the colors so they are opposite one another. Click the outlines on the Inner Bevel layer and arrange the gradient to go from dark at the top to light at the bottom. Then arrange the outlines on the Outer Bevel layer to be light at the top and dark at the bottom. Garnish to taste.

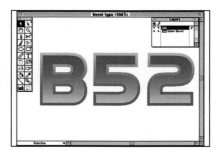

Quilted Type

Davida

Quilted text creates the look of quilted fabric. This technique is, perhaps, a bit more limited than some of the others, but it is useful nonetheless, and demonstrates some techniques you might want to use in other applications.

1 CREATE TYPE AND GRAPHICS
Since we start with line art and type, I created the art in Illustrator. Some artwork can be created just as easily in Photoshop. It's your call.

2 MAKE A PHOTOSHOP DOCUMENT
The document should be a grey-scale file with a white background. In the Black channel, place the graphic you created in Illustrator or create one from scratch. Invert the channel so you have white type and graphics on a black background.

3 DUPLICATE BLACK CHANNEL
Create a duplicate of the Black channel by dragging its name to the middle icon in the Channels palette. Name the new channel "Original copy" so I can refer to it later.

4 APPLY GAUSSIAN BLUR FILTER
Select the original Black channel and apply the Gaussian Blur filter (Filter-Blur-Gaussian Blur) with a radius setting around 3.

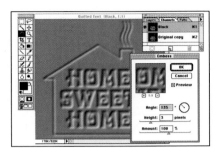

5 APPLY EMBOSS FILTER

Apply the Emboss filter (Filter-Stylize-Emboss) to the Black channel. The settings can vary but start with an Angle of 135 degrees, a Height of 3 pixels, and an Amount of 100%.

8 LOAD THE "ORIGINAL COPY" CHANNEL AS A SELECTION

With the Black channel still selected, Option-click on the "Original copy" name in the Channels palette. This is the same technique as in Step 6.

6 LOAD "ORIGINAL COPY" CHANNEL AS A SELECTION AND INVERT

With the Black channel still selected, Option-click on the "Original copy" name in the Channels palette. This will load that channel as a selection. Invert the selection image by choosing Image-Map-Invert. The Quilted effect is complete. Now to colorize it.

9 USE HUE/SATURATION

Choose Image-Adjust-Hue/Saturation. Click on the "Colorize" checkbox in the lower right corner. Adjust the top slider to the color required. If the "Preview" checkbox is also selected, you should be able to see the image change as you adjust the slider. When you have the color you wish, click OK.

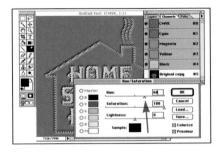

7 CHANGE THE MODE TO CMYK

Choose CMYK color under Mode. In the Channels palette, you should see all four CMYK channels instead of just the one Black channel.

10 INVERSE THE SELECTION AND COLORIZE

With the image still selected, choose Select-Inverse. The un-colorized portions of your image should now be selected. Again choose Image-Adjust-Hue/Saturation and change the color as in Step 9.

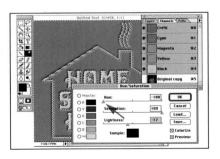

Ghosted Type

*Goudy Handtooled &
Function Condensed Bold*

Ghosted type adds a dramatic touch to your designs. When done right, it almost always looks classy and sophisticated. Of course, this depends on the photo as much as the type. You'll see ghosted type used in all sorts of designs, but it is especially well suited for multimedia and video, or any design where the image or photo occupies the entire design space — CD album covers and liners are a good example — leaving no room for type except to be placed directly on the image.

Start with a photo or image appropriate to your design, and create your type in Illustrator or FreeHand. You can enter type directly in Photoshop, but we recommend preparing it in one of these applications; Photoshop lets you enter formatted type, but you can't edit it or change its format later. If your type exists in an Illustrator document, for example, you can always make changes to it in Illustrator, and re-import it to Photoshop.

1 OPEN PHOTO AND CREATE NEW CHANNEL

Open the photo or image file in Photoshop and create a new blank channel (click on the middle icon at the bottom of the Channel palette). Name the new channel "Type." Still in the new channel, choose Select All from the Select menu, make sure your background color is white, and press Delete.

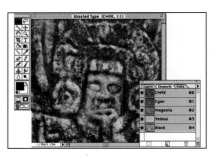

2 PLACE THE TYPE IN THE "TYPE" CHANNEL

With the "Type" channel selected, choose File-Place and select the file from the dialog box.

If you want your type to be centered in your channel, after placing it or typing it, while it is still selected, choose Cut. Now when you choose Paste, it will be centered horizontally and vertically within your image.

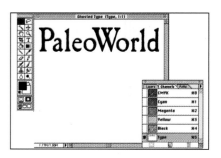

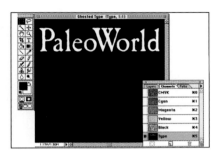

3 INVERT "TYPE" CHANNEL

Deselect the type and invert the entire channel by choosing Image-Map-Invert so you will have white type on a black background.

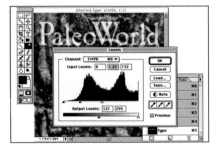

4 LOAD "TYPE" CHANNEL
AS A SELECTION

Select the image channel and load the "Type" channel as a selection. Option-click on the "Type" channel name.

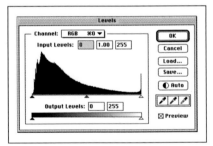

5 ADJUST CONTRAST OF
SELECTED IMAGE

At this point you can use either the Levels control or the Curves control to adjust the contrast of the "Type" channel. I like the Levels control because it offers a bit more control over the image lightness, darkness, and contrast.

Before you bring up the Levels control, choose Select-Hide Edges to hide the selection outline, or *the marching ants* as it is commonly referred to. The selection is still selected, but the outline won't get in the way as you visually control the levels.

Interlapping Type

Phyllis Swash & URW Antiqua Bold

Interlapping type adds a subtle and elegant appearance to type logos, creating the illusion of weaved characters. This can enhance a simple text-only design proving the adage that the whole is greater than the sum of the parts.

This techniques relies on Illustrator 5.0's Divide filter. This filter can also be used in FreeHand 5.0 (yes, Macromedia FreeHand can load and use Adobe Illustrator filters.)

☹ Unfortunately you will not be able follow the steps in this technique using Illustrator 4.0 for Windows.

1 CREATE TYPE IN ILLUSTRATOR
Design an award winning logo. Create the type in Illustrator and position the letters so they overlap. Color each letter with different colors. It could also be different shades of grey. Convert the letters to graphic outlines.

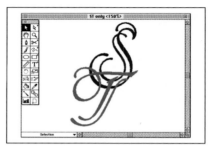

2 APPLY THE DIVIDE FILTER
Select the letters you wish to interlap. Choose the Divide filter (Filter-Pathfinder-Divide). This filter looks at all the selected elements and where there is overlap, it creates a new closed path. You can select any of these new pieces and modify them any way you wish. The newly created segments are colored red so you can see the results of the filter. You don't need to color them as it shows in the example to the right.

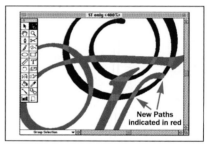

3 CHANGE THE COLOR OF INTERLAPPING SEGMENTS
Determine which segments need to be recolored. Choose the Direct Select tool (the white arrow), select the first segment and apply the new color. You can redefine the color a couple of different ways. After you

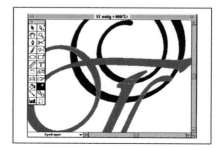

make the selection, you can simply adjust the color faders in the Paint Style palette to the new color. If the new color is a custom color, click on the new color in the Paint Style palette under the custom color list.

down the Option key and your cursor turns into the Paint Bucket tool. Place the Paint Bucket cursor over the area you wish to fill with the new color and click. Repeat the same process for all other segments that need to be recolored.

4 USING THE EYEDROPPER TOOL
I like using this tool for changing colors of elements because of how quick and easy it is. First make sure you have the Direct Select tool selected (the white arrow). Then select the Eyedropper tool. Zoom in on the area you wish to modify. Hold down the Command key. The tool temporarily changes to the Direct Select tool. (This is why you first select the Direct Select tool before selecting the Eyedropper tool. If you had the regular selection tool selected last— the solid black arrow—and you held down the Command key, the tool would become the regular select tool and would not allow to select just certain segments of your letters). Select the segment you wish to recolor. Release the Command key and the tool returns to the Eyedropper tool. Click on any other segment that has the same color you wish to change the select segment to. Now hold

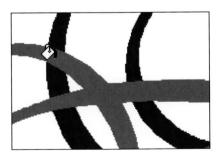

Engraved Type

GOURMET BURGERS & SPIRITS

Copperplate Gothic Bold & Franklin Gothic

This technique is very simple, yet adds a remarkably sophisticated appearance to your type. It's not used all that often, so it tends to attract a good deal of attention.

Illustrator was used for this example, but you could just as easily accomplish the same thing with FreeHand.

2 OFFSET THE COPY

The easiest way to move items in precise units is by using the arrow keys on your keyboard. Open the General Preferences dialog box under the File menu, and change the Cursor key option to 1 point if it's not already (this value can be anything you wish so you can change it later if it is not giving you the results you want). The Arrow keys move your selection in the direction of the arrow and by the amount in the Cursor key setting. Make sure that the letters are selected, then move them down and to the right by simply pressing the Down and Right arrow keys. The final amount that you move the type will depend on the size of your type. Change the type's fill color to white.

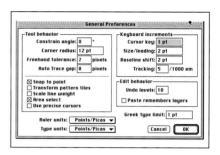

1 CREATE YOUR TYPE

Create the type you want to engrave. Some letterspacing is appropriate here to accommodate the effect. Change its fill color to black. Copy the type to the Clipboard, and then choose Edit-Paste in Back.

3 COPY OFFSET TYPE AND PASTE IN BACK

With the second copy still selected, copy it and paste it behind as we did with the original. With this third copy selected, move it down and to the right as we did the second copy, and change its fill color to black.

After you have created three copies, you can adjust the positioning to achieve just the right amount of engraving effect. You can also change the color of the first and third copies to any color you want. If your design uses a background color under the type, however, you'll need to change the color of the second copy to the same color as the background. This effect works only if the background contains a single solid color. If your background is a texture or photo, for instance, or uses multiple colors, then you must create the engraved type with filters.

4 CREATE TYPE OUTLINES
Start as before with your type. Convert the type to graphic outlines by selecting the type and choosing Create Outlines from the Type menu.

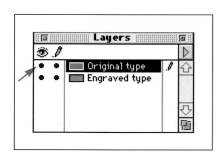

5 COPY THE OUTLINES TO A NEW LAYER
In the Layers palette, double-click the Layer 1 name, rename it "Engraved type" and click OK. In the Layers palette submenu choose New Layer and name it "Original type." Select and Copy the letter

outlines. With the "Original type" layer selected, choose Paste In Front from the Edit menu. Hide the layer by clicking the Eyeball bullet next to the layer name in the Layers palette. We'll come back to this layer later.

6 OFFSET TYPE
The "Engraved type" layer should be the only layer visible. Select the outlines and offset them from their original position the amount appropriate to the design. For smaller text, this may only be a point or two; for larger text you will probably want a more significant offset.

7 COPY AND PASTE IN BACK
Copy the type again and select Paste in Back from the Edit menu. Offset these letters with the Down and Right arrow keys like you did before. Each letter should now have two copies.

8 APPLY MINUS FRONT FILTER
Select each set of letters one at a time and apply the Minus Front filter from the Patherfinder submenu in the Filter menu. That is, select both copies of the first letter and apply the filter, then select both copies of the second letter and

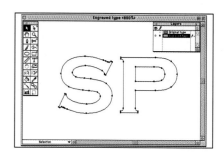
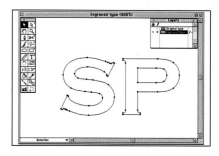
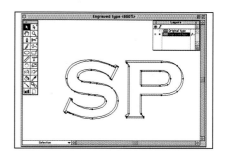

apply the filter, etc. In other words, don't select both copies of all the letters and apply the filter. This would be bad.

If you are using a version of Illustrator that doesn't sport Layers (like Illustrator 4 for Windows) you can use the Hide and Show commands instead of layering.

NOTE The words California and Authority were modified by using a plug-in filter called Infinite FX/1. It's extremely easy to use. Just select an object and apply one of the 55 different effects available. You can find a demo version of the plug-in on the companion CD. Ordering information is also provided if you are interested in purchasing the full version.

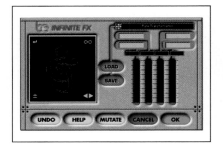

9 SHOW ALL LAYERS

Show the "Original type" layer to see the completed design. Here you can adjust the colors as necessary. We added a gradient behind the letters to show that you can see background elements between the cracks of the letters.

Reflective Type

Plakette Demi Bold

As its name suggests, this technique creates the wavy, reflective quality of metal. Actually, the technique I discuss here generates an effect not quite as irregular looking as real metal. Because of this, it is also useful for a wider range of applications, specifically those requiring colors other than the typical metallic colors. For this technique, it's not really feasible to create your type directly in Photoshop because of special letterspacing needed to create the bevel. I instead used Illustrator to create my type. FreeHand can also be used. Illustrator files can be regular Illustrator or EPS file formats. In FreeHand, however, you must export the file in Illustrator format (any one will do). If you experience problems placing an Illustrator file created by FreeHand, convert the type to paths prior to exporting it as an Illustrator document.

1 CREATE A PHOTOSHOP DOCUMENT

In the Photoshop document, create a new channel from the Channels palette and name it "Type original." Press the D key to make sure the foreground and background are the default colors. Note the channel is filled with black. Select the entire channel by choosing All from the Select menu, press the delete key, and deselect the channel by choosing None from the Select menu. The channel should be filled with white.

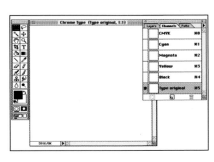

2 PLACE YOUR TEXT

Place your text from Illustrator or FreeHand into the "Type original" channel (File-Place). Size and position appropriately. Deselect the type. Invert the channel by choosing Image-Map-Invert. You should now have white type on a black background.

3 DUPLICATE ORIGINAL CHANNEL

In the Channels palette, make a duplicate of the "Type original" channel by dragging the name to the middle icon at the bottom of the palette and rename it "Type thickened." This new channel allows us to create a bevel.

4 APPLY MAXIMUM FILTER

With this channel selected, apply the Maximum filter (Filter-Other-Maximum). The higher the radius value, the thicker the bevel. I used a value of 2 pixels.

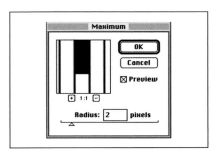

5 CREATE FIRST GRADIENT

Select the original color channel, and load the new "Type thickened" channel as a selection. Drag the name to the left-most icon. Choose the two colors you'll be using to graduate back and forth. In this example, I chose a dark blue

and a light blue, and assigned them to the foreground and background colors. I usually assign the lighter of the two colors as the foreground but it really doesn't matter. With the gradient tool, apply the two colors to the selection with the lighter color on top.

To constrain the gradient vertically, hold down the Shift key while applying the gradient tool.

7 SELECT ORIGINAL TYPE

In the Channels palette, make sure the color channel is selected (the RGB or CMYK channel) and load "Type original" as a selection. Go back to the Paths palette, and with the Split path selected, apply the Make Selection command from the Paths palette submenu.

8 DELETE LOWER PORTION OF TYPE FROM SELECTION

In the Make Selection dialog box, choose the Subtract from Selection operation. Change the Feather Radius to 0, if it isn't already, and click OK. You should now have the upper portion (above the wavy line) selected.

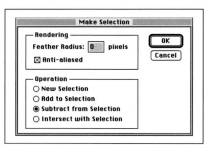

6 DRAW THE PATH

Go into the Paths palette and select the pen tool. Draw a free form wavy line that splits the type in two and name it Split (you name paths just like you do layers). It's important that the path be closed. Notice how I closed the path by drawing outside and below the image. Remember, this is just a path — only the wavy line will have an effect on the image; the lines drawn outside and below the text will not change it in any way.

9 CREATE UPPER GRADIENT

Using the gradient tool, reverse the gradient, that is, using the same two colors, create a gradient from dark to light with dark on top.

10 CREATE LOWER GRADIENT

Go back to the Channels palette and load the "Type original" channel as a selection. From the Paths palette, choose the Make Selection command again from the Paths palette submenu, and choose the Intersect with Selection operation from the Make Selection dialog box. You should now have the bottom portion (the stuff below the wavy line) selected. With the gradient tool apply a gradient from dark to light, with dark on top. Deselect the type.

Voilá. You now have reflective type.

Embossed Type

Deanna Flowers, Vendome & Function Condensed

This embossing technique is simple but very strong visually. Almost anything can be used with this technique but the final result will dictate whether or not it's right for the graphic. Type and graphics that have rounded corners and few hor-izontal or vertical straight lines are best suited for this procedure — the leaf symbol graphic used here is a great example of the type of graphic I mean. No straight lines and plenty of curves and rounded corners.

1 CREATE A BACKGROUND COLOR

In this example, I used shades of black to create the emboss effect. In Illustrator draw, a box and fill it with 25% Black. The box should be big enough so the emboss design will fit within its boundaries.

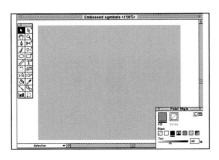

💡 In order for the emboss effect to work, the percentages of black of the background, highlight, and shadow elements need to interact with one another. The background percentage should fall somewhere between the highlight and shadow percentage. Play around with these numbers until you find the right combination.

2 CREATE ARTWORK

Create the type or graphic to be embossed. If there is type involved, convert it to graphic outlines (Type-Create Outlines). I like to work with graphic outlines since they are easier to position when working with multiple copies of the same graphic, which is exactly what we are about to do.

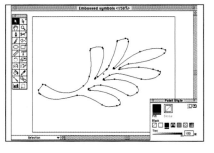

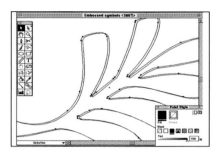

3 DUPLICATE AND REPOSITION HIGHLIGHT

Select the type or graphic and move it up and to the left of the original graphic, but don't let go of the mouse yet. After you have moved the copy into the correct position, hold down the Option key and let go of the mouse. You should now see two copies of the original type or graphic.

ment is on top of the other two elements. Select the original element and select Bring to Front from the Arrange menu.

After you create the effect, play with the percentages of black for the different elements. A small percentage differential between elements will create a more subtle effect. If you want a more defined effect, make the highlight lighter and the shadow darker.

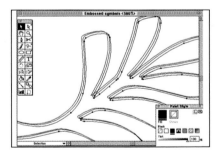

4 DUPLICATE AND REPOSITION SHADOW

Using the same technique as in Step 3, create a copy that is down and to the right of the original. Remember to hold down the Option key before releasing the mouse. There should be three copies of the original graphic.

5 APPLY BLACK PERCENTAGES TO THE ELEMENTS

Select the highlight element and change it to 10% Black. Select the original element and change it to 40% Black. Select the shadow element and change it to 60% Black. Also make sure the original ele-

Debossed Type

Adobe Helvetica Black & Industria Solid

This is a really cool, if somewhat complex, procedure combining lots of different effects. It is excellent for use in multimedia and video applications. I used a texture with a file size of 640 by 480 pixels for the background. After adjusting its color, I then created the spot light shooting across it. You can use any texture you like for the background, and thousands are available from a variety of sources.

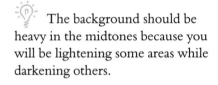

1 PREPARE YOUR TYPE

The type in this example was created in Illustrator, where both the words "Midnight" and "Matinee" were positioned and sized relative to one another, and then saved as a regular Illustrator document.

2 CREATE A BACKGROUND

Create the background or open a background texture in Photoshop. Create a new channel called "Type." In the Channels palette, click the middle icon at the bottom. Make the entire channel white by choosing Select All from the Select menu and pressing the Delete key. Your background color should be white.

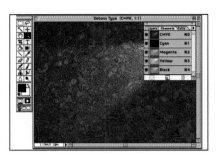

The background should be heavy in the midtones because you will be lightening some areas while darkening others.

3 IMPORT YOUR TYPE

If you created your text in Illustrator, choose Place from the File menu and select the file that contains the text. If you are creating the type in Photoshop, do so in the Type channel.

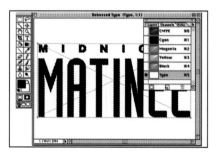

When placing the type and before actually allowing Photoshop to rasterize it, you can adjust the size. When you place a file, a box with an 'X' through it appears. If you wait just a moment longer, a preview of the imported file will show in the box. At this point you can adjust the size and position.

Size is more important than positioning since you can move the type to any location after it's placed without degrading the quality.

4 INVERT "TYPE" CHANNEL

In this sample, we are working the word "Matinee" only. For steps on applying a drop shadow like the word "Midnight," see the *Drop Shadow* section earlier in this chapter. Invert the "Type" channel by choosing Image-Map-Invert. You should end up with white type on a black background.

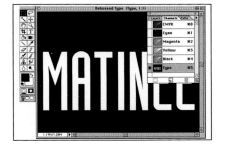

5 DUPLICATE THE "TYPE" CHANNEL

In the Channels palette, click and hold the "Type" channel name and drag it to the middle icon at the bottom of the palette. Name this duplicate channel "Hilite."

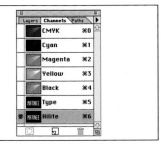

6 DUPLICATE THE "HILITE" CHANNEL

Use the same technique as in Step 5. Name the new channel "Shadow." You should now have three channels in addition to the normal color channels in the file (a total of six if the file uses RGB color, seven if it uses CMYK).

7 APPLY OFFSET FILTER TO "HILITE" CHANNEL

Make sure the "Hilite" channel is selected in the Channels palette and choose Filter-Other-Offset. Change the Horizontal to -1 pixel and the Vertical to 1 pixel. This should move the entire channel 1 pixel down and 1 pixel to the left. Select the Wrap Around option under Undefined Areas.

The direction you move the "Hilite" and "Shadow" channels is determined by the imaginary light source. In the Midnight Matinee sample, I had a spot light coming from the upper right corner. So the highlight on the type should be on the lower left sides.

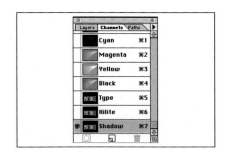

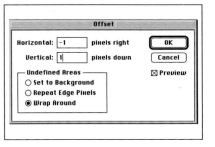

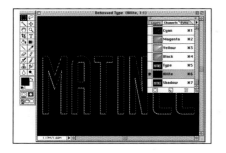

8 LOAD "TYPE" CHANNEL AND FILL WITH BLACK

With the "Hilite" channel selected, load the "Type" channel as a selection. Hold down the Option key and click once on the "Type" channel name in the Channels palette. You should see the selection come up after a moment. Make sure your foreground color is black, and then hold down the Option key again and press Delete. This fills your selection with black. Choose Select-None to deselect the channel.

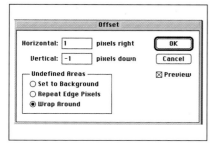

9 APPLY OFFSET FILTER TO "SHADOW" CHANNEL

Make sure the "Shadow" channel is selected in the Channels palette and choose Filter-Other-Offset. Change the Horizontal to 1 pixel and the Vertical to -1 pixel. This should move the entire channel 1 pixel up and 1 pixel to the right. Select the Wrap Around option under Undefined Areas.

10 LOAD "TYPE" CHANNEL AND FILL WITH BLACK

This is the same as Step 8 except you should have the "Shadow" channel selected. We now have three of the four channels needed to complete the type effect.

11 DUPLICATE "TYPE" CHANNEL

Select the "Type" channel and duplicate it by dragging it to the middle icon at the bottom of the Channels palette. Double-click the name and rename it "Inside Shadow." Invert the "Inside Shadow" channel (Image-Map-Invert). You should have black type on a white background.

12 APPLY THE GAUSSIAN BLUR AND OFFSET FILTERS

Apply a Gaussian Blur (Filter-Blur-Gaussian Blur) at a setting of 3. Apply the Offset filter (Filter-Other-Offset) with a Horizontal setting of -4 and a Vertical setting of 4.

13 LOAD "TYPE" CHANNEL AND INVERSE THE SELECTION

Load the "Type" channel by Option-clicking its name and Select-Inverse. Make sure your foreground color is black, hold down the Option key, and press Delete and deselect.

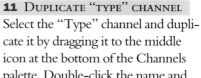

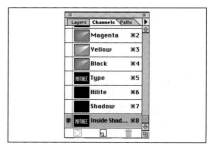

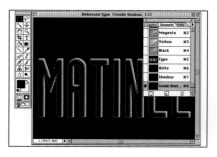

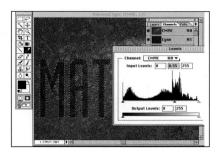

14 ADJUST LEVELS OF THE
BACKGROUND TEXTURE

In the Channels palette, select the original background texture channel. Load the "Type" channel (Option-click the channel name). Choose Image–Adjust–Levels to bring up the Levels control. Adjust the top middle slider by moving it to the right to slightly darken the inside of the letters. It should be just dark enough to read the type but not much darker. We need to add a darker shadow in a later step.

the Option key this time. Remember that pressing the Delete key fills the selected area with the current *background* color and Option-Delete fills with the current *foreground* color.)

For both the shadow and the hilite, if they are not dark enough or light enough, press the key combination twice. For example, if you press Option-Delete twice in Step 15, the shadow will appear darker; if you press the Delete key twice in Step 16, the hilite will appear brighter.

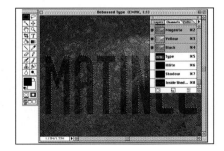

15 LOAD "SHADOW" CHANNEL AND
FILL WITH BLACK

Load the "Shadow" channel by Option-clicking its name in the Channels palette. Make sure your foreground color is black, then hold down the Option key and press Delete. This fills the selection with black.

16 LOAD "HILITE" CHANNEL AND
FILL WITH WHITE

Load the "Hilite" channel by Option-clicking its name in the Channels palette. Make sure your background color is white by pressing the letter D, and then press Delete. (Do not hold down

17 LOAD "INSIDE SHADOW"
CHANNEL AND ADJUST LEVELS

Load the "Inside Shadow" channel. Bring up the Levels control (Image–Adjust–Levels) and adjust the top left slider to the right to slightly darken the selection area. You can also adjust the middle slider to the right to further darken the selection area. Congratulations, you can breathe now!

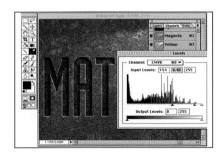

Type in Flames

Typewriter Condensed Bold & Franklin Gothic Heavy

Fire is nothing if not attention grabbing. In nature, I think it's safe to say that things on fire tend to catch our eye. Have you ever seen a man on fire? He is focused. His attention is grabbed. Almost as if nothing else really matters. This technique mimics the appearance of flames around type. We found it trollin' the net one evening (thanks DoctorW@aol.com). There are many good ideas to be found on the Internet, and especially in some of the graphics and desktop publishing forums on CompuServe and America Online.

Type in flames is wonderful for advertising purposes and cover art (or in any application where you're using words like "hot" or "spicy" or "Hell" or…you get the picture).

This technique requires a completed graphic. For example, the graphic in Step 1 was created in Illustrator.

1 START WITH A GREYSCALE FILE

In Photoshop, create a greyscale file appropriate for the size of the final type. In the New document

dialog box, change the Contents option to White. Use the Type tool to enter your text, or import a graphic from an Illustrator or Free-Hand file. You're basically starting this technique with a completed image — all we're showing you is how to torch it. After your image is placed, deselect the graphic and invert it. Choose Image-Map-Invert. See the *Type on a Path* technique for steps on how to wrap type around objects.

2 DUPLICATE THE CHANNEL

In the Channels palette, drag the channel name to the middle icon at the bottom of the Channels palette. You should now see two channels.

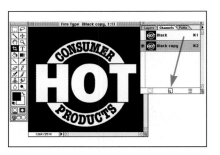

3 ROTATE ORIGINAL CHANNEL

Select the original channel, and rotate the entire image 90 degrees counter clockwise. Choose Image-Rotate-90° CCW.

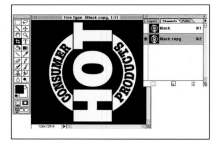

4 APPLY WIND FILTER

With the original channel selected, choose Filter-Stylize-Wind. Change the parameters to Blast and Left.

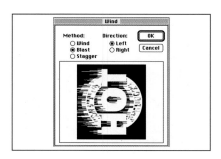

5 APPLY DIFFUSE FILTER

Choose Filter-Stylize-Diffuse and change the mode to Normal.

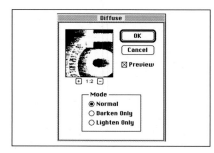

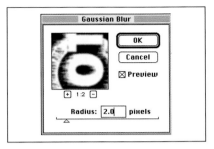

6 APPLY GAUSSIAN BLUR

Apply a Gaussian Blur to the image (Filter-Blur-Gaussian Blur). This setting is variable and some experimentation should be used here. A small radius value around 3 pixels should do it. You might want to save your file at this point. If you don't like this blur setting, you can come back to this step and try again. Write down the settings used at each step if you think you might need to backtrack later.

7 ROTATE IMAGE TO ORIGINAL ORIENTATION

Choose Image-Rotate-90°CW.

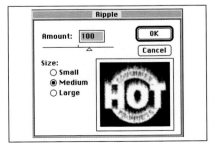

8 APPLY RIPPLE FILTER

The final filter is Ripple (Filter-Distort-Ripple). Adjust the amount to 100 and the Size to Medium. Again, experimentation is encouraged.

Your image should now look something like this:

9 LOAD SECOND CHANNEL AND FILL WITH BLACK

With the original channel selected, load the second channel as a selection by dragging its name to the left icon at the bottom of the Channels palette (or Option-click the name). Then fill the selected area with black.

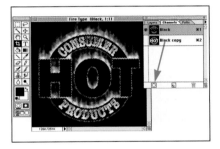

We're going to use the Option-Delete technique (Alt-Delete in Windows) to fill the selection with the foreground color (pressing Delete by itself fills the selection with the background color), but first make sure the foreground color is black. The simplest way to do this is to press the letter D. Then select Option-Delete and deselect the graphic.

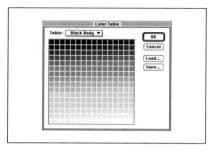

10 CONVERT IMAGE TO
INDEXED COLOR

Choose Mode-Indexed Color and
then select Color Table from the
Mode menu. In the dialog box,
click on the Table pop-up menu,
select Black Body and click OK.

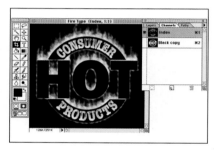

Stick a fork in it, it's done!
Remember you're still in Indexed
Color. In order to print separations
properly, change the Mode to
CMYK. This mode change tends
to desaturate the reds and oranges;
some color manipulation may be
in order. ■

Got my attention!

Picto

Plug-ins & Filters

ANY GRAPHIC PROGRAM WORTH ITS OWN WEIGHT IN RAM offers the ability for other companies to write *extensions* to their program. This extensibility enhances the program's worth and functionality. Extensions can be as simple as file format filters that allow you to read and write formats normally not available to the host program, while others take the user far beyond the software's standard features.

Adobe products refer to these programs as *Plug-ins*, but other products such as Macromedia's FreeHand, for example, refer to them as *Xtras*. Sometimes these extensions are compatible across multiple products (it's possible to use Illustrator Plug-ins with FreeHand), and sometimes they're coded for a particular application.

Many of the techniques in the Type as Graphic Element chapter can be reproduced in a few mouse clicks with extensions. So why did we bother showing you how to do the techniques manually? Even though an extension can produce wonderful effects quickly, you may still want to make changes to it manually after you have applied the filter. Knowing how the graphic is built, gives you the ability to further manipulate it.

The following few pages show examples of stand-out extensions. Most have *demo* versions of the program on the companion CD that came with the book. Check them out and have fun exploring the virtually limitless possibilities these extensions give you.

Plakette Medium distorted with KPT VectorDistort

Adobe Gallery Effects

The text was set in Adobe Illustrator. The KPT Vector Effects 3D Transform was used to create a beveled edge. The type was saved and then opened in Adobe Photoshop where it was colorized. The Gallery Effects Rough Pastels filter was used to finish the effect.

Adobe Mezz & Copperplate Gothic Bold

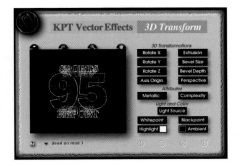

URW Antiqua Bold & Franklin Gothic Heavy

KPT Vector Effects

Sports Report 95 —The words Sports Report were extruded with the 3D Transform filter. The 3D extruded zoom portion was further modified using KPT ColorTweak. You can change the color by increasing or decreasing brightness, contrast and saturation just like you can in Photoshop. The beveled edge on the 95 was created with the KPT 3D Transform. The final logo remained in Illustrator and was saved as an EPS file.

Entertainment News —The word Entertainment was extruded with the KPT 3D Transform filter. The extruded portion was selected separately and KPT ColorTweak was used to remove the color and replace it with greyscale to show dimension. The word News was modified using the KPT ShadowLand filter. It was first filled with black, and then the Halosity variable was adjusted to simulate a blurring effect. Like the previous logo, it remained in Illustrator and was saved as an EPS file.

Function Heavy & Adobe Nueva

These pages showcase Plug-ins for Adobe Photoshop and Adobe Illustrator. The following is a list of the featured products with information on how to contact the manufacturer:

Gallery Effects
Adobe Systems Inc.
1585 Charleston Road
PO Box 7900
Mountain View, CA 94039
800-628-2320

Kai's Power Tools (for Adobe Photoshop)
KPT Vector Effects (for Adobe Illustrator)
MetaTools
6303 Carpinteria Avenue
Carpinteria, CA 93013
805-566-6200

Infinite FX
BeInfinite, Inc.
4651 Woodstock Road
Suite 203, #210
Roswell, GA 30075-1686
800-554-6624
404-552-6624

TypeCaster
Xaos Tools, Inc.
600 Townsend Street
Suite 270 East
San Francisco, CA 94103
415-487-7000

Adobe Nueva

KPT Vector Effects

Nova Vacation & Travel — The text was set in Illustrator and the multi-color fill pattern was created with KPT ShatterBox. The reflection was created using KPT 3D Transform. A light grey-to-white gradient was then applied to create the shadow effect. This is an Illustrator file that can be scaled to any size without loss in quality.

Flowers — This graphic used the KPT Emboss filter in Illustrator to simulate a raised surface. The manual version (explained earlier in this book) required five steps to complete in Illustrator. Using a filter specially design for this effect, it required only a few clicks.

Moe's Tavern — Do you remember this graphic from the Neon Type section? It took six steps to create in Photoshop using channels and paths from Illustrator. Here, the same effect is accomplished with a few clicks of the mouse with KPT Neon and KPT ShadowLand. Unlike the Moe's Tavern graphic created with Photoshop, this version is an Illustrator file based on vector elements as opposed to raster elements.

Deanna Flowers, Vendome & Function Condensed

Salut, VAG Rounded Bold

Goudy Sans Bold

Plakette Medium

Function Heavy & Regular

Xaos TypeCaster

This Photoshop plug-in gives you exceptional control over extruding type in 3D. You simply enter the text, choose a font and adjust the controls for face color, bevel, extrusion and light source and then click Apply. The results can be amazing. You can color the type with flat colors or apply textures normally referred to as texture mapping. Like the KPT filters, the interface takes some time to get used to, but it is very logical. I was setting type in minutes with no documentation because I was working on a beta version. The plug-in should be available by the time you read this.

Kai's Power Tools

KPT Power Tools is another Photoshop plug-in. It may not be perfectly suited to manipulate type, per se, but as you can see from the example, you can dress it up a bit. I couldn't even begin to describe each step I took to achieve the final result. I used a combination of two KPT Power Tool filters, Gradients on Path and Texture Explorer. I also used Gaussian Blur, Stroke and Invert on selected portions. Basically, I kept on playing until I ended up with what you see above. This is what makes these programs with plug-ins fun to work with.

BeInfinite Infinite FX

There are 55 different filters in the Infinite FX package for Adobe Illustrator. In the sample above, I started with text in Illustrator and converted it to paths. With the type selected, I chose the Cylinder Wrap filter. Using the sliders on the right of the filter window (see below), I adjusted the variables to achieve the results I was looking for. I then pasted the globe behind the type to finish the logo.

CHAPTER 10

Choosing
Typefaces

Choosing Typefaces

Bridal Shower ~~Bridal Shower~~

BRIDAL SHOWER ~~BRIDAL SHOWER~~

BRIDAL SHOWER ~~BRIDAL SHOWER~~

𝕭𝖗𝖎𝖉𝖆𝖑 𝕾𝖍𝖔𝖜𝖊𝖗 ~~Bridal Shower~~

Bridal Shower ~~Bridal Shower~~

Bridal Shower ✓

PEOPLE NEW TO TYPE AND TYPOGRAPHY OFTEN ASK "What typeface should I use for such-and-such?" I usually respond with more questions than I do answers, but eventually we get the selection down to a handful. After that, it's purely a matter of personal taste. In the typeface descriptions section in the next chapter, I list some suggestions for the types of documents particular fonts might be well-suited for, but these are just general guidelines, and by no means hard and fast rules.

Perhaps the most important guiding principle to keep in mind is that typography exists to enhance the subject matter, or the content. In other words, typography does not exist for typography's sake. Every typographic action — the typeface you choose, the point size, leading, and line width, for example — should enhance, or at the very least, not distract from what you're writing about or what you're trying to say. Easier said than done. How does one go about this? Well, follow me on this.

1 *Match the typeface to the content.*

Before choosing a typeface, examine it, print out some samples of it, and be aware of any images it brings to mind. What is the first thing it reminds you of? Chances are this typeface would have a similar effect on your readers. So then, logically you must ask yourself whether the image this typeface projects has anything to do with your subject matter. Is it similar? Neutral? Or opposite? If you're writing a paper about the 18th century philosopher Immanuel Kant, for example, the typeface Futura will be out of time and out of character, but New Baskerville might fit in nicely. If you're designing wedding invitations, typefaces with an elegant or formal air such as URW Palladio, Galliard, or script faces such as Vivaldi or Zapf Chancery would be more appropriate than, say, Hobo

or Ad Lib. The latter with their playful and casual appearance might be quite effective when used in birthday party invitations. Of course, these are no-brainers, but you'd be surprised how many documents I see with these kinds of mismatches.

2 *Consider the basics before the exotics.*

For most text such as newsletters, reports, books, correspondence, and so on, it's hard to go wrong with Oldstyle designs such as Garamond, Bembo, or Sabon, to name a few, but these fonts might look somewhat stuffy if used in a rock magazine or techno-trendoid publication. The choice is never easy, nor is anyone going to be able to offer the ultimate suggestion without having seen the text printed with it. But if you start with basic fonts, it's easy to make changes and substitutions. There are more options available to you in terms of alternate font choices, styles changes, leading options, and so on.

3 *Pick a typeface and get to know it.*

Use it for everything. Memos, correspondence, fax covers, flyers, whatever. Try using it for every type of document you might have to create. Set it in wide columns and narrow, at large point sizes and small, with lots of leading and with minimal leading. Choose it for every conceivable situation. Better yet, try to avoid combining it with other fonts if you can, instead using the same font in a different style (bold or italic) or point size where you might otherwise opt to combine it with another font. This might be for headlines, subheads, page footers, captions for illustrations, and so on. For example, if you were to choose an extended typeface family such as Franklin Gothic, you could use the

Heavy weight for headlines and subheads, the Light to Regular weights for body text, and the Regular to Bold weights for captions and callouts. The goal here is to use the same typeface family, and push it to its limits. You'll discover a lot about it. You'll notice certain characters, features and quirks that simply reading about would not have revealed to you at a personal level. You'll understand, first hand, how well or how poorly it works in certain situations, whether it's a space-saver or a line-hog, for instance, or whether it looks dark at small sizes or light.

As with most things in life, practice makes perfect. Setting type is no different, but the discipline required to do it — that is, to select a single face and use it for everything — is somewhat at odds with having type libraries of a few hundred fonts or more. The knowledge you gain about the font, however, will help you design better looking documents than owning a type library of several thousand fonts.

Wax on, wax off.

Of course, this exercise applies primarily to text fonts. I wouldn't suggest using the display font Davida for all your documents. Start with a serif text font and run it through the paces for a few weeks, or maybe even a few months. Then move on to some of the sans serif text fonts. Tell people *"I'm in a Transitional phase. Divorce? No, Baskerville."* or *"I'm doing the Syntax thing these days."*

It will take time, but after a while, you'll no longer feel wishy-washy or uncertain about your font choices. In fact, you'll know exactly what font to use for any given document. And the knowledge and experience will apply to new fonts you've never before used as well; you'll know what to look for when you do use them. The time it takes for you to form an opinion

about a new typeface, or the types of documents where you might want to apply it, will be much shorter and won't require quite as much experimentation; that is, you'll get it right the first time.

4 *Consider all technical limitations.*

The text font used throughout this book is Bergamo (SoftMaker's version of Bembo, available on the companion CD) 10-point. Bergamo is a beautiful Oldstyle, or Renaissance typeface that looks great when printed at resolutions above 300 dpi. This book, for example, was printed from an imagesetter at 2400 dpi. Below say 600 dpi, however, Bergamo loses much of its refinement and detail. Resolution must be considered before deciding on something as important as the main text font for a publication.

By comparison, some faces look good at almost any size and at any resolution. URW Antiqua, Futura, and New Baskerville are good choices for text fonts when printing at low resolutions. Of course, the PostScript resident fonts Times, New Century Schoolbook, Palatino, and Bookman are also adequate for low-res printing. Baskerville, Bodoni, Garamond, and Sabon look increasingly better as resolution increases. At 10 points and above, these faces will even reproduce well on 300 dpi laser printers, but they look considerably better at 600 dpi.

Display and script faces are less affected by resolution constraints because they are typically printed at large point sizes (14 points and above), where printer resolution has less effect on overall character detail. At small sizes, however, many display faces will suffer regardless of printer resolution. Fette Fraktur, for example, would be ineffective at 8 points even when printed from a 2400 dpi imagesetter.

What kind of paper will you be using? Light fonts with fine detail tend to "sponge out" on standard printer or photocopier paper. A glossy paper stock can improve appearance considerably, and there are specially formulated papers that improve laser-printed output, but such paper is substantially more expensive.

Will you even be printing to paper at all? That is, are your documents intended for on-screen display (read: multimedia)? If they are, your font choices may be somewhat limited. Well, you can choose whatever font you like, but your *optimal* choices will be limited. First, are you preparing your type in a program such as Adobe Photoshop, which has the ability to *anti-alias* type, greatly improving its appearance at screen resolution (72 dpi)? Anti-aliasing smoothes the edges of type and graphics by blending them into the background colors. It's an optical illusion, but it works.

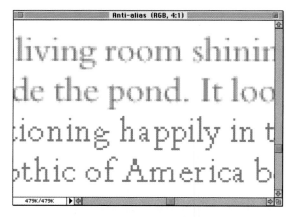

If we zoom in on the text, we can see how the anti-aliasing process really works. Notice how the edges of the anti-aliased text have been blended into the background to create the illusion of smoothness. It's really no more smooth, but anti-aliasing creates the illusion that it is.

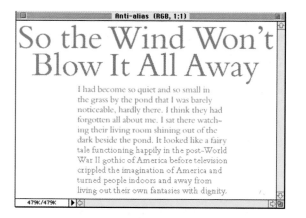

The first line of the title was anti-aliased in Adobe Photoshop. The second line was not. The first few lines of body text were also anti-aliased, and the bottom lines were left alone. This is how it would appear in any other application.

If you will be using an anti-aliasing application such as Photoshop to create your text for on-screen display, you can use just about any font and it will look good. Just remember that for reading text on-screen, you shouldn't choose a point size below 12 points. The anti-aliasing benefits are lost at small point sizes, and in many cases can even make text look worse.

If you're not anti-aliasing your text, then your font choices for on-screen documents are considerably more limited. You'll have little luck creating an attractive, easy-to-read multimedia application, for example, that uses 10-point Garamond for on-screen text. Your audience will hate you for forcing them to try to read it. Your best choices are the fonts that came with your operating system. On the Macintosh, the typeface Geneva is very readable at small sizes (9 to 12 points), and is a good choice for text you won't be anti-aliasing. In Windows, I would suggest using bitmap system fonts for the same reasons, although screen resolution is greater on the PC, so text tends to look better than on Macintosh screens. On either system, if your text will be 12 points or above, your font choices are a little better, but not much. The typefaces Times (or Times New Roman) and Helvetica (or Arial) are readable at 12 points and higher for on-screen documents.

Generally speaking, loosely spaced sans serif typefaces such as Geneva and MS Sans Serif are easier to read on-screen than serif types. Serifs are really intended for printed output, and lose much of their readability on-screen. This is almost the opposite of printed documents. If you choose to use serif fonts for on-screen documents, consider increasing the point size.

If all of these decisions seem too much, consider using Adobe Acrobat to create on-screen documents. Acrobat eliminates some of the problems associated with choosing readable fonts for on-screen display, because it automatically substitutes fonts using special Acrobat Multiple Master fonts. These special fonts, Adobe Sans and Adobe Serif, are automatically installed when you install the Acrobat software, and are automatically substituted when you create an Acrobat document…regardless what fonts you used to originally create the document.

The idea here is that you can focus your energy on creating good looking documents for printed output, i.e., paper, and let Acrobat worry about making it readable on-screen. Of course, if the screen is the ultimate intended output device for your documents, that is, if you don't plan on printing them, then design for the screen.

Acrobat documents are portable, too. They can be opened on any system — Mac, Windows, DOS and Unix — that has the Acrobat software installed. It's a bit too soon to tell whether Acrobat documents will change the way we work, whether we'll be ushering in the era of the paperless office any time soon, but they are becoming much more common for use as *ReadMe* files and online documentation. I imagine several books will soon be dedicated to designing Acrobat documents, perhaps even distributed as Acrobat files. ■

Typefaces

Typeface Classification

WHEN ASSEMBLING THE TYPEFACES FOR THIS BOOK, SoftMaker provided me with over 3,000 typefaces to choose from. I didn't want the selection to be gratuitous or haphazard, a packaging approach so common among low-cost type vendors, but rather meaningful and useful. My goal was to create a wide selection, yet provide depth in the right places, most notably in the category of text fonts — fonts you'll use everyday in all sorts of applications and documents. I also wanted to provide typefaces representative of the major historical and functional classifications so that I could better discuss those classifications.

And that is the purpose of this chapter — the classification of type. Classification is not as important to the field of typography as it is to, say, biology, but it is important. It's important to know your Oldstyles from your Moderns, your Geometrics from your Humanists, not just for cocktail party and online conversations, but for the effects these designs have on your documents, be they newsletters, advertisements, logos or letterhead. Type is central to design. The two can't be separated. Type must work with the page design, graphics and illustrations in a cohesive way. Sure, you could just start with any typeface for your newsletter, picking different ones at random until you find one you like, but that's not a very efficient approach. It would help to have a general idea about the kind of type you're looking at, and it is my goal to help you refine the part of your experience that formulates those general ideas.

Not that I have come up with these classifications on my own! Of course I didn't. Serif text fonts, for example, have been around for about 500 years, and they tend to fall into historical classification schemes quite nicely — typefaces from the 15th and 16th centuries are known as Oldstyles, and share many similar characteristics; typefaces from the 18th century fall into a category known as Transitionals; and typefaces from the late-18th and early-19th centuries are known as Moderns. I'll discuss these periods and the major typefaces associated with them in the following pages. You'll see that the lines of classification are fairly apparent, and a familiarity with them should help your type selection decisions. Sans serif typefaces, on the other hand, have only been around for the past century, so it wouldn't be very meaningful to classify these types on an historical basis, but a functional or descriptive approach will prove quite useful. This is particularly true as it relates to helping you choose sans serif fonts to combine with serif fonts, a common practice you'll no doubt engage in.

The first part of this section discusses the basic classifications, what they are and the general principles associated with them. It then moves on to the specifics, showing you samples of typefaces belonging to the various categories, and provides suggestions for how you might want to use these fonts, or which fonts you might consider combining them with. Each font discussed is also provided on the companion CD.

Some of the SoftMaker fonts have different names than the original typefaces, but the basic designs are similar, if not identical. The quality of these faces is outstanding, better than what you would find in any of the low-cost typeface packages on the market, and in most cases, approaches the quality of packages from high-end vendors. My hope is that if you become sufficiently excited about the world of type, you will migrate to some of these higher-end vendors such as Adobe, Monotype, and Agfa.

Parts of a Letter

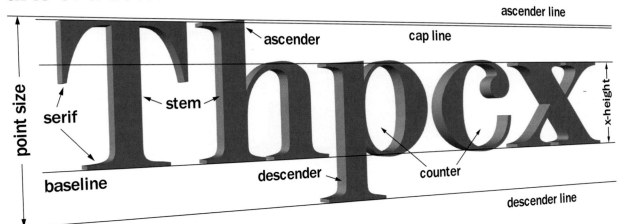

It's impossible to talk about typefaces without at some point resorting to some fairly technical terms. Fortunately these terms are also quite descriptive, and sometimes even make sense. The illustration above should give you a good idea as to what these terms mean. It's generalized, however. Even though I point out what a serif is, for example, there are several different types of serifs; for my purposes, however, these distinctions are not significant.

ASCENDER: The part of a lowercase letter that extends above the x-height, as in b, h, l.

BASELINE: The imaginary line on which all characters in a typeface rest (more or less).

COUNTER: The enclosed (or partially enclosed) parts of a letter such as p, g, C.

DESCENDER: The parts of such letters as g, p, q that extend below the baseline.

CAP HEIGHT: The height of the uppercase or capital letters. This is usually slightly less than the height of the ascenders of the lowercase letters.

POINT: A typographic unit of measure equal to $\frac{1}{12}$ th of a pica or $\frac{1}{72}$ nd of an inch. Font sizes are stated in points.

POINT SIZE: Refers to an imaginary bounding box extending from the descender line to the ascender line. The actual character sizes may vary greatly within the bounding box, which is why two fonts of the same point size can be very different in optical size.

SERIF: The finishing strokes, or feet, on a letter. Serifs help guide the eye from letter to letter, making them generally easier to read. Body text is usually set in a serif typeface.

STEM: The upright part of a letter such as K, L, T.

X-HEIGHT: The height of the lowercase letters, not including the ascenders or descenders.

All three type samples are set at 24 points, but notice the variance in optical size.

Oldstyles

Bergamo (aka Bembo)

The height of the lower-case letters, or *x-height*, is small in relation to the uppercase letters.

Serifs are bracketed, meaning that the stem slopes gently down to the serif.

Transitionals

Times Roman

The x-height is larger in relation to the uppercase letters.

Different Strokes...

Oldstyles The relationship between thick and thin strokes is fairly pronounced.

Bergamo

Transitionals The relationship between thick and thin strokes is less apparent.

Baskerville

Moderns The relationship between thick and thin strokes is highly exaggerated.

Bodoni

Although the distinctions are primarily historical — Oldstyles are based on designs from the 15th & 16th centuries, Transitionals from the 17th & 18th centuries, Moderns from the 18th & 19th centuries — they are also somewhat visceral. Oldstyles are friendly, warm, romantic, classical yet often quirky. Transitionals are rational, matter-of-fact and more even in terms of design and emotion. Moderns are stylized, refined, cool and sophisticated. Keep these characteristics in mind when designing documents and choosing fonts.

Moderns

Bodoni

The x-height is similar in proportion to Oldstyle designs—small in relation to the uppercase letters.

Thick and thin parts of letters are distributed along a vertical axis.

Serifs are thin and usually unbracketed. Sometimes referred to as "hairline" serifs.

Slab Serifs

Clarendon

The x-height is large in relation to uppercase letters.

Slab serifs have an even stroke width and large, bracketed serifs.

Slab Serifs

Slab Serif is a very broad category that includes typefaces such as Clarendon (above), New Century Schoolbook, and Glypha (available on the CD as *Glytus*), which is essentially a sans serif design with slab serifs.

Stress is the orientation upon which the thin and thick strokes of a character are aligned. It is most noticeable in closed characters such as the letters o, p, and b, but is reflected in all of the characters in a typeface. The stress of Oldstyles is oblique, Transitionals less so, approaching vertical, and Moderns have perfect vertical stress.

Geometric

Function (aka Futura)

The x-height is similar in proportion to modern designs—small in relation to the uppercase letters.

Sans serif literally means "without feet."

Grotesque

Franklin Gothic

Large proportional x-height.

Humanist

Chantilly (aka Gill Sans)

x-height is similar in proportion to that of Oldstyle serif types.

Historically speaking, sans serif types have only been around since the last century, so their classification is based entirely on form. Sans serif designs appear more linear and less fluid than serif designs, there is little variation in stroke width, and the stress is nearly vertical. For Geometric sans serifs such as Futura (on the CD as *Function*), the monowidth stroke is quite apparent, and the curves remain nearly identical from letter to letter, enhancing the strict geometry upon which this face is designed. Grotesques such as Franklin Gothic (shown here), Arial, and Helvetica, have slightly more variation in stroke, a larger x-height, and their proportions are not quite so geometric. Humanists are sans serif designs based on serif proportions, primarily Oldstyle serifs. To illustrate this, compare the lowercase 'a' of Chantilly (second from right) with that of Bergamo (right):

a a a a

Function, Franklin Gothic, Chantilly & Bergamo

American Uncial

uncial

Uncial types are based on the handwritten letters of Irish scribes dating to the 5th century. The *Book of Kells*, for example, an illuminated manuscript of the Gospels in Latin written in a monastery in County Meath during the 7th century, is probably the most well-known and most beautiful example of the uncial form.

Fette Fraktur

Black Letter

Black Letter type originated as a written form in northern Europe and dates to the late mediæval period. This style was also referred to as "Gothic," a derogatory term applied after the Renaissance when people assumed anything from the Middle Ages to be barbaric or Goth-like (Goths apparently weren't very hip).

Phyllis Swash et al.

Script

Larry
Moe
Curly

Script faces are based on handwriting, and as such tend to defy strict classification. Script fonts generally have joining characters, like cursive handwriting, and are generally difficult to read (like handwriting). Script faces are good for documents in which legibility is not your primary concern.

Stop et al.

DECORATIVE

G G G G G G

Decorative typefaces, also referred to as Display faces, are not designed for legibility or readability, but rather for their ability to attract attention. Decorative fonts are used for corporate logos, signs, advertisements, headlines in publications, multimedia, video and movie titles. Like script faces, they defy rigid classification. The only rule here is no rules.

Oldstyles

150-pt. Gareth

 Indicates font has matching small caps and Oldstyle figures.

 Indicates font has matching expert sets, which include ligatures, fractions, inferior and superior numerals.

OLDSTYLE TYPEFACES ARE DESIGNATED AS SUCH because, well, they're old. Actually, that's not entirely true. There are classic Oldstyle and revival Oldstyle typefaces. The classic Oldstyle typefaces, that is, those designs upon which all other Oldstyles are based, were designed between the 15th and 18th centuries by such printers and designers as Aldus Manutius (1450–1515), the designer of Bembo (on the companion CD as *Bergamo*), Claude Garamond (1480–1561), and William Caslon, whose designs bear their names. Obviously these men were not practicing their craft using computers, so it's safe to assume that someone had to transfer their designs to the PostScript and TrueType manifestations we use today.

And that's exactly what happened. Through the years, the designs of Manutius, Garamond, Caslon, et al. have been continually upgraded and refined as they migrate from one technological platform to the next. For example, the Garamond typeface on the companion CD was an adaptation made in the early 1970s of Claude Garamond's original designs from the early 1530s. It was later digitized in the 1980s, and no doubt changed to some degree, however small, before it found its way to your personal computer. Quite often these refinements represent improvements, but this is not always the case.

But other Oldstyles are revivals, typefaces designed to look like the centuries old originals, or perhaps simply inspired by them. Garamond Condensed and Sabon (on the companion CD as *Savoy*) were designed in the 1960s and 70s, but are Oldstyles nonetheless.

Oldstyles are based on the hand-drawn lettering and type of Renaissance designers long since dead.

Most have beautiful italics. This category is ideal for just about any text that is meant for extended reading: books, reports, articles, newsletters, user manuals, memos, correspondence, journals. At larger point sizes, Oldstyle typefaces work well as display fonts in head-lines, logos, signs, etc.

There are several Oldstyle typefaces on the com-panion CD: Bergamo, Caslon, Garamond, Garamond Condensed, Gareth, URW Palladio and Savoy.

Generally speaking, Oldstyle faces combine very well with sans serif typefaces such as Gill Sans (on the companion CD as *Chantilly*) and Syntax because they share similarly shaped characters and proportions. For example, if you are writing an operator manual, you might consider using a typeface like Bergamo for the main text, Chantilly for captions in figures and illustra-tions, and Chantilly Heavy for section headings. Such a combination would be complementary, consistent, and yet pleasing to the eye. There are hundreds of such combinations, far too many in fact to present them all, but presenting some of the general features and "rules" (if you want to call them that) will help develop and refine your sense for choosing them on your own.

Aldus Manutius designed this trademark to be printed in all of his books. It first appeared in 1502. (We added the drop shadow 493 years later.)

THE PLEASANT HISTORY OF
Lazarillo de Tormes

15-pt. Bergamo & 36-pt. Italic

THE PLEASANT HISTORY OF
Lazarillo de Tormes

15-pt. Caslon & 36-pt. Italic

THE PLEASANT HISTORY OF
Lazarillo de Tormes

15-pt. Garamond & 36-pt. Italic

THE PLEASANT HISTORY OF
Lazarillo de Tormes

15-pt. Garamond Condensed & 36-pt. Italic

THE PLEASANT HISTORY OF
Lazarillo de Tormes

15-pt. Gareth & 36-pt. Italic

THE PLEASANT HISTORY OF
Lazarillo de Tormes

15-pt. Savoy & 36-pt. Italic

BEMBO

SUGGESTED USES: text, books, journals, reports, memos

CONSIDER COMBINING WITH: Syntax, Gill Sans, Franklin Gothic

Bembo (available as *Bergamo* on the companion CD) is one of the most popular typefaces of all time for book printing. It is a true classic designed by the Venetian printer Aldus Manutius, and dates back to the Italian Renaissance of the 15th and 16th centuries. Aldus had a very interesting motto, *Festina lente*, or "make haste slowly," which I think captures the spirit of this

Bergamo 10·13

design: timelessness. Bembo is nearly 500 years old, and yet readers never seem to grow tired of it.

Bembo has always been one of my favorite typefaces, so I rely on it more than any other single text face. It's as natural as say, khaki pants, loafers, and that well-worn, but classic tweed blazer — at home in almost any situation. Comfortably classic.

Use Bembo for everything from book printing to office correspondence, but keep in mind that it suffers at low resolution (300 dpi or less). For that reason, I would only recommend using it if you plan on printing to a 600 dpi or greater printer, unless you are printing it at large point sizes for use as a titling or display face, for example.

In Xanadu did Kubla Khan 1492

52-pt. Bergamo & 52-pt. Bergamo Small Caps

Bergamo Regular & Italic 9·11

The chief virtue of a style is perspicuity, and nothing so vicious in it as to need an interpreter. Words borrowed of antiquity do lend a kind of majesty to style, and are not without their delight sometimes. For they have the authority of years, and out of their intermission do win themselves a kind of grace-like newness. But the eldest of the present, and newest of past language, is the best. *A strict and succinct style is that, where you can take away nothing without loss, and that loss to be manifest. The chief virtue of a style is perspicuity, and nothing so vicious in it as*

Bergamo Regular & Italic 11·13

The chief virtue of a style is perspicuity, and nothing so vicious in it as to need an interpreter. Words borrowed of antiquity do lend a kind of majesty to style, and are not without their delight sometimes. For they have the authority of years, and out of their intermission do win themselves a kind of grace-like newness. But the eldest of the present, and newest of past language, is the best. *A strict and succinct style is that, where you can take away nothing without loss, and that loss to be manifest. The chief virtue of a style is perspicuity, and nothing so vicious in it as to need an interpreter.*

Bergamo Regular & Italic 12·14

The chief virtue of a style is perspicuity, and nothing so vicious in it as to need an interpreter. Words borrowed of antiquity do lend a kind of majesty to style, and are not without their delight sometimes. For they have the authority of years, and out of their intermission do win themselves a kind of grace-like newness. But the eldest of the present, and *newest of past language, is the best. A strict and succinct style is that, where you can take away nothing without loss, and that loss to be manifest.*

Bergamo Bold & Bold Italic 9·11

The chief virtue of a style is perspicuity, and nothing so vicious in it as to need an interpreter. Words borrowed of antiquity do lend a kind of majesty to style, and are not without their delight sometimes. For they have the authority of years, and out of their intermission do win themselves a kind of grace-like newness. But the eldest of the present, and newest of past lan- *guage, is the best. A strict and succinct style is that, where you can take away nothing without loss, and that loss to be*

Bergamo Bold & Bold Italic 11·13

The chief virtue of a style is perspicuity, and nothing so vicious in it as to need an interpreter. Words borrowed of antiquity do lend a kind of majesty to style, and are not without their delight sometimes. For they have the authority of years, and out of their intermission do win themselves a kind of grace-like newness. But the eldest of the present, and newest of past language, is the best. *A strict and succinct style is that, where you can take away nothing without loss, and that loss to be manifest. The chief virtue of a style is perspicuity,*

Bergamo Bold & Bold Italic 12·14

The chief virtue of a style is perspicuity, and nothing so vicious in it as to need an interpreter. Words borrowed of antiquity do lend a kind of majesty to style, and are not without their delight sometimes. For they have the authority of years, and out of their intermission do win themselves a kind of grace-like newness. But the eldest of the present, and *newest of past language, is the best. A strict and succinct style is that, where you can take away nothing without loss,*

ABCDEFGHIJKLMNOPQRSTUVWXYZ1234567890

| CHAPTER II: OLDSTYLES

CASLON

SUGGESTED USES: all-purpose text face, books, magazines, journals, correspondence, etc.

CONSIDER COMBINING WITH: Futura and other bold sans serif geometric designs.

Designed by William Caslon in 1725, this face's classic lines, sturdiness and legibility has made it one of the most popular text faces of all time. Suitable for long text passages as well as headlines and titles, Caslon's versatility leads to an adage among designers and typographers that says "when in doubt, set in Caslon."

Caslon saw wide use in the United States during the 18th century. In fact the Declaration of Independence was originally set in Caslon.

Caslon 10-13

When in the course of human 1234

45-pt. Caslon

Caslon Regular & Italic 9·11

The chief virtue of a style is perspicuity, and nothing so vicious in it as to need an interpreter. Words borrowed of antiquity do lend a kind of majesty to style, and are not without their delight sometimes. For they have the authority of years, and out of their intermission do win themselves a kind of grace-like newness. But the eldest of the present, and newest of past language, is the best. *A strict and succinct style is that, where you can take away nothing without loss, and that loss to be manifest. The chief virtue*

Caslon Regular & Italic 11·13

The chief virtue of a style is perspicuity, and nothing so vicious in it as to need an interpreter. Words borrowed of antiquity do lend a kind of majesty to style, and are not without their delight sometimes. For they have the authority of years, and out of their intermission do win themselves a kind of grace-like newness. But the eldest of the present, and newest of past language, is the best. *A strict and succinct style is that, where you can take away nothing without loss, and that loss to be manifest. The chief virtue of a style is perspicuity, and nothing so*

Caslon Regular & Italic 12·14

The chief virtue of a style is perspicuity, and nothing so vicious in it as to need an interpreter. Words borrowed of antiquity do lend a kind of majesty to style, and are not without their delight sometimes. For they have the authority of years, and out of their intermission do win themselves a kind of grace-like newness. *But the eldest of the present, and newest of past language, is the best. A strict and succinct style is that, where you can take away nothing without loss,*

Caslon Bold & Bold Italic 9·11

The chief virtue of a style is perspicuity, and nothing so vicious in it as to need an interpreter. Words borrowed of antiquity do lend a kind of majesty to style, and are not without their delight sometimes. For they have the authority of years, and out of their intermission do win themselves a kind of grace-like newness. But the eldest of the present, and *newest of past language, is the best. A strict and succinct style is that, where you can take away nothing without loss, and that loss*

Caslon Bold & Bold Italic 11·13

The chief virtue of a style is perspicuity, and nothing so vicious in it as to need an interpreter. Words borrowed of antiquity do lend a kind of majesty to style, and are not without their delight sometimes. For they have the authority of years, and out of their intermission do win themselves a kind of grace-like newness. But the eldest of the present, and newest of past language, is the best. A strict *and succinct style is that, where you can take away nothing without loss, and that loss to be manifest. The chief virtue of a style is per-*

Caslon Bold & Bold Italic 12·14

The chief virtue of a style is perspicuity, and nothing so vicious in it as to need an interpreter. Words borrowed of antiquity do lend a kind of majesty to style, and are not without their delight sometimes. For they have the authority of years, and out of their intermission do win themselves a kind of grace-like newness. But the eldest *of the present, and newest of past language, is the best. A strict and succinct style is that, where you can take away*

ABCDEFGHIJKLMNOPQRSTUVWXYZ1234567890

GALLIARD

SUGGESTED USES: general purpose
text, books, magazines

CONSIDER COMBINING WITH:
Syntax

Galliard (available as *Gareth* on the companion CD) is a true modern day
Oldstyle. It was inspired by the typeface designs of Robert Granjon, a
16th-century French typefounder and printer whose designs were based
on those of his predecessor, Claude Garamond.

Created in the late 1970s by Matthew Carter, Galliard is the first of the
many Garamond-Granjon-Jannon-inspired typefonts to be designed using
computer technology (URW's *Ikarus* program), perhaps contributing to its
success and usefulness on the desktop.

Galliard is a wonderful typeface for extended or lengthy text (e.g.,
books). It is highly legible, yet rich with interesting detail. The italics are
particularly interesting, reminiscent of Chancery-style typefaces, and the
bold weights work well as display text.

Gareth 10·13

Yr oedd elfen o *gymodi* y tu ôl 123

46-pt. Gareth Bold & Bold Italic

Gareth Regular & Italic 9·11

The chief virtue of a style is perspicuity, and nothing so vicious in it as to need an interpreter. Words borrowed of antiquity do lend a kind of majesty to style, and are not without their delight sometimes. For they have the authority of years, and out of their intermission do win themselves a kind of grace-like newness. But the eldest of the present, and newest of past language, is the best. A *strict and succinct style is that, where you can take away nothing without loss, and that loss to be manifest. The chief virtue of a style is perspicuity, and noth-*

Gareth Regular & Italic 11·13

The chief virtue of a style is perspicuity, and nothing so vicious in it as to need an interpreter. Words borrowed of antiquity do lend a kind of majesty to style, and are not without their delight sometimes. For they have the authority of years, and out of their intermission do win themselves a kind of grace-like newness. But the eldest of the present, and newest of past language, is the best. *A strict and succinct style is that, where you can take away nothing without loss, and that loss to be manifest. The chief virtue of a style is perspicuity, and nothing so vicious in it as to need an inter-*

Gareth Regular & Italic 12·14

The chief virtue of a style is perspicuity, and nothing so vicious in it as to need an interpreter. Words borrowed of antiquity do lend a kind of majesty to style, and are not without their delight sometimes. For they have the authority of years, and out of their intermission do win themselves a kind of grace-like *newness. But the eldest of the present, and newest of past language, is the best. A strict and succinct style is that, where you can take away nothing without loss, and that loss to be*

Gareth Bold & Bold Italic 9·11

The chief virtue of a style is perspicuity, and nothing so vicious in it as to need an interpreter. Words borrowed of antiquity do lend a kind of majesty to style, and are not without their delight sometimes. For they have the authority of years, and out of their intermission do win themselves a kind of grace-like newness. But the eldest of the present, and newest of *past language, is the best. A strict and succinct style is that, where you can take away nothing without loss, and that loss to be manifest. The chief*

Gareth Bold & Bold Italic 11·13

The chief virtue of a style is perspicuity, and nothing so vicious in it as to need an interpreter. Words borrowed of antiquity do lend a kind of majesty to style, and are not without their delight sometimes. For they have the authority of years, and out of their intermission do win themselves a kind of grace-like newness. But the eldest of the present, and newest of *past language, is the best. A strict and succinct style is that, where you can take away nothing without loss, and that loss to be manifest. The chief virtue of a style is perspicuity, and nothing*

Gareth Bold & Bold Italic 12·14

The chief virtue of a style is perspicuity, and nothing so vicious in it as to need an interpreter. Words borrowed of antiquity do lend a kind of majesty to style, and are not without their delight sometimes. For they have the authority of years, and out of their intermission do win themselves a kind *of grace-like newness. But the eldest of the present, and newest of past language, is the best. A strict and succinct style is that, where you can take away nothing without loss, and*

ABCDEFGHIJKLMNOPQRSTUVWXYZ1234567890

GARAMOND

SUGGESTED USES: newsletters, correspondence, business documents, manuals, books

CONSIDER COMBINING WITH: Futura Heavy, Franklin Gothic

KLM
OPR
QST
XYZ

For a long time I thought Garamond was French for "everyone and their dog uses this typeface." Throughout most of the 1980s it was the most popular text face used in the computer industry, thanks to companies like Apple Computer, which adopted it as a standard for user manuals, brochures, mailings, newsletters, in fact just about all of their printed

Garamond 10·13

material. From the beginning Garamond has been a perennial favorite among desktop publishers because it works so well in so many different applications.

There are many versions of Garamond, some based on the original designs of Claude Garamond such as the Garamond family included on the companion CD,

others based on the work of Jean Jannon, another 16th-century French type designer whose work was later mistakenly attributed to Monsieur Garamond. The Garamond Condensed typeface on the companion CD, for example, is based on a Jannon design rather than one of Garamond's.

Qui vitam gucci & more versaci 5674

Garamond Regular & Italic 9-11

The chief virtue of a style is perspicuity, and nothing so vicious in it as to need an interpreter. Words borrowed of antiquity do lend a kind of majesty to style, and are not without their delight sometimes. For they have the authority of years, and out of their intermission do win themselves a kind of grace-like newness. But the eldest of the present, and newest of past language, is the best. A *strict and succinct style is that, where you can take away nothing without loss, and that loss to be manifest. The chief virtue of a style is perspicuity, and nothing so vicious in it as to*

Garamond Regular & Italic 11-13

The chief virtue of a style is perspicuity, and nothing so vicious in it as to need an interpreter. Words borrowed of antiquity do lend a kind of majesty to style, and are not without their delight sometimes. For they have the authority of years, and out of their intermission do win themselves a kind of grace-like newness. But the eldest of the present, and newest of *past language, is the best. A strict and succinct style is that, where you can take away nothing without loss, and that loss to be manifest. The chief virtue of a style is perspicuity, and nothing so vicious in it as to need an interpreter.*

Garamond Regular & Italic 12-14

The chief virtue of a style is perspicuity, and nothing so vicious in it as to need an interpreter. Words borrowed of antiquity do lend a kind of majesty to style, and are not without their delight sometimes. For they have the authority of years, and out of their intermission do win themselves a kind of grace-like newness. *But the eldest of the present, and newest of past language, is the best. A strict and succinct style is that, where you can take away nothing without loss, and that loss to be manifest.*

Garamond Bold & Bold Italic 9-11

The chief virtue of a style is perspicuity, and nothing so vicious in it as to need an interpreter. Words borrowed of antiquity do lend a kind of majesty to style, and are not without their delight sometimes. For they have the authority of years, and out of their intermission do win themselves a kind of grace-like newness. But the eldest of the present, and newest of past language, is the best. A *strict and succinct style is that, where you can take away nothing without loss, and that loss to be manifest. The chief virtue of a style is perspicuity,*

Garamond Bold & Bold Italic 11-13

The chief virtue of a style is perspicuity, and nothing so vicious in it as to need an interpreter. Words borrowed of antiquity do lend a kind of majesty to style, and are not without their delight sometimes. For they have the authority of years, and out of their intermission do win themselves a kind of grace-like newness. But the eldest of the present, and newest of past language, is the best. A *strict and succinct style is that, where you can take away nothing without loss, and that loss to be manifest. The chief virtue of a style is perspicuity, and nothing so vicious in it as to need an*

Garamond Bold & Bold Italic 12-14

The chief virtue of a style is perspicuity, and nothing so vicious in it as to need an interpreter. Words borrowed of antiquity do lend a kind of majesty to style, and are not without their delight sometimes. For they have the authority of years, and out of their intermission do win themselves a kind of grace-like *newness. But the eldest of the present, and newest of past language, is the best. A strict and succinct style is that, where you can take away nothing without loss, and that loss to*

A B C D E F G H I J K L M N O P Q R S T U V W X Y Z 1 2 3 4 5 6 7 8 9 0

GARAMOND CONDENSED

Suggested uses: general purpose text, advertisements, brochures, correspondence, corporate identity

Consider combining with: Futura Heavy, Franklin Gothic, Bodoni (when used as a display type)

This condensed version of Garamond is quite distinct from the original Garamond. This is true not only in terms of metrics and width, but it is actually a different design, a re-design if you will, based loosely on the designs of Jean Jannon, a 16th-century type designer and contemporary of Claude Garamond.

Garamond Condensed has a significantly greater x-height, that is, the proportion of the lowercase letters to the uppercase is greater. This makes it quite legible, and its condensed width makes it quite economical for setting text in narrower columns.

Do not mix Garamond Condensed with the standard Garamond—you won't like the results.

Garamond Condensed Light is elegant and graceful, and is appropriate for just about any text.

Garamond Condensed 10-13

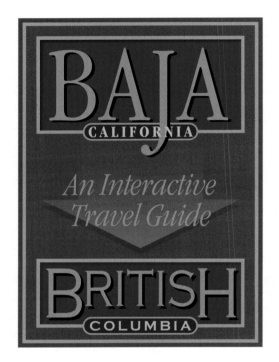

Garamond Condensed Regular, Italic & Bold
Copperplate Gothic & Bold

April showers do bring May flowers

53-pt. Garamond Condensed Italic

Garamond Condensed Light & Italic 9·11

The chief virtue of a style is perspicuity, and nothing so vicious in it as to need an interpreter. Words borrowed of antiquity do lend a kind of majesty to style, and are not without their delight sometimes. For they have the *authority of years, and out of their intermission do win themselves a kind of grace-like newness. But the eldest of the present, and*

Garamond Condensed Light & Italic 11·13

The chief virtue of a style is perspicuity, and nothing so vicious in it as to need an interpreter. Words borrowed of antiquity do lend a kind of majesty to style, and are not without their delight sometimes. For they have the authority of *years, and out of their intermission do win themselves a kind of grace-like newness. But the eldest of the present, and newest of past language, is the best.*

Garamond Condensed Light & Italic 12·14

The chief virtue of a style is perspicuity, and nothing so vicious in it as to need an interpreter. Words borrowed of antiquity do lend a kind of majesty to style, and are not without their delight sometimes. For they have the *authority of years, and out of their intermission do win themselves a kind of grace-like newness. But the eldest of the present, and newest of past language, is*

Garamond Condensed Regular & Italic 9·11

The chief virtue of a style is perspicuity, and nothing so vicious in it as to need an interpreter. Words borrowed of antiquity do lend a kind of majesty to style, and are not without their delight sometimes. For they have *the authority of years, and out of their intermission do win themselves a kind of grace-like newness. But the eldest of the*

Garamond Condensed Regular & Italic 11·13

The chief virtue of a style is perspicuity, and nothing so vicious in it as to need an interpreter. Words borrowed of antiquity do lend a kind of majesty to style, and are not without their delight sometimes. For they have the *authority of years, and out of their intermission do win themselves a kind of grace-like newness. But the eldest of the present, and newest of past language, is*

Garamond Condensed Regular & Italic 12·14

The chief virtue of a style is perspicuity, and nothing so vicious in it as to need an interpreter. Words borrowed of antiquity do lend a kind of majesty to style, and are not without their delight some-*times. For they have the authority of years, and out of their intermission do win themselves a kind of grace-like newness. But the eldest of the*

Garamond Condensed Bold & Italic 9·11

The chief virtue of a style is perspicuity, and nothing so vicious in it as to need an interpreter. Words borrowed of antiquity do lend a kind of majesty to style, and are not without their delight sometimes. For they have the authority *of years, and out of their intermission do win themselves a kind of grace-like newness. But the eldest of the present,*

Garamond Condensed Bold & Italic 11·13

The chief virtue of a style is perspicuity, and nothing so vicious in it as to need an interpreter. Words borrowed of antiquity do lend a kind of majesty to style, and are not without their delight sometimes. For they have the authority of years, and out of *their intermission do win themselves a kind of grace-like newness. But the eldest of the present, and newest of past language, is the best.*

Garamond Condensed Bold & Italic 12·14

The chief virtue of a style is perspicuity, and nothing so vicious in it as to need an interpreter. Words borrowed of antiquity do lend a kind of majesty to style, and are not without their delight sometimes. For they have the *authority of years, and out of their intermission do win themselves a kind of grace-like newness. But the eldest of the present, and*

ABCDEFGHIJKLMNOPQRSTUVWXYZ1234567890

URW PALLADIO

SUGGESTED USES: general text, newsletters, brochures

CONSIDER COMBINING WITH: Optima, Futura Heavy, Franklin Gothic, Syntax, Goudy Sans

URW Palladio was designed by Hermann Zapf, the designer of the type-faces Palatino, Optima (available on the companion CD as *Opus*), Zapf Chancery, and Zapf Dingbats. URW Palladio is in fact very similar to Palatino—the typeface has a chiseled appearance, giving it a formal, slightly calligraphic look—but is perhaps better suited as a text face than Palatino. URW Palladio is useful for a wide range of documents and at larger sizes is a elegant display font.

URW Palladio 10-13

The marriage of Princess Aoife & the Earl of Pembroke

52-pt. URW Palladio & 46-pt. URW Palladio Italic (ampersand)

URW Palladio Regular & Italic 9·11

The chief virtue of a style is perspicuity, and nothing so vicious in it as to need an interpreter. Words borrowed of antiquity do lend a kind of majesty to style, and are not without their delight sometimes. For they have the authority of years, and out of their intermission do win themselves a kind of grace-like newness. But the eldest of the present, and newest of past language, is the best. *A strict and succinct style is that, where you can take away nothing without loss, and that loss to be manifest. The chief virtue of a style is per-*

URW Palladio Regular & Italic 11·13

The chief virtue of a style is perspicuity, and nothing so vicious in it as to need an interpreter. Words borrowed of antiquity do lend a kind of majesty to style, and are not without their delight sometimes. For they have the authority of years, and out of their intermission do win themselves a kind of grace-like newness. But the eldest of the present, and newest of past language, is the *best. A strict and succinct style is that, where you can take away nothing without loss, and that loss to be manifest. The chief virtue of a style is perspicuity, and nothing so vicious in it as to need an interpreter.*

URW Palladio Regular & Italic 12·14

The chief virtue of a style is perspicuity, and nothing so vicious in it as to need an interpreter. Words borrowed of antiquity do lend a kind of majesty to style, and are not without their delight sometimes. For they have the authority of years, and out of their intermission do win themselves a kind of grace-*like newness. But the eldest of the present, and newest of past language, is the best. A strict and succinct style is that, where you can take away nothing without loss, and that loss to be mani-*

URW Palladio Bold & Italic 9·11

The chief virtue of a style is perspicuity, and nothing so vicious in it as to need an interpreter. Words borrowed of antiquity do lend a kind of majesty to style, and are not without their delight sometimes. For they have the authority of years, and out of their intermission do win themselves a kind of grace-like newness. But the eldest of the present, and newest of past *language, is the best. A strict and succinct style is that, where you can take away nothing without loss, and that loss to be manifest. The chief virtue of*

URW Palladio Bold & Italic 11·13

The chief virtue of a style is perspicuity, and nothing so vicious in it as to need an interpreter. Words borrowed of antiquity do lend a kind of majesty to style, and are not without their delight sometimes. For they have the authority of years, and out of their intermission do win themselves a kind of grace-like newness. But the eldest of the present, and newest of past language, is the *best. A strict and succinct style is that, where you can take away nothing without loss, and that loss to be manifest. The chief virtue of a style is perspicuity, and nothing so vicious in it as to*

URW Palladio Bold & Italic 12·14

The chief virtue of a style is perspicuity, and nothing so vicious in it as to need an interpreter. Words borrowed of antiquity do lend a kind of majesty to style, and are not without their delight sometimes. For they have the authority of years, and out of their intermission do win themselves a kind of grace- *like newness. But the eldest of the present, and newest of past language, is the best. A strict and succinct style is that, where you can take away nothing without loss, and that*

A B C D E F G H I J K L M N O P Q R S T U V W X Y Z 1 2 3 4 5 6 7 8 9 0

SABON

SUGGESTED USES: general text, newsletters, brochures

CONSIDER COMBINING WITH: Optima, Futura Heavy, Copperplate Gothic

Sabon is a modern day Oldstyle designed by Jan Tschichold in 1964. Loosely based on the 16th-century designs of Claude Garamond, Sabon (available on the companion CD as *Savoy*) is a great choice when you're bored working with other text fonts. It is lively and interesting, but not overly so (as opposed to faces such as Goudy Oldstyle). A Romantic design married to Teutonic sensibility. Sabon is almost always a good choice for documents where you want to create a classical and elegant look.

Savoy 10·13

Savoy Regular, Italic & Bold modified in Adobe Illustrator

The primary art *is* writing 465

58-pt. Savoy & Small Caps

Savoy Regular & Italic 9·11

The chief virtue of a style is perspicuity, and nothing so vicious in it as to need an interpreter. Words borrowed of antiquity do lend a kind of majesty to style, and are not without their delight sometimes. For they have the authority of years, and out of their intermission do win themselves a kind of grace-like newness. But the eldest of the present, and newest of past language, is the best. *A strict and succinct style is that, where you can take away nothing without loss, and that loss to be manifest. The chief virtue of a style is perspicuity, and*

Savoy Regular & Italic 11·13

The chief virtue of a style is perspicuity, and nothing so vicious in it as to need an interpreter. Words borrowed of antiquity do lend a kind of majesty to style, and are not without their delight sometimes. For they have the authority of years, and out of their intermission do win themselves a kind of grace-like newness. But the eldest of the present, and newest of past language, is the best. *A strict and succinct style is that, where you can take away nothing without loss, and that loss to be manifest. The chief virtue of a style is perspicuity, and nothing so vicious in it as to need an inter-*

Savoy Regular & Italic 12·14

The chief virtue of a style is perspicuity, and nothing so vicious in it as to need an interpreter. Words borrowed of antiquity do lend a kind of majesty to style, and are not without their delight sometimes. For they have the authority of years, and out of their intermission do win themselves a kind of grace-like newness. *But the eldest of the present, and newest of past language, is the best. A strict and succinct style is that, where you can take away nothing without loss, and that loss to be manifest.*

Savoy Bold 9·11

The chief virtue of a style is perspicuity, and nothing so vicious in it as to need an interpreter. Words borrowed of antiquity do lend a kind of majesty to style, and are not without their delight sometimes. For they have the authority of years, and out of their intermission do win themselves a kind of grace-like newness. But the eldest of the present, and newest of past language, is the best. A strict and succinct style is that, where you can take away nothing without loss, and that loss to be manifest. The chief virtue of a style

Savoy Bold 11·13

The chief virtue of a style is perspicuity, and nothing so vicious in it as to need an interpreter. Words borrowed of antiquity do lend a kind of majesty to style, and are not without their delight sometimes. For they have the authority of years, and out of their intermission do win themselves a kind of grace-like newness. But the eldest of the present, and newest of past language, is the best. A strict and succinct style is that, where you can take away nothing without loss, and that loss to be manifest. The chief virtue of a style is perspicuity, and nothing so vicious in it as to need an inter-

Savoy Bold 12·14

The chief virtue of a style is perspicuity, and nothing so vicious in it as to need an interpreter. Words borrowed of antiquity do lend a kind of majesty to style, and are not without their delight sometimes. For they have the authority of years, and out of their intermission do win themselves a kind of grace-like newness. But the eldest of the present, and newest of past language, is the best. A strict and succinct style is that, where you can take away nothing without loss, and that loss to be manifest.

A B C D E F G H I J K L M N O P Q R S T U V W X Y Z 1 2 3 4 5 6 7 8 9 0

Transitionals

168-pt. Baskerville Italic

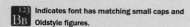

TRANSITIONAL TYPEFACES ARE MORE MECHANICAL AND geometric in design than Oldstyles, resulting in a more businesslike appearance. In terms of documents intended for business use (memos, annual reports, and the like) however, Transitional typefaces are not necessarily better suited than Oldstyle designs; they just have a more rational or less romantic appearance.

Historically, Transitional typefaces were designed during the late 18th century during a period referred to as the Neoclassical. The modifier "neo" suggests that it is not quite classical, in fact coming after that period, but before some other period—in this case the Modern period—hence the classification Transitional.

But what is meant by "more rational" or "less romantic"? Transitional designs tend to be less complex than romantic designs, based more on mathematics than hand-drawn lettering. The serifs tend to be symmetrical and the stress, that is, the degree to which the thick parts and the thin parts of a character are distributed, is slightly less oblique. The relationship of the height of the lowercase characters to the uppercase is also less pronounced. Precisely because of these reasons, Transitional designs reproduce better at lower resolutions than do Oldstyle faces—yet another reason to consider them if you will be outputting your documents using printers with resolutions below 600 dots per inch.

Times, Baskerville, and URW Antiqua (the latter two are available on the companion CD) are good examples of Transitional typefaces.

Transitionals combine well with sans serif typefaces such as Avant Garde, Helvetica, and Franklin Gothic.

Transitional typefaces such as Baskerville, Times Roman, Bookman, Perpetua, Utopia and many others, are supposed to be rational and business-like, and in France they even call these typefaces "Reales," which sounds pretty business-like to me. And so they

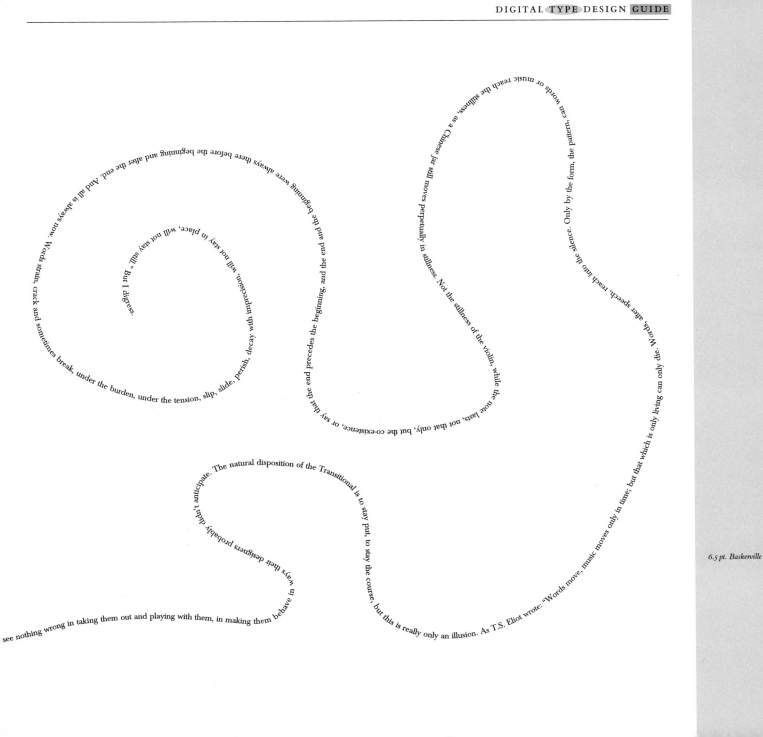

see nothing wrong in taking them out and playing with them, in making them behave in ways their designers probably didn't anticipate. The natural disposition of the Transitional is to stay put, to stay the course, but this is really only an illusion. As T.S. Eliot wrote: "Words move, music moves only in time; but that which is only living can only die. Words, after speech, reach into the silence. Only by the form, the pattern, can words or music reach the stillness, as a Chinese jar still moves perpetually in stillness. Not the stillness of the violin, while the note lasts, not that only, but the co-existence, or say that the end precedes the beginning, and the end and the beginning were always there before the beginning and after the end. And all is always now. Words strain, crack and sometimes break, under the burden, under the tension, slip, slide, perish, decay with imprecision, will not stay in place, will not stay still." But I digress.

6.5 pt. Baskerville ir-Regular

URW ANTIQUA

SUGGESTED USES: books, reports, articles, headlines

CONSIDER COMBINING WITH: Franklin Gothic, Futura

URW Antiqua is a revival of the Transitional form typified by the typefaces Baskerville and New Baskerville. It was designed by the eminent German type designer Hermann Zapf, the creator of such popular typefaces as Palatino, URW Palladio, and

Optima (the latter two are on the companion CD). As a neo-classical design, URW Antiqua tends more toward the neo than the classical, something of a transition between the Transitionals and the Moderns. It's as rational in appearance as the Baskervilles, yet

slightly more geometric, a feature that also makes it perhaps a bit more fashionable. URW Antiqua is especially useful if you print to lower-resolution printers such as the Apple Laserwriter Plus or Hewlett-Packard LaserJet II printers (300 dpi).

URW Antiqua 10·13

Necessity knows no law.

I know some attorneys of the same.

48-pt. URW Antiqua Regular & 10-pt. Bold

URW Antiqua Regular & Italic 9·11

The chief virtue of a style is perspicuity, and nothing so vicious in it as to need an interpreter. Words borrowed of antiquity do lend a kind of majesty to style, and are not without their delight sometimes. For they have the authority of years, and out of their intermission do win themselves a kind of grace-like newness. But the eldest *of the present, and newest of past language, is the best. A strict and succinct style is that, where you can take away nothing without loss, and*

URW Antiqua Regular & Italic 11·13

The chief virtue of a style is perspicuity, and nothing so vicious in it as to need an interpreter. Words borrowed of antiquity do lend a kind of majesty to style, and are not without their delight sometimes. For they have the authority of years, and out of their intermission do win themselves a kind of grace-like newness. But the eldest *of the present, and newest of past language, is the best. A strict and succinct style is that, where you can take away nothing without loss, and that loss to be manifest. The chief*

URW Antiqua Regular & Italic 12·14

The chief virtue of a style is perspicuity, and nothing so vicious in it as to need an interpreter. Words borrowed of antiquity do lend a kind of majesty to style, and are not without their delight sometimes. For they have the authority of years, and out of their intermission *do win themselves a kind of grace-like newness. But the eldest of the present, and newest of past language, is the best. A strict and succinct style is that, where*

URW Antiqua Bold & Bold Italic 9·11

The chief virtue of a style is perspicuity, and nothing so vicious in it as to need an interpreter. Words borrowed of antiquity do lend a kind of majesty to style, and are not without their delight sometimes. For they have the authority of years, and out of their intermission do win themselves a kind of grace-like *newness. But the eldest of the present, and newest of past language, is the best. A strict and succinct style is that, where you*

URW Antiqua Bold & Bold Italic 11·13

The chief virtue of a style is perspicuity, and nothing so vicious in it as to need an interpreter. Words borrowed of antiquity do lend a kind of majesty to style, and are not without their delight sometimes. For they have the authority of years, and out of their intermission do win themselves a kind of grace-like newness. But the *eldest of the present, and newest of past language, is the best. A strict and succinct style is that, where you can take away nothing without loss, and that loss to be*

URW Antiqua Bold & Bold Italic 12·14

The chief virtue of a style is perspicuity, and nothing so vicious in it as to need an interpreter. Words borrowed of antiquity do lend a kind of majesty to style, and are not without their delight sometimes. For they have the authority of years, and out of their *intermission do win themselves a kind of grace-like newness. But the eldest of the present, and newest of past language, is the best. A strict and succinct*

A B C D E F G H I J K L M N O P Q R S T U V W X Y Z 1 2 3 4 5 6 7 8 9 0

BASKERVILLE

SUGGESTED USES: books, journals, formal presentations, general text

CONSIDER COMBINING WITH: Futura and other geometric sans serif fonts, especially in bold weights.

Baskerville is the prototypical Transitional typeface. This face takes its name from its designer, John Baskerville, an English printer and contemporary of the famous American printer Benjamin Franklin. It's no mistake that this typeface was more popular among revolutionaries in the American colonies and in France—what is a revolution after all if not a

Baskerville 10/13

transition?—than it was in its native England. Some two centuries later, however, Baskerville is now one of the most popular typefaces used for book printing in Great Britain.

Baskerville, including the typeface New Baskerville, is a very clear, easy-to-read typeface with gently sloping italics best described as understated elegance.

DON QUIJOTE
de la
MANCHA

"En un lugar de la Mancha," de cuyo no quiero acordarme, no ha mucho tiempo que vivía un hidalgo de los de lanza en astillero, adarga antigua, rocín flaco y galgo corredor. Una olla de algo más vaca que carnero, salpicón las más noches, duelos y quebrantos los sábados, lantejas los viernes, algún palomino de añadidura los domingos, consumían las tres partes de su hacienda. El resto dell conchuían sayo de velarte, calzas de velludo para las fiestas, con sus pantuflos de lo mesmo, y los días de entre semana se honraba con su vellorí de lo más fino. Tenía en su casa una ama que pasaba de los cuarenta, y una sobrina que no llegaba a los veiente, y un mozo de campo y plaza, que así ensillaba el rocín como tomaba la podadera. Frisaba la edad de nuestro hidalgo con los cincuenta años: era de complexión recia, seco de carnes, enjuto de rostro, gran madrugador y amigo de la caza. Quieren decir que tenía el sobrenombre de Quijada, o Quesada, que en esto hay alguna diferencia en los autores que deste caso escriben; aunque por conjeturas verosímiles se deja entender que se llamaba Quejana. Pero esto impor-

34

Whate'er's begun in *anger,* ends in shame.

40-pt. Baskerville

Baskerville Regular & Italic 9·11

The chief virtue of a style is perspicuity, and nothing so vicious in it as to need an interpreter. Words borrowed of antiquity do lend a kind of majesty to style, and are not without their delight sometimes. For they have the authority of years, and out of their intermission do win themselves a kind of grace-like newness. But the eldest of the present, and newest of past language, is the best. *A strict and succinct style is that, where you can take away nothing without loss, and that loss to be manifest. The chief virtue of a style is perspicuity, and nothing*

Baskerville Regular & Italic 11·13

The chief virtue of a style is perspicuity, and nothing so vicious in it as to need an interpreter. Words borrowed of antiquity do lend a kind of majesty to style, and are not without their delight sometimes. For they have the authority of years, and out of their intermission do win themselves a kind of grace-like newness. But the eldest of the present, and newest of past language, is the best. *A strict and succinct style is that, where you can take away nothing without loss, and that loss to be manifest. The chief virtue of a style is perspicuity, and nothing so vicious in it as to need an interpreter.*

Baskerville Regular & Italic 12·14

The chief virtue of a style is perspicuity, and nothing so vicious in it as to need an interpreter. Words borrowed of antiquity do lend a kind of majesty to style, and are not without their delight sometimes. For they have the authority of years, and out of their intermission do win themselves a kind of grace-like newness. *But the eldest of the present, and newest of past language, is the best. A strict and succinct style is that, where you can take away nothing without loss, and that loss to be manifest.*

Baskerville Bold & Bold Italic 9·11

The chief virtue of a style is perspicuity, and nothing so vicious in it as to need an interpreter. Words borrowed of antiquity do lend a kind of majesty to style, and are not without their delight sometimes. For they have the authority of years, and out of their intermission do win themselves *a kind of grace-like newness. But the eldest of the present, and newest of past language, is the best. A strict and succinct style is that, where you can*

Baskerville Bold & Bold Italic 11·13

The chief virtue of a style is perspicuity, and nothing so vicious in it as to need an interpreter. Words borrowed of antiquity do lend a kind of majesty to style, and are not without their delight sometimes. For they have the authority of years, and out of their intermission do win themselves a kind of grace-like newness. *But the eldest of the present, and newest of past language, is the best. A strict and succinct style is that, where you can take away nothing without loss, and that loss to be manifest. The chief virtue*

Baskerville Bold & Bold Italic 12·14

The chief virtue of a style is perspicuity, and nothing so vicious in it as to need an interpreter. Words borrowed of antiquity do lend a kind of majesty to style, and are not without their delight sometimes. For they have the authority of years, and *out of their intermission do win themselves a kind of grace-like newness. But the eldest of the present, and newest of past language, is the best. A strict and succinct style is that,*

ABCDEFGHIJKLMNOPQRSTUVWXYZ1234567890

NEW BASKERVILLE

SUGGESTED USES: books, journals, lengthy text

CONSIDER COMBINING WITH: Futura and other geometric sans serif faces

New Baskerville is an ideal font for publications or documents with lots of text. It has a very traditional and rational appearance, but not at the expense of elegance, and it is definitely not boring like Times Roman. New Baskerville is not quite as compact as Baskerville, and has a somewhat larger x-height, perhaps making it somewhat easier to read in long passages of text. For these reasons, do not combine New Baskerville with Baskerville in the same document.

New Baskerville 10&13

Better a witty fool than a foolish wit. 12390

40-pt. New Baskerville Italic

New Baskerville Regular & Italic 9/11

The chief virtue of a style is perspicuity, and nothing so vicious in it as to need an interpreter. Words borrowed of antiquity do lend a kind of majesty to style, and are not without *their delight sometimes. For they have the authority of years, and out of their intermission do win themselves a kind of*

New Baskerville Regular & Italic 11/13

The chief virtue of a style is perspicuity, and nothing so vicious in it as to need an interpreter. Words borrowed of antiquity do lend a kind of majesty to style, and are not without *their delight sometimes. For they have the authority of years, and out of their intermission do win themselves a kind of grace-like newness. But the eldest of*

New Baskerville Regular & Italic 12/14

The chief virtue of a style is perspicuity, and nothing so vicious in it as to need an interpreter. Words borrowed of antiquity do lend a kind of majesty to style, and are *not without their delight sometimes. For they have the authority of years, and out of their intermission do win themselves a kind of grace-*

New Baskerville Semi-bold & Semi-bold Italic 9/11

The chief virtue of a style is perspicuity, and nothing so vicious in it as to need an interpreter. Words borrowed of antiquity do lend a kind of majesty to style, and are not with*out their delight sometimes. For they have the authority of years, and out of their intermission do win themselves a*

New Baskerville Semi-bold & Semi-bold Italic 11/13

The chief virtue of a style is perspicuity, and nothing so vicious in it as to need an interpreter. Words borrowed of antiquity do lend a kind of majesty to style, and are not without *their delight sometimes. For they have the authority of years, and out of their intermission do win themselves a kind of grace-like newness. But the eldest of*

New Baskerville Semi-bold & Semi-bold Italic 12/14

The chief virtue of a style is perspicuity, and nothing so vicious in it as to need an interpreter. Words borrowed of antiquity do lend a kind of majesty to style, and are *not without their delight sometimes. For they have the authority of years, and out of their intermission do win themselves a kind of grace-*

New Baskerville Bold & Bold Italic 9/11

The chief virtue of a style is perspicuity, and nothing so vicious in it as to need an interpreter. Words borrowed of antiquity do lend a kind of majesty to style, and are not without their delight sometimes. *For they have the authority of years, and out of their intermission do win themselves a kind of grace-like new-*

New Baskerville Bold & Bold Italic 11/13

The chief virtue of a style is perspicuity, and nothing so vicious in it as to need an interpreter. Words borrowed of antiquity do lend a kind of majesty to style, and are not without their delight sometimes. For they have the *authority of years, and out of their intermission do win themselves a kind of grace-like newness. But the eldest of the present, and newest of past*

New Baskerville Bold & Bold Italic 12/14

The chief virtue of a style is perspicuity, and nothing so vicious in it as to need an interpreter. Words borrowed of antiquity do lend a kind of majesty to style, and are not without their delight sometimes. For *they have the authority of years, and out of their intermission do win themselves a kind of grace-like newness. But the eldest of the*

ABCDEFGHIJKLMNOPQRSTUVWXYZ1234567890

Moderns

200-pt. Walbaum

 Indicates font has matching small caps and Oldstyle figures.

 Indicates font has matching expert sets, which include ligatures, fractions, inferior and superior numerals.

THE TERM "MODERN" REFLECTS THE TIME SCALE ON which art forms such as typography operate: the so-called Modern designs date back to the early 18th century, yet some 200 years later, we still refer to them as Moderns. Get used to it. The prototypical Modern typeface was first conceived and designed by Giambattista Bodoni (1740–1813), and the various designs that bear his name share the same characteristics: exaggerated thick and thin strokes (some parts of a character are very thin while others are quite thick by comparison) and perfect vertical stress (the exaggerated thin and thick strokes are distributed in an up and down fashion and not in an oblique fashion as with Oldstyle and Transitional typefaces).

Modern typefaces have a very elegant appearance—almost unnaturally so—and are very popular in advertising, magazine, and fashion design. They demand attention in an aloof sort of way, rather like the beauty queen (whatever gender he or she may be) we can't help but gaze upon, but at the same time we realize is not quite natural or realistic. For this reason modern typefaces such as Bodoni may present problems if you intend to use them for extended reading. Not that it can't be done; I've seen many books, for example, set with modern designs, but it is not forgiving in terms of environment; the paper stock, size, ink, point size, leading, character spacing, margins, and so on must be perfect.

Moderns work well for short articles and captions, in addition to their common application in headlines, posters, and signs.

Consider combining them with Geometric sans serifs such as Futura (available on the companion CD as *Function*), especially the extra bold or heavy variations—the heavier weight tends to complement the exaggerated stroke of the Moderns.

Note the difference in stress between the Oldstyle typeface on the left and the Modern typeface on the right.

GIAMBATTISTA

"King of Typographers and the Typographer of Kings."

Bodoni

1740–1813

Bodoni Regular & Bodoni Small Caps

BODONI

SUGGESTED USES: headlines, titling, advertising, presentations

CONSIDER COMBINING WITH: Futura and other geometric sans serif faces

Designed by Giambattista Bodoni in the 18th century, Bodoni is a modern typeface, characterized by flat, unbracketed serifs, high contrast between thick and thin strokes, and perfect vertical stress. Bodoni is an elegant and beautiful typeface, but I would not recommend using it for large amounts of text because, aesthetics aside, it just isn't an easy typeface to read. The high degree of contrast confuses the eye, forcing it to pause and re-read. At least it does this to my eyes.

Bodoni 10½/13

Quousque tandem abutêre, Catilina, patientiâ nostrâ?

48-pt. Bodoni

Bodoni Regular & Italic 9/Æ11

The chief virtue of a style is perspicuity, and nothing so vicious in it as to need an interpreter. Words borrowed of antiquity do lend a kind of majesty to style, and are not without their delight sometimes. For they have the authority of years, and out of their intermission do win themselves a kind of grace-like newness. But the eldest of the present, and newest of *past language, is the best. A strict and succinct style is that, where you can take away nothing without loss, and that loss to be manifest. The chief*

Bodoni Regular & Italic 11/Æ13

The chief virtue of a style is perspicuity, and nothing so vicious in it as to need an interpreter. Words borrowed of antiquity do lend a kind of majesty to style, and are not without their delight sometimes. For they have the authority of years, and out of their intermission do win themselves a kind of grace-like newness. But the eldest of the present, and newest of past *language, is the best. A strict and succinct style is that, where you can take away nothing without loss, and that loss to be manifest. The chief virtue of a style is perspicuity, and nothing so vicious in*

Bodoni Regular & Italic 12/Æ14

The chief virtue of a style is perspicuity, and nothing so vicious in it as to need an interpreter. Words borrowed of antiquity do lend a kind of majesty to style, and are not without their delight sometimes. For they have the authority of years, and out of their intermission do win themselves a kind of grace-*like newness. But the eldest of the present, and newest of past language, is the best. A strict and succinct style is that, where you can take away nothing without loss, and that*

Bodoni Bold & Bold Italic 9/Æ11

The chief virtue of a style is perspicuity, and nothing so vicious in it as to need an interpreter. Words borrowed of antiquity do lend a kind of majesty to style, and are not without their delight sometimes. For they have the authority of years, and out of their intermission do win themselves a kind of grace-like newness. But the eldest of the present, and *newest of past language, is the best. A strict and succinct style is that, where you can take away nothing without loss, and that loss to be man-*

Bodoni Bold & Bold Italic 11/Æ13

The chief virtue of a style is perspicuity, and nothing so vicious in it as to need an interpreter. Words borrowed of antiquity do lend a kind of majesty to style, and are not without their delight sometimes. For they have the authority of years, and out of their intermission do win themselves a kind of grace-like newness. But the eldest of the present, and *newest of past language, is the best. A strict and succinct style is that, where you can take away nothing without loss, and that loss to be manifest. The chief virtue of a style is perspicuity,*

Bodoni Bold & Bold Italic 12/Æ14

The chief virtue of a style is perspicuity, and nothing so vicious in it as to need an interpreter. Words borrowed of antiquity do lend a kind of majesty to style, and are not without their delight sometimes. For they have the authority of years, and out of their intermission do win themselves *a kind of grace-like newness. But the eldest of the present, and newest of past language, is the best. A strict and succinct style is that, where you can take away nothing without*

A B C D E F G H I J K L M N O P Q R S T Y V W X Y Z 1 2 3 4 5 6 7 8 9 0

MODERN 216

SUGGESTED USES: advertising, logos, headlines, display

CONSIDER COMBINING WITH: Futura and other geometric sans serif faces

Modern 216 owes much of its design to the definitive modern typeface Bodoni, but has even more variation in stroke width and is considerably wider than Bodoni. Modern 216 is a good face for advertising and display purposes.

Modern 216 10·13

...my thoughts go out to you my Immortal Beloved...

–Ludwig

Modern 216 Regular & Italic (various sizes)

Modern 216 Regular & Italic 9·11

The chief virtue of a style is perspicuity, and nothing so vicious in it as to need an interpreter. Words borrowed of antiquity do lend a kind of majesty to style, and are not without their delight sometimes. For they have the authority of years, and out of their intermission do win themselves a kind of grace-like newness. *But the eldest of the present, and newest of past language, is the best. A strict and succinct style is that, where you*

Modern 216 Regular & Italic 11·13

The chief virtue of a style is perspicuity, and nothing so vicious in it as to need an interpreter. Words borrowed of antiquity do lend a kind of majesty to style, and are not without their delight sometimes. For they have the authority of years, and out of their intermission do win themselves a kind of grace-like newness. But the *eldest of the present, and newest of past language, is the best. A strict and succinct style is that, where you can take away nothing without loss, and that loss*

Modern 216 Regular & Italic 12·14

The chief virtue of a style is perspicuity, and nothing so vicious in it as to need an interpreter. Words borrowed of antiquity do lend a kind of majesty to style, and are not without their delight sometimes. For they have the authority of years, and out of their *intermission do win themselves a kind of grace-like newness. But the eldest of the present, and newest of past language, is the best. A strict*

Modern 216 Bold & Bold Italic 9·11

The chief virtue of a style is perspicuity, and nothing so vicious in it as to need an interpreter. Words borrowed of antiquity do lend a kind of majesty to style, and are not without their delight sometimes. For they have the authority of years, and out of their intermission do win themselves a kind of grace-like newness. *But the eldest of the present, and newest of past language, is the best. A strict and succinct style is that, where*

Modern 216 Bold & Bold Italic 11·13

The chief virtue of a style is perspicuity, and nothing so vicious in it as to need an interpreter. Words borrowed of antiquity do lend a kind of majesty to style, and are not without their delight sometimes. For they have the authority of years, and out of their intermission do win themselves a kind of grace-like newness. But *the eldest of the present, and newest of past language, is the best. A strict and succinct style is that, where you can take away nothing without loss, and*

Modern 216 Bold & Bold Italic 12·14

The chief virtue of a style is perspicuity, and nothing so vicious in it as to need an interpreter. Words borrowed of antiquity do lend a kind of majesty to style, and are not without their delight sometimes. For they have the authority of years, and out of *their intermission do win themselves a kind of grace-like newness. But the eldest of the present, and newest of past language, is the best.*

A B C D E F G H I J K L M N O P Q R S T U V W X Y Z 1 2 3 4 5 6 7 8 9 0

WALBAUM

Suggested uses: logos, titles, headlines

Consider combining with: Futura and other geometric sans serif faces

For information on how to weave type with Adobe Illustrator, see Chapter 9

Walbaum was one of the first typefaces to imitate the style originated by Bodoni. The capital letters are somewhat wider than Bodoni, and interestingly the lowercase 'b' and 'q' have no foot serifs. The difference between the thick and thin strokes are also more exaggerated than Bodoni. I'm really impressed with this font's geometric appearance combined with its very smooth curves. At large sizes, Walbaum is an exceptional display face for use in headlines, signs and logos. At smaller sizes it even works well as a text font, especially for limited use, such as the first page of a magazine article, for example, or in captions. Consider giving it extra leading at text sizes.

Walbaum 10·14

300-pt. Walbaum

GIOVANNI'S
CUCINA ITALIANA

64-pt. Walbaum condensed 70% & 14-pt. normal

Walbaum 9·11

The chief virtue of a style is perspicuity, and nothing so vicious in it as to need an interpreter. Words borrowed of antiquity do lend a kind of majesty to style, and are not without their delight sometimes. For they have the authority of years, and out of their intermission do win themselves a kind of grace-like newness. But the eldest of the pre- sent, and newest of past language, is the best. A strict and succinct style is that, where you can take away nothing without loss, and that loss to be manifest. The chief

Walbaum 11·13

The chief virtue of a style is perspicuity, and nothing so vicious in it as to need an interpreter. Words borrowed of antiquity do lend a kind of majesty to style, and are not without their delight sometimes. For they have the authority of years, and out of their intermission do win themselves a kind of grace-like newness. But the eldest of the present, and newest of past language, is the best. A strict and succinct style is that, where you can take away nothing without loss, and that loss to be manifest. The chief virtue of a style is perspicuity, and nothing so

Walbaum 12·14

The chief virtue of a style is perspicuity, and nothing so vicious in it as to need an interpreter. Words borrowed of antiquity do lend a kind of majesty to style, and are not without their delight sometimes. For they have the authority of years, and out of their intermission do win themselves a kind of grace-like newness. But the eldest of the present, and newest of past language, is the best. A strict and succinct style is that, where you can take away nothing without loss, and that

Walbaum Bold 9·11

The chief virtue of a style is perspicuity, and nothing so vicious in it as to need an interpreter. Words borrowed of antiquity do lend a kind of majesty to style, and are not without their delight sometimes. For they have the authority of years, and out of their intermission do win themselves a kind of grace-like newness. But the eldest of the present, and newest of past language, is the best. A strict and succinct style is that, where you

Walbaum Bold 11·13

The chief virtue of a style is perspicuity, and nothing so vicious in it as to need an interpreter. Words borrowed of antiquity do lend a kind of majesty to style, and are not without their delight sometimes. For they have the authority of years, and out of their intermission do win themselves a kind of grace-like newness. But the eldest of the present, and newest of past language, is the best. A strict and succinct style is that, where you can take away nothing without loss, and that loss to be

Walbaum Bold 12·14

The chief virtue of a style is perspicuity, and nothing so vicious in it as to need an interpreter. Words borrowed of antiquity do lend a kind of majesty to style, and are not without their delight sometimes. For they have the authority of years, and out of their intermission do win themselves a kind of grace-like newness. But the eldest of the present, and newest of past language, is the best. A strict and succinct

ABCDEFGHIJKLMNOPQRSTUVWXYZ1234567890

Slab Serifs

SLAB SERIFS, DEVELOPED IN THE 19TH CENTURY FOR use as display faces, share the same proportions as the Moderns, typefaces such as Bodoni and Modern 216 for example, but have less contrast between thick and thin strokes.

Consider using slab serifs for logo type and corporate identity, or in any situation where high legibility for short amounts of text is your primary concern.

A slab serif such as Clarendon combines well with a sans serif typeface like Helvetica, Univers or Franklin Gothic (the latter is on the companion CD).

A slab ⟶

192-pt. Clarendon Light

EGYPTIAN

TYPE & GRAPHICS

This logo was created in Illustrator using KPT Vector Effects from MetaTools (formerly HSC Software). I used the 3D Transform filter to extrude and bevel the main title. The Vector Effects package includes 11 other mind-blowing plug-ins for Illustrator and FreeHand.

Clarendon Heavy & Bold

Clarendon Regular & Heavy

CLARENDON

SUGGESTED USES: headlines, captions, advertising, posters, signs, spreadsheet column heads

CONSIDER COMBINING WITH: Franklin Gothic

Slab serif typefaces such as Clarendon were designed in the 19th century, and typify the industrialist society of the time. They are reminiscent of advertisements, bills, and posters hawking new inventions and magnificent developments of the time—the building of the first subways or the Brooklyn bridge, for example, or newspaper headlines attracting readers to fantastic stories of the wild west.

Understated is not a word you'd use to describe this typeface; Clarendon is a good attention getter. It is also quite legible, making it a good choice for column headlines in spreadsheet documents, for example.

Reversing the usual practice of combining a sans serif headline with a serif text face, you might consider using Clarendon for heads and a sans serif face such as Franklin Gothic or Franklin Gothic Condensed for text or numbers.

Clarendon Light 10 · 13

Income Statement

	1995		
	JAN	FEB	MAR
Sales	$1,295	$1,594	$1,200
Cost of Goods Sold:			
Material	210	309	104
Direct Labor	198	305	295
Direct Overhead	208	269	310
Total Cost of Goods Sold	617	883	709
Gross Profit	760	987	1,083

Clarendon Light, Bold & Heavy and Franklin Gothic

Clarendon Regular & Bold 9·11

The chief virtue of a style is perspicuity, and nothing so vicious in it as to need an interpreter. Words borrowed of antiquity do lend a kind of majesty to style, and are not without their delight sometimes. For they have the authority of years, and out of their intermission do win themselves a kind of grace-like newness. But the eldest of the present, and newest of past language, is the best. A strict and succinct style is that, where you can take away

Clarendon Regular & Bold 11·13

The chief virtue of a style is perspicuity, and nothing so vicious in it as to need an interpreter. Words borrowed of antiquity do lend a kind of majesty to style, and are not without their delight sometimes. For they have the authority of years, and out of their intermission do win themselves a kind of grace-like newness. But the eldest of the present, and newest of past language, is the best. A strict and succinct style is that, where you can take away nothing without loss, and that loss to be

Clarendon Regular & Bold 12·14

The chief virtue of a style is perspicuity, and nothing so vicious in it as to need an interpreter. Words borrowed of antiquity do lend a kind of majesty to style, and are not without their delight sometimes. For they have the authority of years, and out of their intermission do win themselves a kind of grace-like newness. But the eldest of the present, and newest of past language, is the best. A strict and succinct style

Clarendon Light & Heavy 9·11

The chief virtue of a style is perspicuity, and nothing so vicious in it as to need an interpreter. Words borrowed of antiquity do lend a kind of majesty to style, and are not without their delight sometimes. For they have the authority of years, and out of their intermission do win themselves a kind of grace-like newness. But the eldest of the present, and newest of past language, is the best. A strict and succinct style is that, where you

Clarendon Light & Heavy 11·13

The chief virtue of a style is perspicuity, and nothing so vicious in it as to need an interpreter. Words borrowed of antiquity do lend a kind of majesty to style, and are not without their delight sometimes. For they have the authority of years, and out of their intermission do win themselves a kind of grace-like newness. But the eldest of the present, and newest of past language, is the best. A strict and succinct style is that, where you can take away nothing without loss, and that loss

Clarendon Light & Heavy 12·14

The chief virtue of a style is perspicuity, and nothing so vicious in it as to need an interpreter. Words borrowed of antiquity do lend a kind of majesty to style, and are not without their delight sometimes. For they have the authority of years, and out of their intermission do win themselves a kind of grace-like newness. But the eldest of the present, and newest of past language, is the best.

ABCDEFGHIJKLMNOPQRSTUVWXYZ1234567890

GLYPHA

SUGGESTED USES: general text, magazine and newsletter copy, logos, advertising, display

CONSIDER COMBINING WITH: Franklin Gothic Heavy

Think of Glypha (available on the companion CD as *Glytus*) as a sans serif text face that happens to have slab serifs attached to it. As such, it shares little with the traditional slab serif designs of the 19th century, such as Clarendon.

Glypha is an exceptionally legible text face that also works well as a display for use in headlines, captions, and subheads.

Glytus 10-13

Sometimes a cigar is just a cigar.

SIGMUND FREUD

Glytus Light & Regular

A woman is only a woman, but a good cigar is a **Smoke.**

36-pt. Glytus Light Italic & Bold

Glytus Light & Italic 9·11

The chief virtue of a style is perspicuity, and nothing so vicious in it as to need an interpreter. Words borrowed of antiquity do lend a kind of majesty to style, and are not without their delight sometimes. *For they have the authority of years, and out of their intermission do win themselves a kind of grace-like*

Glytus Light & Italic 11·13

The chief virtue of a style is perspicuity, and nothing so vicious in it as to need an interpreter. Words borrowed of antiquity do lend a kind of majesty to style, and are not without their delight sometimes. *For they have the authority of years, and out of their intermission do win themselves a kind of grace-like newness. But the eldest of the present,*

Glytus Light & Italic 12·14

The chief virtue of a style is perspicuity, and nothing so vicious in it as to need an interpreter. Words borrowed of antiquity do lend a kind of majesty to style, and are not without *their delight sometimes. For they have the authority of years, and out of their intermission do win themselves a kind of grace-like new-*

Glytus Regular & Italic 9·11

The chief virtue of a style is perspicuity, and nothing so vicious in it as to need an interpreter. Words borrowed of antiquity do lend a kind of majesty to style, and are not without *their delight sometimes. For they have the authority of years, and out of their intermission do win them-*

Glytus Regular & Italic 11·13

The chief virtue of a style is perspicuity, and nothing so vicious in it as to need an interpreter. Words borrowed of antiquity do lend a kind of majesty to style, and are not without *their delight sometimes. For they have the authority of years, and out of their intermission do win themselves a kind of grace-like new-*

Glytus Regular & Italic 12·14

The chief virtue of a style is perspicuity, and nothing so vicious in it as to need an interpreter. Words borrowed of antiquity do lend a kind of majesty to style, and are *not without their delight sometimes. For they have the authority of years, and out of their intermission do win themselves a*

Glytus Bold & Bold Italic 9·11

The chief virtue of a style is perspicuity, and nothing so vicious in it as to need an interpreter. Words borrowed of antiquity do lend a kind of majesty to style, and are not without their delight sometimes. ***For they have the authority of years, and out of their intermission do win themselves a kind of***

Glytus Bold & Bold Italic 11·13

The chief virtue of a style is perspicuity, and nothing so vicious in it as to need an interpreter. Words borrowed of antiquity do lend a kind of majesty to style, and are not without their delight sometimes. For they have ***the authority of years, and out of their intermission do win themselves a kind of grace-like newness. But the eldest of the present,***

Glytus Bold & Bold Italic 12·14

The chief virtue of a style is perspicuity, and nothing so vicious in it as to need an interpreter. Words borrowed of antiquity do lend a kind of majesty to style, and are not without their delight sometimes. ***For they have the authority of years, and out of their intermission do win themselves a kind of grace-like newness. But***

A B C D E F G H I J K L M N O P Q R S T U V W X Y Z 1 2 3 4 5 6 7 8 9 0

Sans Serifs

96-point Function Regular

Indicates font has matching small caps and Oldstyle figures.

Indicates font has matching expert sets, which include ligatures, fractions, inferior and superior numerals.

UNLIKE SERIF DESIGNS, THE CLASSIfiCATION OF SANS serifs is primarily descriptive and functional rather than historical. And even though letter forms without serifs have occasionally appeared throughout history as scribal letters or inscriptions, they never made it into type until the latter part of the 19th century. There is no Oldstyle sans serif classification, for example. Such a distinction is historical, and sans serif typefaces do not have centuries of history to draw upon. In fact the oldest sans serif typefaces have only been around for a hundred years or so. That is not to say that historical influences are not apparent in sans serif types, but they only appeared in recent history.

Sans serif typefaces fall into three basic categories: Grotesque, Geometric, and Humanist. Grotesque designs have similar proportions to serif faces, but without serifs, of course. Helvetica, clearly the most popular sans serif design in the world, and Franklin Gothic (available on the companion CD) are the standards of Grotesque sans serifs.

Geometric designs are based on simple geometric principles: the horizontal and vertical parts of letters (ascenders, descenders, and crosses) are very straight lines with little or no variation in stroke width; and the curved parts of letters follow paths that are nearly circular. Typefaces such as Avant Garde, designed in 1970, and Futura, designed in the mid-1920s (available on the companion CD as *Function*) clearly demonstrate the characteristics of geometric design.

Think of Humanist sans serifs as Oldstyle serifs, but without the serifs. Humanist typefaces such as Gill Sans (available on the companion CD as *Chantilly*) and

Syntax are examples. Of all the sans serifs, the Humanists are probably the most versatile and well-suited for a variety of tasks. For example, they work equally well as text faces as they do in headlines and subheads or in callouts and captions. In fact, books and magazine articles are often set in Gill Sans. It is not surprising that the bulk of the Humanists have been designed by some of the most prominent and influential type designers of this century: Hermann Zapf (*Optima*), Frederic Goudy (*Goudy Sans*) and Eric Gill (*Gill Sans*).

Most sans serifs, especially when used in heavier, bold weights, combine well with most serif typefaces for accent. Of course, this is a generalization, but it is difficult to go wrong with such combinations. Even though Humanist sans serifs may combine with Oldstyle serifs more effectively than might Geometrics, for example — where similarities in proportion, axis and stroke modulation complement — it is a matter of degree and not one of rule. For example, Geometrics are often used with Oldstyles when strong contrast is desired rather than subtle complement.

Function Light & Heavy

FRANKLIN GOTHIC

SUGGESTED USES: headlines, callouts, captions, labels, packaging

CONSIDER COMBINING WITH: Bembo, Clarendon, most text fonts

Typefaces like Franklin Gothic capture the realist movement of the late-19th and early-20th centuries. They are simple designs, yet more often than not, bold and strong. In Europe these designs are referred to as Grotesques, and include typefaces such as Helvetica and its many variants, Akzidenz Grotesk (the forerunner of this genre) and Franklin Gothic.

Franklin Gothic is always a good substitute for the ubiquitous and overused Helvetica. It combines well with most text faces,

and if you haven't figured it out already, is the typeface used for the captions, lead-ins, headlines, and page numbers for this book.

The heavier weights of this face are standards in advertising, newspaper and magazine design.

That old saw among typesetters and designers that goes "When in doubt, use Caslon," I think applies equally well to Franklin Gothic.

Franklin Gothic Regular 10·13

The Return of Professor Hawkline.

46-pt. Franklin Gothic Regular

standard

110-pt. Franklin Gothic Heavy

12345
67890

36-pt. Franklin Gothic Condensed Small Caps

The chief virtue of a style i
s *perspicuity, and nothing*
so vicious in it as to need
an interpreter. Words borro
wed of antiquity do lend
a kind of majesty to styl

21-pt. Franklin Gothic Regular, Bold & Heavy with Obliques

the

machine

that

changed

the

world

16-pt. Franklin Gothic Condensed Bold

van • guard (van'gärd') *n.*
[< OFr] **1** *from the old French*
meaning one who guards
the van.

18-pt. Franklin Gothic Regular & Heavy

CAMERON&GREER

30-pt. Franklin Gothic Regular & Heavy

400-pt. Franklin Gothic Regular

ABCDEFGHIJKLMNOPQRSTUVWXYZabc
defghijklmnopqrstuvwxyz1234567890

32-pt. Franklin Gothic Heavy

Franklin Gothic Regular & Oblique 9·11

The chief virtue of a style is perspicuity, and nothing so vicious in it as to need an interpreter. Words borrowed of antiquity do lend a kind of majesty to style, and are not without their delight sometimes. For they have the authority of years, and out of their intermission do win themselves a kind of grace-like newness. But the eldest of the present, and newest of past language, is the best. *A strict and succinct style is that, where you can take away nothing without loss, and that loss to be manifest. The chief virtue of*

Franklin Gothic Regular & Oblique 11·13

The chief virtue of a style is perspicuity, and nothing so vicious in it as to need an interpreter. Words borrowed of antiquity do lend a kind of majesty to style, and are not without their delight sometimes. For they have the authority of years, and out of their intermission do win themselves a kind of grace-like newness. But the eldest of the present, and newest of past language, is the best. *A strict and succinct style is that, where you can take away nothing without loss, and that loss to be manifest. The chief virtue of a style is perspicuity, and nothing so vicious in it as to need an*

Franklin Gothic Regular & Oblique 12·14

The chief virtue of a style is perspicuity, and nothing so vicious in it as to need an interpreter. Words borrowed of antiquity do lend a kind of majesty to style, and are not without their delight sometimes. For they have the authority of years, and out of their intermission do win themselves a kind of grace-like *newness. But the eldest of the present, and newest of past language, is the best. A strict and succinct style is that, where you can take away nothing without loss, and that loss to be*

Franklin Gothic Bold & Bold Oblique 9·11

The chief virtue of a style is perspicuity, and nothing so vicious in it as to need an interpreter. Words borrowed of antiquity do lend a kind of majesty to style, and are not without their delight sometimes. For they have the authority of years, and out of their intermission do win themselves a kind of grace-like newness. But the eldest of the present, and newest of past *language, is the best. A strict and succinct style is that, where you can take away nothing without loss, and that loss to be manifest. The chief virtue of*

Franklin Gothic Bold & Bold Oblique 11·13

The chief virtue of a style is perspicuity, and nothing so vicious in it as to need an interpreter. Words borrowed of antiquity do lend a kind of majesty to style, and are not without their delight sometimes. For they have the authority of years, and out of their intermission do win themselves a kind of grace-like newness. But the eldest of the present, and newest of past language, is the ***best. A strict and succinct style is that, where you can take away nothing without loss, and that loss to be manifest. The chief virtue of a style is per-spicuity, and nothing so vicious in it as to need an***

Franklin Gothic Bold & Bold Oblique 12·14

The chief virtue of a style is perspicuity, and nothing so vicious in it as to need an interpreter. Words borrowed of antiquity do lend a kind of majesty to style, and are not without their delight sometimes. For they have the authority of years, and out of their intermission do win themselves a kind of grace-like newness. But the eldest of the present, and newest of past language, is the best. ***A strict and succinct style is that, where you can take away nothing without loss, and that***

A B C D E F G H I J K L M N O P Q R S T U V W X Y Z 1 2 3 4 5 6 7 8 9 0

Franklin Gothic Condensed Regular & Oblique 9-11

The chief virtue of a style is perspicuity, and nothing so vicious in it as to need an inter- preter. Words borrowed of antiquity do lend a kind of majesty to style, and are not without their delight sometimes. For they have the authority of years, and out of their intermis- sion do win themselves a kind of grace-like newness. But the eldest of the present, and newest of past language, is the best. A strict and succinct style is that, where you can take *away nothing without loss, and that loss to be manifest. The chief virtue of a style is per- spicuity, and nothing so vicious in it as to need an interpreter. Words borrowed of*

Franklin Gothic Condensed Regular & Oblique 11-13

The chief virtue of a style is perspicuity, and nothing so vicious in it as to need an interpreter. Words borrowed of antiquity do lend a kind of majesty to style, and are not without their delight sometimes. For they have the author- ity of years, and out of their intermission do win them- selves a kind of grace-like newness. But the eldest of the present, and newest of past language, is the best. A strict and succinct style is that, where you can take away noth- *ing without loss, and that loss to be manifest. The chief virtue of a style is perspicuity, and nothing so vicious in it as to need an interpreter. Words borrowed of antiquity do lend a kind of majesty to style, and are not without their*

Franklin Gothic Condensed Regular & Oblique 12-14

The chief virtue of a style is perspicuity, and nothing so vicious in it as to need an interpreter. Words bor- rowed of antiquity do lend a kind of majesty to style, and are not without their delight sometimes. For they have the authority of years, and out of their intermis- sion do win themselves a kind of grace-like newness. But the eldest of the present, and newest of past lan- *guage, is the best. A strict and succinct style is that, where you can take away nothing without loss, and that loss to be manifest. The chief virtue of a style is perspicuity, and nothing so vicious in it as to need an*

Franklin Gothic Condensed Bold & Bold Oblique 9-11

The chief virtue of a style is perspicuity, and nothing so vicious in it as to need an inter- preter. Words borrowed of antiquity do lend a kind of majesty to style, and are not without their delight sometimes. For they have the authority of years, and out of their intermis- sion do win themselves a kind of grace-like newness. But the eldest of the present, and newest of past language, is the best. A strict and succinct style is that, where you can take *away nothing without loss, and that loss to be manifest. The chief virtue of a style is per- spicuity, and nothing so vicious in it as to need an interpreter. Words borrowed of*

Franklin Gothic Condensed Bold & Bold Oblique 11-13

The chief virtue of a style is perspicuity, and nothing so vicious in it as to need an interpreter. Words borrowed of antiquity do lend a kind of majesty to style, and are not without their delight sometimes. For they have the author- ity of years, and out of their intermission do win them- selves a kind of grace-like newness. But the eldest of the present, and newest of past language, is the best. A strict and succinct style is that, where you can take away noth- *ing without loss, and that loss to be manifest. The chief virtue of a style is perspicuity, and nothing so vicious in it as to need an interpreter. Words borrowed of antiquity do lend a kind of majesty to style, and are not without their*

Franklin Gothic Condensed Bold & Bold Oblique 12-14

The chief virtue of a style is perspicuity, and nothing so vicious in it as to need an interpreter. Words bor- rowed of antiquity do lend a kind of majesty to style, and are not without their delight sometimes. For they have the authority of years, and out of their intermis- sion do win themselves a kind of grace-like newness. But the eldest of the present, and newest of past lan- *guage, is the best. A strict and succinct style is that, where you can take away nothing without loss, and that loss to be manifest. The chief virtue of a style is perspicuity, and nothing so vicious in it as to need*

A B C D E F G H I J K L M N O P Q R S T U V W X Y Z 1 2 3 4 5 6 7 8 9 0

FUTURA

SUGGESTED USES: headlines, callouts, captions, labels, packaging

CONSIDER COMBINING WITH: Bodoni, Modern 216

Futura (available on the companion CD as *Function*) has a clean, distinct appearance that has made it one of the most commonly used faces in advertising and graphic design in recent years. A crisp face that is highly readable at both text and display sizes, Futura reproduces well on low-resolution printers and contrasts nicely with many serif faces.

Use the light and heavy versions to add drama or contrast. Futura Light delivers great print results at minimal sizes. The heavy weight is a real attention grabber.

Function 10-13

Futura Condensed works well in documents where space is at a premium. Use it at larger point sizes though—below 14 points Futura Condensed can be difficult to read. The bold version of this face is used extensively in advertising in the U.S. and Europe. Great for short callouts and captions.

Futura is one of the few sans serif designs with complementary small caps and Oldstyle figures (which are also available on the CD).

192-pt. Function

88-pt. Function Heavy & Light

progressive

110-pt. Function Regular

1 2 3 4 5 6 7 8 9 0

36-pt. Function Small Caps

The chief virtue of a style is perspicuity, and nothing so vic ious in it as to need an interpr eter. Words borrowed of anti **quity do lend a kind of maj esty to style, and are not wit hout their delight someti mes. For they have the a**

21-pt. Function Light, Regular, Bold & Heavy with Obliques

THE

SHAPE

OF

THINGS

TO

COME

16-pt. Function Heavy

The chief virtue of a style is perspicuity, a nd nothing so vicious in it as to need an in terpreter. Words borrowed of antiquity d o lend a kind of majesty to style, and ar **e not without their delight sometim es. For they have the authority of y ears, and out of their inter mission do win themselves**

21-pt. Function Condensed Light, Regular, Bold & Heavy with Obliques

MODERNGEOMETRICLINEAR

52-pt. Function Light, Bold, Heavy

A B C D E F G H I J K L M N O P Q R S T U V W X Y Z 1 2 3 4 5 6 7 8 9 0 a b c d e f g h i j k l m n o p q r s t u v w x y z & $ % ? ( ) ! #

24-pt. Function Display

Function Regular & Oblique 9-11

The chief virtue of a style is perspicuity, and nothing so vicious in it as to need an interpreter. Words borrowed of antiquity do lend a kind of majesty to style, and are not without their delight sometimes. For they have the authority of years, and out of their intermission do win themselves a kind of grace-like newness. But the eldest of the present, and newest of past language, is the best. A strict and succinct *style is that, where you can take away nothing without loss, and that loss to be manifest. The chief virtue of a style is perspicuity, and nothing so vicious in it as to*

Function Regular & Oblique 11-13

The chief virtue of a style is perspicuity, and nothing so vicious in it as to need an interpreter. Words borrowed of antiquity do lend a kind of majesty to style, and are not without their delight sometimes. For they have the authority of years, and out of their intermission do win themselves a kind of grace-like newness. But the eldest of the present, and newest of past language, is the best. A strict and succinct style is that, *where you can take away nothing without loss, and that loss to be manifest. The chief virtue of a style is perspicuity, and nothing so vicious in it as to need an interpreter. Words borrowed of antiquity do lend a*

Function Regular & Oblique 12-14

The chief virtue of a style is perspicuity, and nothing so vicious in it as to need an interpreter. Words borrowed of antiquity do lend a kind of majesty to style, and are not without their delight sometimes. For they have the authority of years, and out of their intermission do win themselves a kind of grace-like newness. But the eldest of the *present, and newest of past language, is the best. A strict and succinct style is that, where you can take away nothing without loss, and that loss to be manifest. The chief virtue of a style is perspicu-*

Function Bold & Bold Oblique 9-11

The chief virtue of a style is perspicuity, and nothing so vicious in it as to need an interpreter. Words borrowed of antiquity do lend a kind of majesty to style, and are not without their delight sometimes. For they have the authority of years, and out of their intermission do win themselves a kind of grace-like newness. But the eldest of the present, and newest of past language, is the best. A strict and suc- *cinct style is that, where you can take away nothing without loss, and that loss to be manifest. The chief virtue of a style*

Function Bold & Bold Oblique 11-13

The chief virtue of a style is perspicuity, and nothing so vicious in it as to need an interpreter. Words borrowed of antiquity do lend a kind of majesty to style, and are not without their delight sometimes. For they have the authority of years, and out of their intermission do win themselves a kind of grace-like newness. But the eldest of the present, and newest of past language, is the best. ***A strict and succinct style is that, where you can take away nothing without loss, and that loss to be manifest. The chief virtue of a style is perspicuity, and nothing so vicious in it as to need an interpreter.***

Function Bold & Bold Oblique 12-14

The chief virtue of a style is perspicuity, and nothing so vicious in it as to need an interpreter. Words borrowed of antiquity do lend a kind of majesty to style, and are not without their delight sometimes. For they have the authority of years, and out of their intermission do win themselves a kind of grace-like newness. ***But the eldest of the present, and newest of past language, is the best. A strict and succinct style is that, where you can take away nothing without loss, and that loss***

A B C D E F G H I J K L M N O P Q R S T U V W X Y Z 1 2 3 4 5 6 7 8 9 0

Function Light & Light Oblique 9·11

The chief virtue of a style is perspicuity, and nothing so vicious in it as to need an interpreter. Words borrowed of antiquity do lend a kind of majesty to style, and are not without their delight sometimes. For they have the authority of years, and out of their intermission do win themselves a kind of grace-like newness. But the eldest of the present, and newest of past language, is the best. A strict and succinct style is that, *where you can take away nothing without loss, and that loss to be manifest. The chief virtue of a style is perspicuity, and nothing so vicious in it as to need an interpreter.*

Function Light & Light Oblique 11·13

The chief virtue of a style is perspicuity, and nothing so vicious in it as to need an interpreter. Words borrowed of antiquity do lend a kind of majesty to style, and are not without their delight sometimes. For they have the authority of years, and out of their intermission do win themselves a kind of grace-like newness. But the eldest of the present, and newest of past language, is the best. A strict and succinct style is that, *where you can take away nothing without loss, and that loss to be manifest. The chief virtue of a style is perspicuity, and nothing so vicious in it as to need an interpreter. The chief virtue of a style is perspicuity, and nothing so vicious in it as to*

Function Light & Light Oblique 12·14

The chief virtue of a style is perspicuity, and nothing so vicious in it as to need an interpreter. Words borrowed of antiquity do lend a kind of majesty to style, and are not without their delight sometimes. For they have the authority of years, and out of their intermission do win themselves a kind of grace-like newness. But the eldest of the present, and newest *of past language, is the best. A strict and succinct style is that, where you can take away nothing without loss, and that loss to be manifest. The chief virtue of a style is perspicuity, and nothing so vicious*

Function Heavy & Heavy Oblique 9·11

The chief virtue of a style is perspicuity, and nothing so vicious in it as to need an interpreter. Words borrowed of antiquity do lend a kind of majesty to style, and are not without their delight sometimes. For they have the authority of years, and out of their intermission do win themselves a kind of grace-like newness. But the eldest of the present, and newest of past *language, is the best. A strict and succinct style is that, where you can take away nothing without*

Function Heavy & Heavy Oblique 11·13

The chief virtue of a style is perspicuity, and nothing so vicious in it as to need an interpreter. Words borrowed of antiquity do lend a kind of majesty to style, and are not without their delight sometimes. For they have the authority of years, and out of their intermission do win themselves a kind of grace-like newness. But the eldest of the present, *and newest of past language, is the best. A strict and succinct style is that, where you can take away nothing without loss, and that loss to be manifest. The chief virtue of a*

Function Heavy & Heavy Oblique 12·14

The chief virtue of a style is perspicuity, and nothing so vicious in it as to need an interpreter. Words borrowed of antiquity do lend a kind of majesty to style, and are not without their delight sometimes. For they have the authority of years, and out of their intermission do win *themselves a kind of grace-like newness. But the eldest of the present, and newest of past language, is the best. A strict and succinct style is that, where you*

A B C D E F G H I J K L M N O P Q R S T U V W X Y Z 1 2 3 4 5 6 7 8 9 0

Function Condensed Regular & Oblique 9-11

The chief virtue of a style is perspicuity, and nothing so vicious in it as to need an interpreter. Words borrowed of antiquity do lend a kind of majesty to style, and are not without their delight sometimes. For they have the authority of years, and out of their intermission do win themselves a kind of grace-like newness. But the eldest of the present, and newest of past language, is the best. A strict and succinct style is that, where you can take away nothing without loss, and that loss to be manifest. The chief virtue of a style is perspicuity, and nothing so vicious in it as to need an interpreter. *Words borrowed of antiquity do lend a kind of majesty to style, and are not without their delight sometimes. For they have the authority of years, and out of their intermission do win themselves a kind of*

Function Condensed Regular & Oblique 11-13

The chief virtue of a style is perspicuity, and nothing so vicious in it as to need an interpreter. Words borrowed of antiquity do lend a kind of majesty to style, and are not without their delight sometimes. For they have the authority of years, and out of their intermission do win themselves a kind of grace-like newness. But the eldest of the present, and newest of past language, is the best. A strict and succinct style is that, where you can take away nothing without loss, and that loss to be manifest. The chief virtue of a style is perspicuity, and nothing so vicious in it as to need an interpreter. *Words borrowed of antiquity do lend a kind of majesty to style, and are not without their delight sometimes. For they have the authority of years, and out of their intermission do win themselves a kind of grace-like newness. But the eldest of the present, and newest of past language, is the best.*

Function Condensed Regular & Oblique 12-14

The chief virtue of a style is perspicuity, and nothing so vicious in it as to need an interpreter. Words borrowed of antiquity do lend a kind of majesty to style, and are not without their delight sometimes. For they have the authority of years, and out of their intermission do win themselves a kind of grace-like newness. But the eldest of the present, and newest of past language, is the best. A strict and succinct style is that, where you can take away nothing without *loss, and that loss to be manifest. The chief virtue of a style is perspicuity, and nothing so vicious in it as to need an interpreter. Words borrowed of antiquity do lend a kind of majesty to style, and are not without their delight sometimes. For they have the authority of*

Function Condensed Bold & Bold Oblique 9-11

The chief virtue of a style is perspicuity, and nothing so vicious in it as to need an interpreter. Words borrowed of antiquity do lend a kind of majesty to style, and are not without their delight sometimes. For they have the authority of years, and out of their intermission do win themselves a kind of grace-like newness. But the eldest of the present, and newest of past language, is the best. A strict and succinct style is that, where you can take away nothing without loss, and that loss to be manifest. The *chief virtue of a style is perspicuity, and nothing so vicious in it as to need an interpreter. Words borrowed of antiquity do lend a kind of majesty to style, and are not without their delight sometimes. For*

Function Condensed Bold & Bold Oblique 11-13

The chief virtue of a style is perspicuity, and nothing so vicious in it as to need an interpreter. Words borrowed of antiquity do lend a kind of majesty to style, and are not without their delight sometimes. For they have the authority of years, and out of their intermission do win themselves a kind of grace-like newness. But the eldest of the present, and newest of past language, is the best. A strict and succinct style is that, where you can take away nothing without loss, and that loss to be manifest. The chief virtue of a *style is perspicuity, and nothing so vicious in it as to need an interpreter. Words borrowed of antiquity do lend a kind of majesty to style, and are not without their delight sometimes. For they have the authority of years, and out of their intermission do win them-*

Function Condensed Bold & Bold Oblique 12-14

The chief virtue of a style is perspicuity, and nothing so vicious in it as to need an interpreter. Words borrowed of antiquity do lend a kind of majesty to style, and are not without their delight sometimes. For they have the authority of years, and out of their intermission do win themselves a kind of grace-like newness. But the eldest of the present, and newest of past language, is the best. A strict and suc-*cinct style is that, where you can take away nothing without loss, and that loss to be manifest. The chief virtue of a style is perspicuity, and nothing so vicious in it as to need an interpreter. Words borrowed of antiquity do lend a kind of*

A B C D E F G H I J K L M N O P Q R S T U V W X Y Z 1 2 3 4 5 6 7 8 9 0

Function Condensed Light & Oblique 9-11

The chief virtue of a style is perspicuity, and nothing so vicious in it as to need an interpreter. Words borrowed of antiquity do lend a kind of majesty to style, and are not without their delight sometimes. For they have the authority of years, and out of their intermission do win themselves a kind of grace-like newness. But the eldest of the present, and newest of past language, is the best. A strict and succinct style is that, where you can take away nothing without loss, and that loss to be manifest. *The chief virtue of a style is perspicuity, and nothing so vicious in it as to need an interpreter. Words borrowed of antiquity do lend a kind of majesty to style, and are not without their delight sometimes. For they have the authority of years, and out of their intermission do win themselves a kind of grace-like newness.*

Function Condensed Light & Oblique 11-13

The chief virtue of a style is perspicuity, and nothing so vicious in it as to need an interpreter. Words borrowed of antiquity do lend a kind of majesty to style, and are not without their delight sometimes. For they have the authority of years, and out of their intermission do win themselves a kind of grace-like newness. But the eldest of the present, and newest of past language, is the best. A strict and succinct style is that, where you can take away nothing without loss, and that loss to be manifest. *The chief virtue of a style is perspicuity, and nothing so vicious in it as to need an interpreter. Words borrowed of antiquity do lend a kind of majesty to style, and are not without their delight sometimes. For they have the authority of years, and out of their intermission do win themselves a kind of grace-like newness. But the eldest of the present, and newest of past language, is the best. A strict and succinct style is that, where*

Function Condensed Light & Oblique 12-14

The chief virtue of a style is perspicuity, and nothing so vicious in it as to need an interpreter. Words borrowed of antiquity do lend a kind of majesty to style, and are not without their delight sometimes. For they have the authority of years, and out of their intermission do win themselves a kind of grace-like newness. But the eldest of the present, and newest of past language, is the best. A strict and succinct style is that, where you can take away nothing without loss, and that loss to be *manifest. The chief virtue of a style is perspicuity, and nothing so vicious in it as to need an interpreter. Words borrowed of antiquity do lend a kind of majesty to style, and are not without their delight sometimes. For they have the authority of years, and out of their intermission do*

Function Condensed Heavy & Heavy Oblique 9-11

The chief virtue of a style is perspicuity, and nothing so vicious in it as to need an interpreter. Words borrowed of antiquity do lend a kind of majesty to style, and are not without their delight sometimes. For they have the authority of years, and out of their intermission do win themselves a kind of grace-like newness. But the eldest of the present, and newest of past language, is the best. A strict and succinct style is that, where you can take away nothing without loss, and that loss to be manifest. The chief virtue of a style is perspicuity, and nothing so vicious in it as to

Function Condensed Heavy & Heavy Oblique 11-13

The chief virtue of a style is perspicuity, and nothing so vicious in it as to need an interpreter. Words borrowed of antiquity do lend a kind of majesty to style, and are not without their delight sometimes. For they have the authority of years, and out of their intermission do win themselves a kind of grace-like newness. But the eldest of the present, and newest of past language, is the best. A strict and succinct style is that, where you can take away nothing without loss, and that loss to be manifest. The chief virtue of a style is perspicuity, and nothing so vicious in it as to need an interpreter. Words borrowed of antiquity do lend

Function Condensed Heavy & Heavy Oblique 12-14

The chief virtue of a style is perspicuity, and nothing so vicious in it as to need an interpreter. Words borrowed of antiquity do lend a kind of majesty to style, and are not without their delight sometimes. For they have the authority of years, and out of their intermission do win themselves a kind of grace-like newness. But the eldest of the present, and newest of past language, is the best. A strict and succinct style is that, where you can take away nothing without loss, and that loss to be manifest. The chief virtue

A B C D E F G H I J K L M N O P Q R S T U V W X Y Z 1 2 3 4 5 6 7 8 9 0

GILL SANS

SUGGESTED USES: text, callouts, captions; the heavy version is particularly well suited for headlines and display

CONSIDER COMBINING WITH: Bembo, Garamond, New Baskerville

100-pt. Chantilly Ultra Bold

Gill Sans (available on the companion CD as *Chantilly*) is arguably the most readable and legible sans serif design, and is the standard bearer of the Humanist sans serifs. Designed in the late 1920s by Eric Gill, it is one of the first sans serif typefaces to be used for setting text for continuous reading. Its proportions and letter forms follow the designs of Oldstyle and Transitional serif typefaces very closely, and this is probably one reason it is so easy on the eyes

Chantilly Regular 10·13

(most sans serifs tend to be difficult to read at text sizes and in large amounts).

Gill Sans works well as both a text and a display font. I frequently use it for office correspondence such as letters, memoranda and faxes.

Unlike most sans serif faces, Gill Sans has true italics rather than obliqued roman characters. This is easiest to see with the lowercase *a* and *p*, for example, in the roman and italic forms.

Homo sum; *humani* nihil a *me* alienum puto.

60-pt. Chantilly Regular & Italic

humanists

110-pt. Chantilly Regular

400-pt. Chantilly Regular

The chief virtue of a style is *perspicuity, and nothing so vic* ious in it as to need an interp *reter. Words borrowed of antiq* uity do lend a kind of majes *ty to style, and are not with* **out their delight som etimes. For they have the authority of year**

21-pt. Chantilly Light, Regular, Bold, Heavy with Italics & Ultrabold

FEAR'D

BY

THEIR BREED

&

FAMOUS

BY

THEIR BIRTH

16-pt. Chantilly Regular

Chantilly Regular & Heavy

A B C D E F G H I J K L M N O P Q R S T U V W X Y Z a b c d e f g h i
j k l m n o p q r s t u v w x y z 1 2 3 4 5 6 7 8 9 0 & $ % ? ( ) ! #

19-pt. Chantilly Ultra Bold

Chantilly Regular & Italic 9·11

The chief virtue of a style is perspicuity, and nothing so vicious in it as to need an interpreter. Words borrowed of antiquity do lend a kind of majesty to style, and are not without their delight sometimes. For they have the authority of years, and out of their intermission do win themselves a kind of grace-like newness. But the eldest of the present, and newest of past language, is the best. A strict and succinct style is that, *where you can take away nothing without loss, and that loss to be manifest. The chief virtue of a style is perspicuity, and nothing so vicious in it as to need an*

Chantilly Regular & Italic 11·13

The chief virtue of a style is perspicuity, and nothing so vicious in it as to need an interpreter. Words borrowed of antiquity do lend a kind of majesty to style, and are not without their delight sometimes. For they have the authority of years, and out of their intermission do win themselves a kind of grace-like newness. But the eldest of the present, and newest of past language, is the best. A strict and succinct style is that, *where you can take away nothing without loss, and that loss to be manifest. The chief virtue of a style is perspicuity, and nothing so vicious in it as to need an interpreter. Words borrowed of antiquity do lend a kind*

Chantilly Regular & Italic 12·14

The chief virtue of a style is perspicuity, and nothing so vicious in it as to need an interpreter. Words borrowed of antiquity do lend a kind of majesty to style, and are not without their delight sometimes. For they have the authority of years, and out of their intermission do win themselves a kind of grace-like newness. But the eldest of the *present, and newest of past language, is the best. A strict and succinct style is that, where you can take away nothing without loss, and that loss to be manifest. The chief virtue of a style is perspicuity,*

Chantilly Bold & Bold Italic 9·11

The chief virtue of a style is perspicuity, and nothing so vicious in it as to need an interpreter. Words borrowed of antiquity do lend a kind of majesty to style, and are not without their delight sometimes. For they have the authority of years, and out of their intermission do win themselves a kind of grace-like newness. But the eldest of the present, and newest of past language, is the best. *A strict and succinct style is that, where you can take away nothing without loss, and that loss to be manifest. The chief virtue of a style is perspicuity, and noth-*

Chantilly Bold & Bold Italic 11·13

The chief virtue of a style is perspicuity, and nothing so vicious in it as to need an interpreter. Words borrowed of antiquity do lend a kind of majesty to style, and are not without their delight sometimes. For they have the authority of years, and out of their intermission do win themselves a kind of grace-like newness. But the eldest of the present, and newest of past language, is the best. A strict *and succinct style is that, where you can take away nothing without loss, and that loss to be manifest. The chief virtue of a style is perspicuity, and nothing so vicious in it as to need an interpreter. Words bor-*

Chantilly Bold & Bold Italic 12·14

The chief virtue of a style is perspicuity, and nothing so vicious in it as to need an interpreter. Words borrowed of antiquity do lend a kind of majesty to style, and are not without their delight sometimes. For they have the authority of years, and out of their intermission do win themselves a kind of grace-like newness. *But the eldest of the present, and newest of past language, is the best. A strict and succinct style is that, where you can take away nothing without loss, and that loss to be*

A B C D E F G H I J K L M N O P Q R S T U V W X Y Z 1 2 3 4 5 6 7 8 9 0

Chantilly Light & Italic 9·11

The chief virtue of a style is perspicuity, and nothing so vicious in it as to need an interpreter. Words borrowed of antiquity do lend a kind of majesty to style, and are not without their delight sometimes. For they have the authority of years, and out of their intermission do win themselves a kind of grace-like newness. But the eldest of the present, and newest of past language, is the best. A strict and succinct *style is that, where you can take away nothing without loss, and that loss to be manifest. The chief virtue of a style is perspicuity, and nothing so vicious in it as to need an inter-*

Chantilly Light & Italic 11·13

The chief virtue of a style is perspicuity, and nothing so vicious in it as to need an interpreter. Words borrowed of antiquity do lend a kind of majesty to style, and are not without their delight sometimes. For they have the authority of years, and out of their intermission do win themselves a kind of grace-like newness. But the eldest of the present, and newest of past language, is the best. A strict and succinct style is that, where you can take *away nothing without loss, and that loss to be manifest. The chief virtue of a style is perspicuity, and nothing so vicious in it as to need an interpreter. Words borrowed of antiquity do lend a kind of majesty to style, and are not*

Chantilly Light & Italic 12·14

The chief virtue of a style is perspicuity, and nothing so vicious in it as to need an interpreter. Words borrowed of antiquity do lend a kind of majesty to style, and are not without their delight sometimes. For they have the authority of years, and out of their intermission do win themselves a kind of grace-like newness. But the eldest of the present, *and newest of past language, is the best. A strict and succinct style is that, where you can take away nothing without loss, and that loss to be manifest. The chief virtue of a style is perspicuity, and nothing so vicious in*

Chantilly Heavy & Italic 9·11

The chief virtue of a style is perspicuity, and nothing so vicious in it as to need an interpreter. Words borrowed of antiquity do lend a kind of majesty to style, and are not without their delight sometimes. For they have the authority of years, and out of their intermission do win *themselves a kind of grace-like newness. But the eldest of the present, and newest of past language, is the best. A strict and succinct style is that,*

Chantilly Heavy & Italic 11·13

The chief virtue of a style is perspicuity, and nothing so vicious in it as to need an interpreter. Words borrowed of antiquity do lend a kind of majesty to style, and are not without their delight sometimes. For they have the authority of years, and out of their intermission do win themselves a kind of grace-like newness. *But the eldest of the present, and newest of past language, is the best. A strict and succinct style is that, where you can take away nothing without*

Chantilly Heavy & Italic 12·14

The chief virtue of a style is perspicuity, and nothing so vicious in it as to need an interpreter. Words borrowed of antiquity do lend a kind of majesty to style, and are not without their delight sometimes. For they have the authority of years, *and out of their intermission do win themselves a kind of grace-like newness. But the eldest of the present, and newest of past language, is the best. A strict*

A B C D E F G H I J K L M N O P Q R S T U V W X Y Z 1 2 3 4 5 6 7 8 9 0

GOUDY SANS

SMALL CAPS SUGGESTED USES: text, callouts, captions

SMALL CAPS CONSIDER COMBINING WITH: Goudy Oldstyle, Garamond

Goudy Sans is the quirkiest of the Humanist sans serifs, although its relationship to other designs in this class is quite apparent—Oldstyle proportions, oblique stress, and subtle variations of stroke weight. The roman form is somewhat less geometric than Gill Sans and Syntax, and its italics are significantly more embellished, almost to the point of approaching a script

Goudy Sans Regular 10 13

face. Particularly note the uppercase A and Q, which are beautiful in the italics. You'll also notice that Goudy Sans has very slight hints of serifs on most of its stems.

Like the other Humanists, Goudy Sans' italics are true italics, and not simply obliqued versions of the roman letters.

A Half-Sunday Homage To A Whole Leonardo Da Vinci

60-pt. Goudy Sans Italic

Goudy Sans Regular & Italic 9 11

The chief virtue of a style is perspicuity, and nothing so vicious in it as to need an interpreter. Words borrowed of antiquity do lend a kind of majesty to style, and are not without their delight sometimes. For they have the authority of years, and out of their intermission do win themselves a kind of grace-like newness. But the eldest of the present, and newest of past language, is the best. A strict and succinct *style is that, where you can take away nothing without loss, and that loss to be manifest. The chief virtue of a style is perspicuity, and nothing so vicious in it as to*

Goudy Sans Regular & Italic 11 13

The chief virtue of a style is perspicuity, and nothing so vicious in it as to need an interpreter. Words borrowed of antiquity do lend a kind of majesty to style, and are not without their delight sometimes. For they have the authority of years, and out of their intermission do win themselves a kind of grace-like newness. But the eldest of the present, and newest of past language, is the best. A strict and succinct style is that, *where you can take away nothing without loss, and that loss to be manifest. The chief virtue of a style is perspicuity, and nothing so vicious in it as to need an interpreter. Words borrowed of antiquity do lend a*

Goudy Sans Regular & Italic 12 14

The chief virtue of a style is perspicuity, and nothing so vicious in it as to need an interpreter. Words borrowed of antiquity do lend a kind of majesty to style, and are not without their delight sometimes. For they have the authority of years, and out of their intermission do win themselves a kind of grace-like newness. But the eldest of the present, *and newest of past language, is the best. A strict and succinct style is that, where you can take away nothing without loss, and that loss to be manifest. The chief virtue of a style is perspicuity,*

Goudy Sans Bold & Bold Italic 9 11

The chief virtue of a style is perspicuity, and nothing so vicious in it as to need an interpreter. Words borrowed of antiquity do lend a kind of majesty to style, and are not without their delight sometimes. For they have the authority of years, and out of their intermission do win themselves a kind of grace-like newness. But the eldest of the present, and newest of *past language, is the best. A strict and succinct style is that, where you can take away nothing without loss, and that loss to be manifest. The chief*

Goudy Sans Bold & Bold Italic 11 13

The chief virtue of a style is perspicuity, and nothing so vicious in it as to need an interpreter. Words borrowed of antiquity do lend a kind of majesty to style, and are not without their delight sometimes. For they have the authority of years, and out of their intermission do win themselves a kind of grace-like newness. But the eldest of the present, and newest of past lan-guage, is the best. *A strict and succinct style is that, where you can take away nothing without loss, and that loss to be manifest. The chief virtue of a style is perspicuity, and nothing so vicious in*

Goudy Sans Bold & Bold Italic 12 14

The chief virtue of a style is perspicuity, and nothing so vicious in it as to need an inter-preter. Words borrowed of antiquity do lend a kind of majesty to style, and are not with-out their delight sometimes. For they have the authority of years, and out of their inter-mission do win themselves a kind of grace-like newness. *But the eldest of the present, and newest of past language, is the best. A strict and succinct style is that, where you can take away nothing without loss, and that loss*

A B C D E F G H I J K L M N O P Q R S T U V W X Y Z 1 2 3 4 5 6 7 8 9 0

OPTIMA

Suggested uses: body text, ad copy, headings, correspondence

Consider combining with: Palatino, URW Palladio, Sabon

Optima (available on the companion CD as *Opus*) is not so much a sans serif as a pseudo serif typeface. It appears to have serifs, yet it does not. It works well primarily in body text (another domain usually reserved for serif fonts), but is also a good choice for headings and even display work (I have noticed that several TV and radio stations around the country use Optima for their logos and call letters).

There is a general bias that Optima looks good only at high resolutions. While it's true that it has features (such as the cups on its stems) that benefit from resolutions above 600 dpi (the effect of these cups is partly what gives Optima the illusion of serifs), I think Optima looks good at lower resolutions as well. It is exceptionally readable at all resolutions, and although

it may be slightly less beautiful, somewhat less striking at 600 dpi, for example, it's no ugly duckling. If you're printing at higher resolutions, Optima is classy, elegant, formal, sophisticated. If you're using it at lower resolutions, it is functional, rational in a feminine sort of way (or is that an oxymoron?). Consider using it as your base font for documents such as memos and letters.

In body text, give Optima plenty of line spacing. The standard 10/12 that works with standard serif faces may not be enough. Consider more dramatic line spacing such as 10/15 or 12/18, for example.

Optima set in all caps with letter spacing looks very attractive in many sizes and situations.

Opus Regular 10·15

Opus Regular & Bold

Opus Regular & Italic 9·11

The chief virtue of a style is perspicuity, and nothing so vicious in it as to need an interpreter. Words borrowed of antiquity do lend a kind of majesty to style, and are not without their delight sometimes. For they have the authority of years, and out of their intermission do win themselves a kind of grace-like newness. But the eldest of the present, and newest of past language, is the best. *A strict and succinct style is that, where you can take away nothing without loss, and that loss to be manifest. The chief virtue of a style*

Opus Regular & Italic 11·13

The chief virtue of a style is perspicuity, and nothing so vicious in it as to need an interpreter. Words borrowed of antiquity do lend a kind of majesty to style, and are not without their delight sometimes. For they have the authority of years, and out of their intermission do win themselves a kind of grace-like newness. But the eldest of the present, and newest of past language, is the best. *A strict and succinct style is that, where you can take away nothing without loss, and that loss to be manifest. The chief virtue of a style is perspicuity, and nothing so vicious in it as to need an interpreter. Words*

Opus Regular & Italic 12·14

The chief virtue of a style is perspicuity, and nothing so vicious in it as to need an interpreter. Words borrowed of antiquity do lend a kind of majesty to style, and are not without their delight sometimes. For they have the authority of years, and out of their intermission do win themselves a kind of grace-like newness. *But the eldest of the present, and newest of past language, is the best. A strict and succinct style is that, where you can take away nothing without loss, and that loss to be mani-*

Opus Bold & Bold Italic 9·11

The chief virtue of a style is perspicuity, and nothing so vicious in it as to need an interpreter. Words borrowed of antiquity do lend a kind of majesty to style, and are not without their delight sometimes. For they have the authority of years, and out of their intermission do win themselves a kind of grace-like newness. But the eldest of the present, and newest of past *language, is the best. A strict and succinct style is that, where you can take away nothing without loss, and that loss to be manifest. The chief virtue of*

Opus Bold & Bold Italic 11·13

The chief virtue of a style is perspicuity, and nothing so vicious in it as to need an interpreter. Words borrowed of antiquity do lend a kind of majesty to style, and are not without their delight sometimes. For they have the authority of years, and out of their intermission do win themselves a kind of grace-like newness. But the eldest of the present, and newest of past language, is the best. *A strict and succinct style is that, where you can take away nothing without loss, and that loss to be manifest. The chief virtue of a style is per-spicuity, and nothing so vicious in it as to need*

Opus Bold & Bold Italic 12·14

The chief virtue of a style is perspicuity, and nothing so vicious in it as to need an interpreter. Words borrowed of antiquity do lend a kind of majesty to style, and are not without their delight sometimes. For they have the authority of years, and out of their intermission do win themselves a kind of grace-like newness. *But the eldest of the present, and newest of past language, is the best. A strict and succinct style is that, where you can take away nothing without loss, and that*

A B C D E F G H I J K L M N O P Q R S T U V W X Y Z 1 2 3 4 5 6 7 8 9 0

SYNTAX

SUGGESTED USES: text, captions, headings, display, packaging

CONSIDER COMBINING WITH: Bembo, Sabon, Galliard

I classify Syntax as a rational Humanist. Like other Humanists, it shares the proportions of Oldstyle serif typefaces, but is less affected than typefaces such as Gill Sans, and not quite as quirky. The two typefaces, however, work equally well in similar situations. It is purely a matter of personality, not purpose, that distinguishes them.

Syntax has true italics, meaning that the italic variation is not simply an obliqued version of the roman. This is characteristic of the other Humanists as well (Gill Sans, Optima, and Goudy Sans).

Syntax Regular 10·13

Used Trout Stream For Sale.

MUST BE SEEN TO BE APPRECIATED.

Syntax Regular & Heavy

Syntax Regular & Italic 9·11

The chief virtue of a style is perspicuity, and nothing so vicious in it as to need an interpreter. Words borrowed of antiquity do lend a kind of majesty to style, and are not without their delight sometimes. For they have the authority of years, and out of their intermission do win themselves a kind of grace-like newness. But the eldest of the present, and newest of past language, is the *best. A strict and succinct style is that, where you can take away nothing without loss, and that loss to be manifest. The chief virtue of a style is per-*

Syntax Regular & Italic 11·13

The chief virtue of a style is perspicuity, and nothing so vicious in it as to need an interpreter. Words borrowed of antiquity do lend a kind of majesty to style, and are not without their delight sometimes. For they have the authority of years, and out of their intermission do win themselves a kind of grace-like newness. But the eldest of the present, and newest of past language, is the best. *A strict and succinct style is that, where you can take away nothing without loss, and that loss to be manifest. The chief virtue of a style is perspicuity, and nothing so vicious in it as to need an inter-*

Syntax Regular & Italic 12·14

The chief virtue of a style is perspicuity, and nothing so vicious in it as to need an interpreter. Words borrowed of antiquity do lend a kind of majesty to style, and are not without their delight sometimes. For they have the authority of years, and out of their intermission do win themselves a kind of grace-like new*ness. But the eldest of the present, and newest of past language, is the best. A strict and succinct style is that, where you can take away nothing without loss, and that loss to be*

Syntax Bold 9·11

The chief virtue of a style is perspicuity, and nothing so vicious in it as to need an interpreter. Words borrowed of antiquity do lend a kind of majesty to style, and are not without their delight sometimes. For they have the

Syntax Bold 11·13

The chief virtue of a style is perspicuity, and nothing so vicious in it as to need an interpreter. Words borrowed of antiquity do lend a kind of majesty to style, and are not without their delight sometimes. For they have the authority of years,

Syntax Bold 12·14

The chief virtue of a style is perspicuity, and nothing so vicious in it as to need an interpreter. Words borrowed of antiquity do lend a kind of majesty to style, and are not without their delight sometimes. For they have

Syntax Heavy 9·11

The chief virtue of a style is perspicuity, and nothing so vicious in it as to need an interpreter. Words borrowed of antiquity do lend a kind of majesty to style, and are not without their delight some-

Syntax Heavy 11·13

The chief virtue of a style is perspicuity, and nothing so vicious in it as to need an interpreter. Words borrowed of antiquity do lend a kind of majesty to style, and are not without their delight sometimes. For they

Syntax Heavy 12·14

The chief virtue of a style is perspicuity, and nothing so vicious in it as to need an interpreter. Words borrowed of antiquity do lend a kind of majesty to style, and are not without their delight some-

ABCDEFGHIJKLMNOPQRSTUVWXYZ1234567890

LETTER GOTHIC

SUGGESTED USES: text, columnar data, display, multimedia

CONSIDER COMBINING WITH: just about any type-face as an accent

Letter Gothic is a fixed-pitch typeface useful for form letters and legal docu-ments, or in any document where you want a typewritten appearance but don't want to use Courier. Because it is a monospaced typeface, it's very useful for printing tables, lists, and other forms of columnar data. Over the last couple of years, Letter Gothic has been frequently used as a "grunge" typeface in all sorts of designs, as well as a "techno" face, popular in multimedia and video applications. It is quite effective when used as an accent font for projects such as posters, book and CD covers, and advertisements.

Letter Gothic Regular 10·13

Letter Gothic Bold & Vendome

Letter Gothic Regular & Oblique 9·11

The chief virtue of a style is perspicuity, and nothing so vicious in it as to need an interpreter. Words borrowed of antiquity do lend a kind of majesty to style, and are not without their delight sometimes. For they have the authority of years, and out of their *intermission do win themselves a kind of grace-like newness. But the eldest of the present, and newest of*

Letter Gothic Regular & Oblique 11·13

The chief virtue of a style is perspicuity, and nothing so vicious in it as to need an interpreter. Words borrowed of antiquity do lend a kind of majesty to style, and are not without their delight sometimes. For they have the authority of years, and out of their inter-*mission do win themselves a kind of grace-like newness. But the eldest of the present, and newest of past language, is the best. A strict*

Letter Gothic Regular & Oblique 12·14

The chief virtue of a style is perspicuity, and nothing so vicious in it as to need an interpreter. Words borrowed of antiquity do lend a kind of majesty to style, and are not without their delight sometimes. *For they have the authority of years, and out of their intermission do win themselves a*

Letter Gothic Bold & Bold Oblique 9·11

The chief virtue of a style is perspicuity, and nothing so vicious in it as to need an interpreter. Words borrowed of antiquity do lend a kind of majesty to style, and are not without their delight sometimes. For they have the authority of years, and out of their *intermission do win themselves a kind of grace-like newness. But the eldest of the present, and newest*

Letter Gothic Bold & Bold Oblique 11·13

The chief virtue of a style is perspicuity, and nothing so vicious in it as to need an interpreter. Words borrowed of antiquity do lend a kind of majesty to style, and are not without their delight sometimes. For they have the authority of years, and out of their inter-*mission do win themselves a kind of grace-like newness. But the eldest of the present, and newest of past language, is the best. A strict and*

Letter Gothic Bold & Bold Oblique 12·14

The chief virtue of a style is perspicuity, and nothing so vicious in it as to need an interpreter. Words borrowed of antiquity do lend a kind of majesty to style, and are not without their delight sometimes. *For they have the authority of years, and out of their intermission do win themselves a kind of grace-*

ABCDEFGHIJKLMNOPQRSTUVWXYZ1234567890

Letter Gothic Extra Bold

Script Faces

Script fonts are some of the most beautiful type-faces available, but they are also some of the eas-iest to misuse. Part of the reason for this is emotional: a person might become enamored with a certain script face and attempt to use it for everything—memos, let-ters, brochures, newsletters, etc. Don't let this happen to you. Script faces work very well in formal documents like invitations, and as decorative fonts for use in pack-aging, signs, titles, menus and logos, and as initial drop caps. They do not work well as text fonts, or for long lines of text. Script faces look best with tight letter spacing. Avoid setting them in all caps.

48-pt. Vivaldi & 192-pt. Deanna Flowers

Script faces such as Park Avenue are particularly well-suited for formal documents such as invitations where you want to impart a friendly tone. It has a certain retro feel to it reminiscent of the late 1930s and 40s. This tone is enhanced by its elegant pen-drawn quality, and its small lowercase letters give it a slightly feminine quality. Park Avenue is quite popular in ads for jewelry stores and tuxedo rental shops. Other script faces such as Hudson, Mistral, and Gillies Gothic are friendly and personal, but you wouldn't classify them as elegant or formal. The typefaces Deanna Script and Phyllis are also available with alternate capital letters, called *swash caps*. As the name suggests, swash caps are generally more stylized and decorative than ordinary caps.

Deanna Script & Bodoni Regular

110-pt. Legend

CHICO'S

Bar 'n' Grill

48-pt. Mistral & 20-pt. Garamond Condensed Bold

COMMERCIAL SCRIPT

A B C D E F G H I J K L M N O P Q R S T U V W X Y Z a b c d e f g h i j k l m n o p q r s t u v w x y z 1 2 3 4 5 6 7 8 9 0

DEANNA SCRIPT

A B C D E F G H I J K L M N O P Q R S T U V W X Y Z a b c d e f g h i j k l m n o p q r s t u v w x y z 1 2 3 4 5 6 7 8 9 0

DEANNA SWASH CAPS

A A B C D E F G H I J K L M N O P Q R S T U V W X Y Z

HUDSON

a b c d e f g h i j k l m n o p q r s t u v w x y z a b c d e f g h i j k l m n o p q r s t u v w x y z 1 2 3 4 5 6 7 8 9 0

LEGEND

A B C D E F G H I J K L M N O
P Q R S T U V W X Y Z a b c d e f g h i
j k l m n o p q r s t u v w x y z 1 2 3 4 5 6 7
8 9 0

MISTRAL

ABCDEFGHIJKLMNOPQRSTUVWXY
Zabcdefghijklmnopqrstuvwxyz1
234567890

PARK AVENUE

A B C D E F G H I J K L M N O P Q
R S T U V W X Y Z a b c d e f g h i j k l m
n o p q r s t u v w x y z 1 2 3 4 5 6 7 8 9 0

500-pt. Phyllis Swash

PHYLLIS

A B C D E F G H I J K L M N O P Q R S
T U V W X Y Z a b c d e f g h i j k l m n o p q r s t
u v w x y z 1 2 3 4 5 6 7 8 9 0

PHYLLIS SWASH

A B C D E F G H I J K L M N
O P Q R S T U V W X Y Z a b c d
e f g h i j k l m n o p q r s t u v w x y z 1 2 3 4 5
6 7 8 9 0

VIVALDI

A B C D E F G H I J K L M
N O P Q R S T U V W X Y
Z a b c d e f g h i j k l m n o p q r s t u v w x y z 1 2
3 4 5 6 7 8 9 0

Vivaldi & Deanna Flowers

Uncials

Uncial letters were those used by European scribes, and date back to the 4th century AD. Uncial letters clearly show their reliance upon the quill and hand lettering. They are decorative, but at the same time very readable. Uncials such as American Uncial consist of a single case, as did all European alphabets during the Middle Ages. Use these typefaces for titling, display, and initial drop caps, or as a text font in documents where you want to impart a mediæval or Celtic tone. Uncials combine very well with Oldstyle text faces such as Bembo, Galliard, and Garamond.

The typeface *Rosslaire* is technically not an uncial design, but it is clearly influenced by the uncial form.

ceuo míle fáilte

55-pt. American Uncial

chughat, chugat, a Bhuaine Bhalbh!
marach ó thír na mBan marbh
a'fuaoach an Bhruít uaíne Bhatas.

Awake, awake, thou silent tide!
From the Mortal Women's Land a horseman rides,
From my head the green cloth snatching.

140-pt. American Uncial

aBCOEFghijKlmnopQRStuvw
xyz1234567890

18-pt. American Uncial

ABCDEFGhijKlmnopQRSTuvwxyz
abcdefghijkl mnopqrstuvwxyz1234567890

18-pt. Rosslaire

history &
genealogy
of the
de Burgo
family

by Seán Mac William Burke
16th-century manuscript

24-pt. American Uncial &
10-pt. Bergamo

Black Letter

Black Letter or "Gothic" type originated as a written form in northern Europe in the 12th century. It became so popular throughout all of Europe that it eventually replaced other hand-written styles of lettering such as the many forms of uncials. By the time Gutenberg popularized the concept of printing with moveable type in the mid-15th century, the Black Letter style was ubiquitous. All the early printers modeled their type on Black Letters.

There is no set style among Black Letter typefaces determining the appearance or form of letters — especially uppercase letters — which can make identifying them out of context rather difficult. But for this reason, Black Letters such as Fette Fraktur make very interesting initial drop caps. Black Letters are ideally suited for titles and headlines, but readers from this century will usually find them hard to read as text fonts.

Avoid setting words in all caps with these typefaces (almost impossible to read), and do not add space between letters (Black Letters look best when the letters are as close together as possible).

The Gutenberg family seal

140-pt. Fette Fraktur

UuBbCcDdEeFfGgHhIiJjKtLlMmNnOoPp
QqRrSsTtUuVvWwXxYyZz 1 2 3 4 5 6 7 8 9 0

18-pt. Fette Fraktur

AaBbCcDdEeFfGgHhIiJjKkLlMmNnOo
PpQqRrSsTtUuVvWwXxYyZz 1 2 3 4 5 6 7 8 9 0

18-pt. Fette Gotisch

AaBbCcDdEeFfGgHhIiJjKkLlMmNnOoPpQqRr
SsTtUuVvWwXxYyZz 1 2 3 4 5 6 7 8 9 0

18-pt. Olde English

Death and the Printer

48-pt. Fette Fraktur

You Want It When?

Desktop Publishers of the fifteenth century.

A woodcut from the *Danse Macabre*, printed by Matthies Huss in 1499.

Symbols & Borders

SYMBOL TYPEFACES AND PI FONTS CONTAIN NOT LETTERS of the Roman alphabet but graphic symbols such as arrows, circles, squares, printers hands, bullets, stars, and encircled numbers. Virtually anything. Symbol fonts quite often contain symbols relating to a theme, profession or usage such as mathematical symbols, cartographic symbols, and the pictograms commonly found in roadsigns. Specific symbol fonts exist for just about every purpose.

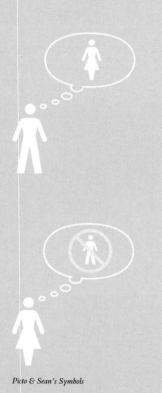

Picto & Sean's Symbols

Celt & American Uncial

CELT

KEY	SYMBOL
1	
2	
Sh-A	
Sh-C	
Sh-D	
Sh-E	
Sh-F	
A	
B	
C	
D	
E	
F	
G	
H	
I	

DEANNA BORDERS

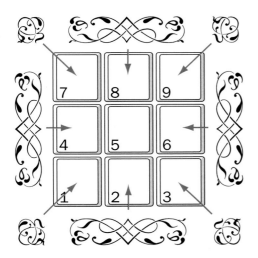

Deanna Borders & Deanna Script

DEANNA FLOWERS

KEY	SYMBOL
A	
B	
C	
D	
E	
F	
G	
H	
I	
J	
K	
L	
M	
N	
O	
P	

The characters that make up the Deanna Borders typeface are encoded in such a way that you could draw a square with them using the numpad keys in the order the numpad keys are arranged on the keyboard. That is, the 7, 9, 3 and 1 keys are the four corners; the 4 and 6 keys are the vertical sides; and the 8 and 2 keys are the horizontal sides. The 5 key creates a space that is the same width as the horizontal sides (in other words, an em space). The spacebar creates a space that is the same width as the vertical sides, or a one-quarter em space (four spacebar spaces equals the width of one 5 key space).

PICTO

The Picto font is a collection of international symbols, or pictogrammes, useful for creating signs, maps, and directions. The meaning of most symbols is apparent. Others may require some imagination. Cognitive scientists may recognize the symbol on the right, for example, as signifying "double-negative," while Latvians use it as a symbol for "Yes." Little known fact.

No, Non, Nyet, Nein

The international symbol for "No" (⊘) and the international symbol for "Sure, what the heck" (○) are designed in such a way that they can be used in conjuction with any other character from any font. First type the character you want placed inside the circle, then type the appropriate keystroke for No (Sh-`) or Yes ( `).

A	📚	P	🍁	Sh-E	✚	Sh-T	🚺
B	🎁	Q	🍁	Sh-F	🧰	Sh-U	🚹
C		R	ℹ	Sh-G		Sh-V	👫
D	🎥	S	✠	Sh-H	🛟	Sh-W	🚶
E	∪	T	☢	Sh-I	🚩	Sh-X	🥾
F	⬆	U	⚕	Sh-J		Sh-Y	⛷
G		V	🚰	Sh-K		Sh-Z	
H	🦌	W	🍎	Sh-L	🎠	1	
I	❄	X	🍴	Sh-M		2	
J		Y	🍷	Sh-N		3	🚲
K	🔥	Z	☕	Sh-O		4	🏍
L	⛺	Sh-A		Sh-P		5	🚌
M	⚓	Sh-B		Sh-Q		6	🚚
N	📞	Sh-C	👶	Sh-R	♿	7	🚕
O	🐕	Sh-D	💯	Sh-S	🚻	8	🚗

9	🛒	]		
0		Sh-]	🍦	
Sh-1	✶	;	✉	
Sh-3		Sh-;		
Sh-4		Comma		
Sh-5		Sh-Comma	✖	
Sh-6		Period		
Sh-7		Sh-Period		
Sh-8	🏃	/		
Sh-9		Sh-/	?	
Sh-Zero		Sh-\`	🚫	
Hyphen	✈	\`	◯	
Equal	P	'		
Sh-Equal		Sh-'		
[		\\		
Sh-[		Sh-\\	🍸	

KEY

Sh = Shift key
Alt = Alt key
Op = Option key

On the Macintosh, certain symbols require a combination of keystrokes in order to access them. Hyphens (–) are used between keystrokes that need to be held down simultaneously. For example, **Sh-Op-M** means that the Shift, Option, and M keys must be held down together to access the proper symbol.

Some symbols require a double sequence of keys to create them. These sequences are shown with a space between each set. For example, **Op-I Sh-A** means you must first press the Option and I keys together, release them, and then press the Shift and A keys together.

In Windows, extended characters are accessed by holding down the Alt key and typing a four-digit sequence beginning with zero. When you release the Alt key, the character appears.

SEAN'S SYMBOLS

I created this symbol collection primarily because I use the circled numbers so often, and have always objected to the way they are organized in Zapf Dingbats, that is, not assigned to number keys. In Sean's Symbols, they are. This font was also designed and encoded for use in a mixed platform environment, meaning that the characters appear the same whether a document using this font is opened on a Mac or from Windows (unlike the Zapf Dingbats font, which encodes characters differently for Mac and Windows). The column on the left shows the keys you need to type on the Mac; the column on the right shows the Windows keystrokes.

MAC		WINDOWS
1	❶	1
2	❷	2
3	❸	3
4	❹	4
5	❺	5
6	❻	6
7	❼	7
8	❽	8
9	❾	9
0	❿	0
Op-1	⓫	Alt-0161
Sh-Op-J	⓬	Alt-0212
Op-3	⓭	Alt-0163
Op-4	⓮	Alt-0162
Sh-Op-I	⓯	Alt-0136

Op-6	⓰	Alt-0167
Op-7	⓱	Alt-0182
Op-F	⓲	Alt-0131
Op-9	⓳	Alt-0170
Sh-1	①	Sh-1
Sh-2	②	Sh-2
Sh-3	③	Sh-3
Sh-4	④	Sh-4
Sh-5	⑤	Sh-5
Sh-6	⑥	Sh-6
Sh-7	⑦	Sh-7
Sh-8	⑧	Sh-8
Sh-9	⑨	Sh-9
Sh-0	⑩	Sh-0
Sh-Equal	☞	Sh-Equal

Hyphen	(pointing hand)	Hyphen
;	(pointing hand)	;
Sh-;	(pointing hand)	Sh-;
Sh-Period	(pointing hand)	Sh-Period
Equal	(pointing hand)	Equal
Sh-\	(hand)	Sh-\
Op-;	(open hand)	Alt-0133
Sh-Op-;	(open hand)	Alt-0218
Period	▶	Period
Comma	◀	Comma
/	▶	/
Sh-`	◀	Sh-`
Sh-]	▶	Sh-]
Sh-[	◀	Sh-[
Sh-N	□	Sh-N
N	■	N
Sh-O	○	Sh-O
O	●	O
Sh-M	▫	Sh-M
M	▪	M
Op-I O	⬠	Alt-0244
Op-` O	⬟	Alt-0242
Op-N O	⬡	Alt-0245

Op-U O	⬢	Alt-0246
Op-` U	(outline octagon)	Alt-0249
Op-E U	(filled octagon)	Alt-0250
Op-'	△	Alt-0230
Sh-Op-'	▲	Alt-0198
Sh-Op-]	△ (dotted)	Alt-0146
Op-]	▲	Alt-0145
Sh-Z	✺	Sh-Z
Sh-Y	✷	Sh-Y
Op-I U	△ (dotted)	Alt-0251
Sh-Op-O	▲	Alt-0216
Sh-Op-Q	⊙	Alt-0140
Op-Q	●	Alt-0156
Sh-Op-/	(gear outline)	Alt-0191
Sh-Op-R	✿ (gear)	Alt-0137
Op-I Sh-A	▽ (starred)	Alt-0194
Op-` A	▼	Alt-0224
Op-E A	◆	Alt-0225
G	✚	G
Op-Zero	✚	Alt-0186
I	△	I
J	□	J
K	▲	K

Key	Symbol	Key/Code
L	◆	L
Op-I Sh-U		Alt-0219
Op-E Sh-E		Alt-0201
Op-U U		Alt-0252
Op-U Sh-U		Alt-0220
D		D
Op-N N		Alt-0241
V		V
W		W
Sh-Op-C	☆	Alt-0199
Sh-W	★	Sh-W
Op-[		Alt-0147
Sh-Op-9		Alt-0183
Sh-Op-Hyphen		Alt-0151
Op-Hyphen		Alt-0150
Sh-J	†	Sh-J
Sh-Op-7		Alt-0135
Op-T		Alt-0134
Sh-Op-A	AMERICAN EXPRESS	Alt-0197
Op-E Sh-A	VISA	Alt-0193
Op-` Sh-O	MasterCard	Alt-0210
Sh-Op-Z	DISCOVER	Alt-0184
Sh-Op-Zero	♂	Alt-0130

Key	Symbol	Key/Code
Sh-Op-W	♀	Alt-0132
Op-U Y		Alt-0255
Op-U Sh-Y		Alt-0159
Op-` Sh-E		Alt-0200
B		B
C	☠	C
Sh-L	⚡	Sh-L
F		F
E		E
Op-E Sh-I	☺	Alt-0205
Op-I Sh-I		Alt-0206
Op-U Sh-I		Alt-0207
Op-` Sh-I		Alt-0204
H	♡	H
Op-E Sh-O		Alt-0211
P	♻	P
Q		Q
R	♻	R
S		S
T		T
Sh-A		Sh-A
Sh-B		Sh-B
Sh-C	↑	Sh-C

Key	Symbol	Key/Code
Sh-D	☂	Sh-D
Sh-H		Sh-H
A	⚠	A
Op-R		Alt-0174
Op-G		Alt-0169
Y		Y
Op-O		Alt-0248
Op-A		Alt-0229
Op-C	⏏	Alt-0231
Op-S		Alt-0223
X	⌘	X
Sh-X		Sh-X
Sh-Comma		Sh-Comma
Op-U Space		Alt-0168
Op-E O		Alt-0243
Sh-E		Sh-E
Sh-F		Sh-F
Sh-G		Sh-G
Op-I A		Alt-0226
Sh-I	🔒	Sh-I
`	☀	`
U		U
Z		Z

Key	Symbol	Key/Code
Sh-/		Sh-/
'		'
Sh-'	☎	Sh-'
Op-Y		Alt-0165
Sh-K	♛	Sh-K
Op-\	○	Alt-0171
Sh-Op-\	⊘	Alt-0187
Sh-Op-2		Alt-0164
Sh-Op-3		Alt-0139
Sh-Op-4		Alt-0155
Op-` Sh-U		Alt-0217
Sh-Op-[	☯	Alt-0148
Op-E Space		Alt-0180
[		[
\		\
]		]
Sh-P		Sh-P
Sh-Q		Sh-Q
Sh-R		Sh-R
Sh-S		Sh-S
Sh-T		Sh-T
Sh-U		Sh-U
Sh-V		Sh-V

Decorative Type

DECORATIVE, OR DISPLAY TYPES AS THEY ARE ALSO known, exhibit the widest range of differences in design. Virtually anything goes, and there are no rules of classification. Display types, with very, very few exceptions, are not intended to be used as text faces for extended reading. This is not one of the criteria a designer considers when developing a display face. Sometimes magazines, for instance, may use them to set the first paragraph of a story, or for callouts, but dramatic visual emphasis is the goal here, not readability.

Decorative types are useful for things like signs, posters and logos, restaurant menus, headlines for advertisements, title pages for books, reports and newsletters, or titles for video or multimedia applications.

As a group, decorative type has the most variation, but in many cases an individual decorative typeface may be suited only for very specific purposes. In contrast, consider an Oldstyle serif design such as Sabon: with few limitations, a designer could use it as a decorative face to create letterhead and business cards for a law firm or a multimedia production company, or use it to create the titles for a motion picture or video. But a decorative type such as Ad Lib, for example, would never work for a law firm, even though a multimedia company may find that it communicates its image quite effectively. It's not to say that decorative types are only useful for one purpose or another, but simply their possibilities are usually more restricted.

I selected 34 display faces for the companion CD. I think this should provide you with a solid starting point for establishing your decorative type library. I won't talk too much about individual display faces; if I tell you how I think one should be used, or am too specific about the circumstances under which you might want to apply it, I might appear to preclude the hundred other ways it could be used, 99 of which

125-pt. Arnold Böcklin

SPRINGFIELD CLINIC
3649 Medical Center Drive
Capital City

Nick Rivera, MD
619-456-7890

Savoy Regular, Savoy Small Caps & Picto

SPRINGFIELD CLINIC
3649 Medical Center Drive
Capital City

Nick Rivera, MD
619-456-7890

Ad Lib & Picto

I might not have considered. So I'll tell you a little bit about some of them, and show you a couple of examples to give you an idea.

I'll start with some descriptions (fonts are listed in alphabetical order):

Ad Lib No, it is not the typeface MTV uses for its Beavis and Butt-Head animated series, but it is very close. Ad Lib was designed by Freeman Craw in 1961. It is probably the only typeface that looks the same flipped upside-down.

Algerian is a dramatic typeface that sees wide use as a logo font for coffee houses. Latte anyone?

Arnold Boecklin (or Böcklin) is a German face from the *Jugendstil* or *Art Nouveau* era of the early 20th century. It is an immensely popular face for posters, signs, logos and other display purposes. For some reason, home beer brewers choose this typeface for their beer bottle labels more often than any other single typeface. Perhaps it is the highly stylized, somewhat drunken appearance of the loopy ascenders and undulating stroke that makes this design popular among beer drinkers. Some of Arnold Boecklin's detail is lost at small sizes on low-resolution printers, but at 600 dpi and above, I have seen it used effectively as a letterhead typeface set at 8 points.

Binner is an all-caps typeface with a decidedly decadent 1930s Berlin cabaret feel about it. It works very well in signs, posters, and menus. Consider using Binner as an alternative to typefaces such as Broadway, which is so stylized it has become nearly a cliché for 1920s Art Deco. Binner is much more flexible, and even works well in documents where an Art Deco tone is neither desired nor intended, such as a headline font for title pages in a book or headings in a newsletter. In fact, my own company, Title Wave, a multimedia design and development firm having nothing to do with Art Deco, uses Binner as its logo type.

Caslon Antique The name Caslon Antique is somewhat of a mystery since there is no connection whatsoever in design or appearance with the various designs based on the types of William Caslon. Caslon Antique is nonetheless a great display and headline face with a worn, rough-shod look. It is quite popular as a "grunge" typeface in designs where a sense of chaos and ugliness is part of the message: rock magazines, books, posters, flyers, and CD album covers, for example.

Chromatic looks as if it's made of chrome-plated tubing. This typeface works well as text font set at small sizes for book and magazine publishing. Say what?!? (Just seeing if you were paying attention.)

Copperplate Gothic was designed by Frederic Goudy in 1901 for American Type Founders. It's a tremendously popular typeface for business card and letterhead design. Copperplate Gothic mixes well with many faces, particularly in logos and graphics. Consider giving this face plenty of letterspacing.

Davida has a distinctive Latino quality to it, making it quite popular as a sign and menu font for taco stands and other fine dining establishments. ¿Cerveza fría?

Delphian Open Titling is a beautiful incised face with a 1920s architectural quality to it. Consider using it for titles and book covers. Delphian Open Titling should only be used at large sizes (24 points and up).

Glaser Stencil is a unique stencil design and good alternative to the overused Stencil font from Adobe. Glaser Stencil is a bit more hip and better suited to modern designs.

Goudy Handtooled was designed by Frederic Goudy in 1922 for American Type Founders. This inline version is based on the bold weight of Goudy Old Style. Goudy Handtooled is a remarkable font for

DECORAT

advertising. Also consider it for magazine and newsletter mastheads, and sign cutting.

Handel Gothic Despite its rather old-world sounding name, it belongs to the Pepsi generation: it is the typeface Pepsi uses for its logo. Because of its heavy weight, gentle curves and simple geometry, Handel Gothic works well in multimedia and video.

Hobo was designed in 1910 by Morris Fuller Benton, but some 85 years later it is one of the most widely used fonts for commercial signs. Hobo is unique in that it contains no straight lines and no descenders (even in the lowercase), giving it an informal, friendly, and downright bouncy feeling.

Horndon shcmorndon bjørndon fjorndon, what can I say about beautiful Horndon?

Mercedes Like VAG Rounded, this typeface was designed for a German automobile manufacturer. Can you guess which one? Mercedes works well in posters and in technical publications.

Mona Lisa shares much in common with Modern typefaces such as Bodoni and Walbaum. It is an inline font with a small x-height and long dramatic ascenders, making it well-suited for things like book jacket designs. Like other inline faces, this font should be used at large point sizes (at least 24 points).

OCR-A OCR is an acronym for Optical Character Recognition. *OCR-A* was the first machine-readable typeface, and was developed in 1968 to conform to U.S. Gov't standards. It is commonly used in forms, identification labels, and other machine-scanned text. Also useful in

any document where you want to impart a cold, impersonal, machine-like tone. OCR-A is another design making a comeback as a grunge font for use in too-hip-for-words rock and techno journals, interactive media designs, video production, book covers, and so on.

OCR-B is just as readable to machines, but is a bit more readable for humans as well. This face appears in most UPC labels, and is the European counterpart to OCR-A. It too is popular in multimedia designs, and imparts an aloof, techno feeling to projects such as letterhead, business cards, logos and advertising.

Plakette is a bold condensed typeface well-suited for advertising headlines, signs and logos.

Reflex My knee-jerk response to this font is that it implies motion and depth. Useful for signs

IVE TYPE

This was typeset by a professional on a closed track. Do not attempt mixing all of your typefaces in a single document at home (or anywhere else for that matter).

and logos, but probably won't win raves in memos and reports.

Salut is great for any design where you want to convey a certain 1950s innocence or "Howdy neighbor!" commercialism.

Stop Designed by Aldo Novarese, Stop is somewhat of an experiment in human cognition and optical illusion. Consider the design of the letter 'K' for example: by itself you might not recognize it as an alphabetic character at all, yet in the presence of other letters it appears quite plainly as a 'K'. The appearance of one letter flows from the character preceding it, giving it a sense of motion. The name "Stop," then, was obviously an ironic choice because the design is so dynamic, and gives such a sense of motion to any text set with it. For this reason, Stop is quite

popular as a logo typeface, and well-suited for a variety of signage and display purposes. It is considerably less dynamic at small point sizes, so keep this in mind if you plan on using it in publications and documents.

Toxica I designed Toxica to be used in a poster for a friend's rock band. This face typifies the grunge school of design: ugly, off-kilter, and disturbed. It attracts attention in the same way piercing one's cheek with a diaper pin attracts attention: that is, through shock value. It is the antithesis of typographic taste, and as such works quite well when *antithesis* is your message.

University Roman (available on the companion CD as *Honeymoon*) is a tremendously popular display typeface useful for posters, signs and advertising. It looks best at large point sizes,

but I have seen it used on menus (restaurants, not operating systems) combined very effectively with Gill Sans (*Chantilly*).

VAG Rounded If this typeface looks familiar, think fahrvergnügen. VAG Rounded is the face used by Volkswagen for its logo and advertising (in fact VAG is an acronym for Volkswagen, A.G.). It has an extraordinary appearance despite its seemingly simple design, and is particularly well-suited for signs and multimedia applications.

Vendome is one of the few display fonts that you might consider using as a text face. Designed in the early 1950s, it is loosely based on the types of Jean Jannon. Vendome is a beautiful titling face.

AD LIB

A B C D E F G H I J K L M N O P Q
R S T U V W X Y Z a b c d e f g h i j
k l m n o p q r s t u v w x y z 1 2 3 4
5 6 7 8 9 0

ALGERIAN

A B C D E F G H I J K L M N O P Q R S T
U V W X Y Z 1 2 3 4 5 6 7 8 9 0

ARNOLD BÖCKLIN

A B C D E F G H I J K L M N O P Q R S T
U V W X Y Z a b c d e f g h i j k l m n o p
q r s t u v w x y z 1 2 3 4 5 6 7 8 9 0

BERLINER GROTESQUE (*regular* & bold)

A B C D E F G H I J K L M N O P Q R S T U V
W X Y Z a b c d e f g h i j k l m n o p q r s t u v
w x y z 1 2 3 4 5 6 7 8 9 0

twice the caffeine

Algerian & Berliner Grotesque
Coffee cup: KPT Power Photos

Arnold Böcklin

BINNER

ABCDEFGHIJKLMNOPQRS
TUVWXYZ1234567890

CASLON ANTIQUE

ABCDEFGHIJKLMNOPQRSTUV
WXYZabcdefghijklmnopqrstuvwx
yz1234567890

CHROMATIC

ABCDEFGHIJKLMNOPQRSTU
VWXYZ1234567890

COPPERPLATE GOTHIC (*regular*, *bold, condensed regular & condensed bold*)

ABCDEFGHIJKLMNOPQ
RSTUVWXYZABCDEFGHIJ
KLMNOPQRSTUVWXYZ123
4567890

Multimedia Development

Binner & Chantilly

Caslon Antique

Wynken Blynken & Nod
LONDON • PARIS • TOKYO • HOBOKEN

Modern 216 & Copperplate Gothic Condensed Bold

DAVIDA

ABCDEFGHIJKLMNOPQRSTU
VWXYZ1234567890

DELPHIAN OPEN TITLING

ABCDEFGHIJKLMNOPQRST
UVWXYZABCDEFGHIJKLMNO
PQRSTUVWXYZ1234567890

GLASER STENCIL

ABCDEFGHIJKLMNOPQRST
UVWXYZ1234567890

GOUDY HANDTOOLED

ABCDEFGHIJKLMNOPQRS
TUVWXYZabcdefghijklmno
pqrstuvwxyz1234567890

Delphian Open Titling, Binner & Franklin Gothic Heavy

Glaser Stencil, Function Condensed Bold & Sean's Symbols

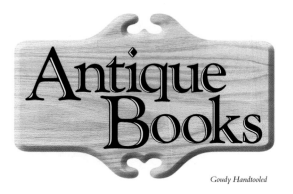

Goudy Handtooled

HANDEL GOTHIC

ABCDEFGHIJKLMNOPQR
STUVWXYZabcdefghijkl
mnopqrstuvwxyz12345
67890

HOBO

ABCDEFGHIJKLMNOPQR
STUVWXYZabcdefghijkl
mnopqrstuvwxyz12345
67890

HONEYMOON

ABCDEFGHIJKLMNOPQRSTUV
WXYZabcdefghijklmnopqrstuv
wxyz1234567890

HORNDON

ABCDEFGHIJKLMNOPQRSTUVWXY
Z1234567890

THE HOME EARTH PLANET

Handel Gothic

Entrees

Mole Poblano

Grilled chicken breast with spicy, chile almond chocolate sauce.
Served with rice and green salad.

11.95

Argentinian Carne a La Parrilla

Flank steak marinated in lime, olive oil and herbs.
Served with red potatoes and cabbage salad.

12.95

Aji de Gallina

Spicy chicken with annato seeds, parmesan cheese and almonds.
Served with red potatoes and green salad.

10.50

Honeymoon & Goudy Sans

MERCEDES *(light & medium)*

A B C D E F G H I J K L M N O P Q R S T
U V W X Y Z a b c d e f g h i j k l m n o p
q r s t u v w x y z 1 2 3 4 5 6 7 8 9 0

MONA LISA

A B C D E F G H I J K L M N O P Q R S T U V W X
Y Z a b c d e f g h i j k l m n o p q r s t u v w x y z 1 2
3 4 5 6 7 8 9 0

OCR A

A B C D E F G H I J K L M N O P
Q R Z T U V W X Y Z a b c d e f
g h i j k l m n o p q r s t u v
w x y z 1 2 3 4 5 6 7 8 9 0

OCR B

A B C D E F G H I J K L M N O P
Q R S T U V W X Y Z a b c d e f
g h i j k l m n o p q r s t u v
w x y z 1 2 3 4 5 6 7 8 9 0

The Regular Division Plane of the

an essay
by
M. C. Escher
commissioned
by the
De Roos
Foundation
in 1957

Mona Lisa & Chantilly Regular & Ultra Bold

OCR A & VAG Rounded

PLAKETTE (*medium & demi bold*)

A B C D E F G H I J K L M N O P Q R S T U V W X Y Z
a b c d e f g h i j k l m n o p q r s t u v w x y z 1 2
3 4 5 6 7 8 9 0

REFLEX

A B C D E F G H I J K L M N O P Q R S T U V W X Y Z
1 2 3 4 5 6 7 8 9 0

SALUT

A B C D E F G H I J K L M N O P Q R S T
U V W X Y Z a b c d e f g h i j k l m n o
p q r s t u v w x y z 1 2 3 4 5 6 7 8 9 0

STOP

A B C D E F G H I J K L M N O P Q R S T U V
W X Y Z 1 2 3 4 5 6 7 8 9 0

Stop & Typewriter Regular

Salut & Typewriter Regular

TOXICA

A B C D E F G H I J K L M N O P
Q R S T U V W X Y Z a b c d e f
g h i j k l m n o p q r s t u v
w x y z 1 2 3 4 5 6 7 8 9 0

TYPEWRITER (_regular_, regular italic, bold, bold italic, condensed & condensed bold)

A B C D E F G H I J K L M N O P Q
R S T U V W X Y Z a b c d e f g h i j
k l m n o p q r s t u v w x y z 1 2 3
4 5 6 7 8 9 0

VAG ROUNDED BOLD

A B C D E F G H I J K L M N O P Q R S T U V
W X Y Z a b c d e f g h i j k l m n o p q r s t u
v w x y z 1 2 3 4 5 6 7 8 9 0

VENDOME

A B C D E F G H I J K L M N O P Q R S
T U V W X Y Z a b c d e f g h i j k l m n o p
q r s t u v w x y z 1 2 3 4 5 6 7 8 9 0

Fashion

Vendome & Vivaldi

urban

art gallery

show times: always   locations: everywhere

Toxica
Graffiti: KPT Power Photos

A RIVER RUNS THROUGH IT

Vendome

BIBLIOGRAPHY

TYPOGRAPHY

BRINGHURST, ROBERT. *The Elements of Typographic Style*. Hartley & Marks, Publishers. 1992.

> The zen and poetry of type and typography, Bringhurst's book is probably my all-time favorite. If I could only recommend one book on typography, this would be it.

DOWDING, GEOFFREY. *Finer Points in The Spacing & Arrangement of Type*. Hartley & Marks, Publishers. Revised edition, 1995.

> Required reading for DTP and printing professionals. The original edition first published by Wace & Company, Ltd is long since out of print, but this revised edition is a classic nonetheless. Detail-freaks will love it.

McLEAN, RUARI. *The Thames and Hudson Manual of Typography*. Thames and Hudson Ltd. 1980. Revised paperback edition, 1992.

> Thorough and practical. The most extensive bibliography available of things typographic.

TSCHICHOLD, JAN. *The Form of The Book: Essays on the Morality of Good Design.* Translated from the original German by Hajo Hadeler. Edited by Robert Bringhurst. Hartley & Marks, Publishers. 1991.

> Originally published in German as *Ausgewählte Aufsätze über Fragen der Gestalt des Buches und der Typographie*, the Hartley & Marks edition is much more than a guide for would-be book designers. It is a feast of typographical information and inspiration for the desktop publisher committed to designing beautiful yet functional, classic yet modern documents and publications.

HISTORY OF TYPE AND TYPE DESIGNERS

EASON, RONALD & ROOKLEDGE, SARAH. *Rookledge's International Handbook of Type Designers*. Sarema Press. 1991.

> The Rookledge guide provides a broad, if not particularly deep, history of individual typeface designers and their typefaces. Recommended reference book for anyone interested in the history of type designs.

HALEY, ALLAN. *Typographic Milestones*. Van Nostrand Reinhold. 1992.

> Well-crafted biographies of leading type designers through history, including a very interesting account of Johann Gutenberg and the earliest days of moveable type.

JASPERT, BERRY & JOHNSON. *Encyclopaedia of Type Faces*. Blanford. 4th ed. 1970.

> Just about every typeface designed before the era of digital typography and desktop publishing is listed in this book. The historical backgrounds provide too little information about any given font—the book is primarily a listing of type specimens in alphabetical order—but it is a useful reference nonetheless to help you identify particular typefaces, as well as the original designers.

LAWSON, ALEXANDER. *Anatomy of a Typeface*. David R. Godine, Publisher, Inc. 1990.

> Lawson's book is destined to become a classic. If you are at all interested in the history of printing and typography, you will enjoy this book. It provides short and informative chapters on all the major typefaces and their designers.

PAGE DESIGN & LAYOUT

COHEN, LUANNE & WENDLING, TANYA. *Design Essentials*. Adobe Press. 1995.

TAPSCOT, SOBERANIS, JEANS, ET AL. *Production Essentials*. Adobe Press. 1994.

> The Adobe Press books are useful, informative, and well-designed publications.

WHITE, JAN V. *Graphic Design for the Electronic Age*. Watson-Guptill Publications/Xerox Press. 1988.

> Despite its rather hokey title, this is an excellent book both for those just getting started in desktop publishing, as well as those who manage DTP departments.

WILSON, ADRIAN. *The Design of Books*. Chronicle Books. 1993.

> What desktop publishing can aspire to become. This is a wonderful and inspiring book.

ELECTRONIC DOCUMENTS

KRISTOF, RAY & SATRAN, AMY. *Interactivity by Design*. Adobe Press. 1995.

> Although it deals with typography only briefly, this book is an excellent resource for anyone designing multimedia applications or documents.

AMES, PATRICK. *Beyond Paper: The Official Guide to Adobe Acrobat.*
Adobe Press. 1993.

> An interesting and well designed book introducing the concept
> of the paperless office as brought to you by Adobe Acrobat.

PERIODICALS

Before & After. Bi-monthly. Page Lab, Inc. Roseville (Calif.).

> This is the best periodical available for desktop publishers. Each
> issue is published in full color on high-quality, high-gloss paper,
> and is a testament to its own design principles regarding layout,
> graphics, color and typography. Each issue is packed with design
> and technique-oriented tips. Be careful about bringing your
> issues to the office, however, because it is the kind of publica-
> tion others will try to steal from you. Keep under lock and key.
> Call 916.784.3880 for information and subscriptions.

U&lc (Upper & lower case). Quarterly. Journal of the International
Typeface Corporation. New York.

> Occasionally features interesting articles on type designers and trends
> in type design and typography. More of a promotional vehicle than an
> editorial one, but well worth subscribing to (especially if you can get
> a free subscription).

ONLINE SOURCES

CompuServe's Desktop Publishing Forum (GO: DTPFOR).

> This is the single best online source for information, suggestions
> and advice on matters of type, typography and desktop publishing
> in general. It's frequented regularly by some of the most experi-
> enced page designers in the world (as well as by representatives from
> many DTP-related software and hardware companies) all of whom
> are more than willing to answer technical and design-oriented
> questions, share tips and tricks, provide product information, etc.
> More than anything, it's a community of desktop publishing practi-
> tioners, professionals and amateurs alike, and anyone is welcome to
> join. A highly recommended resource.

INDEX

accents
    character combinations on Macintosh,
        72, 75−76
    key combinations for, 75−76
acronyms
    using on-line, 119
acute accents
    key combinations for, 75
Ad Lib
    font family, 252
    overview, 249
Adobe
    license agreements, 50
Adobe Acrobat, 163
Adobe Font Metrics files. *See* AFM files
Adobe Gallery Effects, 154, 155
Adobe Illustrator
    creating bevel type with, 130−131
    creating embossed type with, 144−145
    creating engraved type with, 138−140
    creating interlapping type with,
        136−137
    creating type on a path in, 126−127
    Plug-Ins for, 155
Adobe PageMaker
    creating fractions in, 90−91
    extended character keystrokes, 71
    kerning in, 96
    letterspacing in, 99−100
    word spacing in, 110
Adobe Photoshop, 122
    anti-alias accessory, 162
    creating debossed type with, 146−149

creating drop shadows in, 124−125
creating ghosted type with, 134−135
creating quilted type with, 132−133
creating reflective type with, 141−143
creating type in flames with, 150−151
creating type with neon glow in,
    128−129
Plug-Ins for, 155
Adobe Systems, 2
Adobe Type Manager (ATM), 3, 12. *See
    also* SuperATM
    memory of, 16−17, 39
    and Windows, 34
Adobe Type Reunion, 59−60
    and TrueType fonts, 62
AFM files
    on Macintosh, 13−14
    on PC, 34
Algerian
    font family, 252
    overview, 249
Alt key
    accessing extended characters with, 70
    important character combinations,
        71−72
American Standard Code for Information
    Interchange. *See* ASCII
American Uncial, 238−239, 242
ampersands, 86−87
angle brackets
    on-line use of, 116−117
apostrophes
    use of true, 96−97

Apple Computer, 2
applications, open
    installing and uninstalling fonts with
        on Macintosh, 39
        on PC, 39
Arnold Böcklin, 248
    font family, 252
    overview, 249
Æsc character
    key combinatons for, 76
ascender, 167
ASCII, 67−70
ASCII Chart, 73−74
asterisks
    on-line use, 116
ATM. *See* Adobe Type Manager

ballot boxes
    size of, 103−104
baseline, 167
Baskerville, 189
    font family, 193
    overview, 192
Baskerville, John, 192
Bembo. *See also* Bergamo
    font family, 175
    overview, 174
Benton, Morris Fuller
    overview, 250
Bergamo, 173. *See also* Bembo
Berliner Grotesque
    font family, 252
bevel type. *See* type, bevel

Bezier curves, 3–4
Binner
    font family, 253
    overview, 249
bitmap fonts, 2
    identifying in Windows 95 Fonts
        Folder, 32
    and PostScript fonts, 10–11
    removing from Windows 95, 37
    and TrueType fonts, 10–12
    versus TrueType fonts in suitcase files,
        11–12
    in Windows, 33
Black Letter type, 171. *See also* specific
      fonts
    overview, 240
Bodoni
    font family, 199
    overview, 198
Bodoni, Giambattista, 196, 197, 198
body text
    letterspacing, 1
    point size of, 106
boldfacing, 61
    guidelines for, 101
brackets
    created bulleted lists on-line, 117
breve accents
    key combinations for, 75
bullet character, 71–72
bulleted lists
    creating on-line, 117
bullets
    alternatives for, 104

cap height, 167
capitalized text
    letterspacing with, 99–100
    on-line, 115
    point size for, 98–99
caron
    key combinations for, 75

Carter, Matthew, 178
Caslon, 173
    font family, 177
    overview, 176
Caslon, William, 172, 176
Caslon Antique
    font family, 253
    overview, 249
cedilla
    key combinations for, 75
Celt, 242
Chantilly. *See* Gill Sans
character chart
    Macintosh, 68
    Windows, 69
character encoding schemes, 66
    Macintosh versus Windows, 70
characters. *See also* extended characters
    accented
        key combinations for, 75–76
    defined, 66
    8-bit ASCII, 67
    overview, 66–67
    rearranging with FontMonger, 78–81
    7-bit ASCII, 67
Chromatic
    font family, 253
    overview, 249
circumflex
    key combinations for, 75
Clarendon, 205
    font family, 207
    overview, 206
Clinesmith, Stephanie, 123
clipboard suitcase sets, 27
closed suitcase sets, 27
colon
    created bulleted lists on-line, 117
Commercial Script, 235
Compact Pro, 52
control keys
    on Macintosh, 77

Copperplate Gothic
    font family, 253
    overview, 249
copyright symbol, 102
counter, 167

Davida
    font family, 254
    overview, 249
Deanna Borders, 243
Deanna Flowers, 243
Deanna Script, 235
Deanna swash caps
debossed type. *See* type, debossed
decorative type. *See also* specific fonts
    overview, 248–249
Decorative types, 171
default directory
    for PFB files, 34
    for PFM files, 34
Delphian Open Titling
    font family, 254
    overview, 249
descender, 167
design axes, 63
device independence, 3
diacritical marks. *See* accents
diaeresis
    key combinations for, 75
Diffuse filter
    and type in flames, 150
digital typography
    rules of, 94
        ballot box size, 103–104
        boldfacing text, 101
        and bullets, 104
        for copyright, registered trademark,
            and trademark symbols, 102
        ellipses, 103
        hyphenation of proper names and
            titles, 112
        letterspacing, 107

letterspacing with capitalized text
    and small caps, 99–100
line length and margins, 106
line spacing, 104–105
point size for capitalized text, 98–99
point size for numbers, 101
point size of body text, 106
serif versus sans serif typefaces,
    105–106
single space after punctuation,
    94–95
text alignment, 110
underlining, 102
use of em and en dashes, 95–96
use of Oldstyle figures, 100
using true quotation marks and
    apostrophes, 96–98
word spacing, 107–110
word stacks, 111–112
directories
    creating structure
        on PC, 42
    selecting
        for Windows 3.1, 35
        for Windows 95, 36
display type. *See* decorative type
Divide filter
    and interlapping type, 136
double acute accent
    key combinations for, 75
double spacing. *See* line spacing
Downloader, 58
drop shadows, 124–125

8-bit ASCII characters, 67
ellipses, 103
e-mail typography
    rules of, 114
        capitalizing text, 115
        creating bulleted lists, 117
        distinguishing between paragraphs,
            115

double spacing, 115–116
emphasizing text, 116
indicating quotations, 116–117
signing off, 118
using acronyms, 119
using emoticons, 118
embossed type. *See* type, embossed
Emboss filter
and quilted type, 133
em dashes
creating, 70
use of, 95–96
emoticons
using on-line, 118
em-square, 3
en dashes
use of, 95–96
engraved type. *See* type, engraved
Eth characters
key combinatons for, 77
ethel characters
key combinatons for, 76
expert set typefaces
ligatures and, 84
need for, 87–89
using, 87
extended characters, 66–67
accessing, 245
Adobe PageMaker keystrokes, 71
important Alt key character
combinations, 71–72
important keystrokes, 74
key combinations for, 74–77
typing in Windows, 70–72
typing on Macintosh, 72–74
typing on Microsoft Word for
Windows, 70–71
Extract, 52
Eyedropper tool, 137

feet. *See* units of measurement
Fette Fraktur, 240

Fette Gotisch, 240
filters. *See* under specific filters
FOND resource
of Macintosh PostScript fonts, 13
Font/DA Mover, 15
font editors
PostScript editors, 78
font families, 14. *See also* specific fonts
checking, 60–62
displaying by name, 59–60
in FontMinder, 43
FontHandler, 40
FontHopper, 50–51, 53
font managers, 12. *See also* specific
types
Macintosh, 17–18
on PCs, 41–42
FontMinder, 40, 41
deleting fonts with, 44
displaying font samples, 45
installing, 43
installing fonts with, 43–44
managing fonts with, 42–46
organizing font files, 46
printing font samples, 45
using, 43
FontMonger, 50, 51
map characters with, 77
rearranging characters with, 78–81
FontMonster, 32
Fontographer, 50, 51, 53
map characters with, 77
font packs, 42
creating and editing, 41
fonts. *See also* bitmap fonts; PostScript
fonts; printer resident fonts;
TrueType fonts; vector fonts
available, 42
basics versus exotics, 160
building new, 79–80
choosing, 160–163
choosing the best format, 7

converting, 49–53
policies regarding, 50
deleting
with FontMinder, 44
displaying samples, 45
downloading, 57–58
from Macintosh, 58–59
to printers used by Macs and
PCs, 59
from Windows, 59
familiarizing with, 160–161
family-ized, 60
verifying, 60–62
GX smart, 27–29
installing. *See also* installation
with FontMinder, 43–44
with MasterJuggler, 20–21
with Suitcase, 24–25
with System 7.5, 15–16
managing files
on Macintosh, 16–18, 27
in Windows, 39–42
match to text content, 160
minimizing number of, 17
organizing files with FontMinder, 46
printing samples, 45
renaming
while rearranging characters, 79
renaming converted, 53
renaming with ResEdit, 15
stored in printers, 56–57
substituting, 53–54
and Panose Matching, 54
technical limitations of, 161–163
uninstalling
with MasterJuggler, 21
font samples, 42
font scaling, 2–3
font sets
in Suitcase, 24
types of in Suitcase, 26–27
working with

with MasterJuggler, 22–23
with Suitcase, 25–26
fonts folder, 16
fraction bar, 89
fractions
creating in Microsoft Word, 90
creating in PageMaker, 90–91
creating in WordExpress, 91
creating with expert set typefaces,
87–89
creating without expert set typefaces,
89–91
Franklin Gothic
font family, 213–215
overview, 212
Franklin Gothic Condensed. *See* Franklin
Gothic
Function. *See* Futura
Futura, 211
font family, 217–221
overview, 216
Futura Condensed. *See* Futura

Galliard. *See also* Gareth
font family, 179
overview, 178
Garamond, 173
font family, 181
overview, 180
Garamond, Claude, 172, 180
Garamond Condensed, 173
Gareth, 173. *See also* Galliard
Garmond Condensed
font family, 183
overview, 182
Gaussian Blur
and debossed type, 148
for drop shadows, 125
and quilted type, 132
and type in flames, 151
Geometrics, 170, 210. *See also* specific fonts
combining with Moderns, 196

ghosted type. *See* type, ghosted
Gill, Eric, 222
Gill Sans
    font family, 223–225
    overview, 222
Glaser Stencil
    font family, 254
    overview, 249
Glypha
    font family, 209
    overview, 208
Glytus. *See* Glypha
Gothic types. *See* Black Letter
    type
Goudy, Frederic
    overview, 249
Goudy Handtooled
    font family, 254
    overview, 249–250
Goudy Sans
    font family, 227
    overview, 226
Granjon, Robert, 178
graphic programs
    extensions, 154
    vector-based, 122
graphics
    printer treatment of, 55–56
    type as, 122–123
grave accent
    key combinatons for, 76
Grotesques, 170, 210. *See also*
    specific fonts
gutter, 106
    and readability, 108
GX smart fonts, 27–29

Handel Gothic
    font family, 255
    overview, 250
hard drive
    adding to printers, 58

headlines
    leading and, 105
Hewlett-Packard LaserJet 5MP, 6
hinting, 4–6
Hobo
    font family, 255
    overview, 250
Honeymoon. *See* University Roman
Horndon
    font family, 255
    overview, 250
hot keys
    of MasterJuggler, 21–22
Hudson, 235
Humanists, 170, 210. *See also* specific
    fonts
Hungarian umlaut. *See* double acute
    accent
hyphenation
    of proper names and titles, 112
    and word spacing problems, 109–110
hyphens
    versus en dashes, 95
    on-line use, 116

icons
    for PostScript fonts, 12
Illustrator. *See* Adobe Illustrator
inches. *See* units of measurement
Infinite FX, 155, 157
installation
    of FontMinder, 43
    of fonts
        with FontMinder, 43–44
        with MasterJuggler, 20–21
        with Suitcase, 24–25
        using System 7.5, 15–16
    of MasterJuggler, 19
    of Suitcase, 24
    of TrueType fonts
        in Windows 3.1, 34–35
        in Windows 95, 36–37

installed fonts, 42
interlapping type. *See* type, interlapping
italics, 61
    ampersands in, 87
    versus boldfacing, 101
    of Oldstyles, 172
    versus underlining, 102

Jannon, Jean, 180, 182

kerning
    with dashes, 95–96
keyboard, 66
KPT Power Photos, 123
KPT Power Tools, 157
KPT Vector Effects, 155–156, 205
krouzek. *See* ring

LaserJet Utility, 58
Laserwriter Utility, 58
leading. *See* line spacing
Legend, 236
letter
    parts of, 167
Letter Gothic
    font family, 233
    overview, 232
letterspaced type
    using ligatures with, 84–85
letterspacing
    body text, 107
    with small caps and capitalized
        text, 99–100
ligatures. *See also* ampersands
    defined, 84
    non-English, 76, 86
    using, 84–86
line length, 106
line spacing
    double spacing on-line, 115–116
    improving readability with,
        104–105

L slash
    key combinatons for, 77

Macintosh
    AFM files on, 13–14
    character chart, 68
    character combinations for accents, 72
    character translation, 70
    control keys on, 77
    converting fonts from Windows, 50
    converting fonts to Windows, 50
    converting PostScript fonts to/from,
        51–53
    converting TrueType fonts to/from,
        50–51
    distinguishing TrueType fonts from
        PostScript fonts, 48
    downloading fonts from, 58–59
    font names on, 14
    Key Caps accessory, 73
    ligatures on, 84
    managing font files on, 16–18
    organizing by font family name on,
        59–60
    versus PC fonts, 7
    Picto on, 245
    PostScript fonts on, 10, 13–14
    QuickDraw GX, 27–29
    suitcases on, 14–15
    TrueType fonts on, 10–12, 14
    typing extended characters on, 72–74
    using ligatures on, 85
macron
    creating, 80–81
    key combinatons for, 76
Manutius, Aldus, 172, 174
margins, 106
MasterJuggler, 12, 17, 19
    FontShow, 23
    hot keys, 21–22
    installing, 19
    installing fonts with, 20–21

Remember current default dir
    option, 23
uninstalling fonts with, 21
using, 19–23
working with sets, 22–23
Maximum filter
    and reflective type, 141
measurement, units of. *See* units of
    measurement
Mercedes
    font family, 256
    overview, 250
Microsoft Corporation, 2. *See also*
    Microsoft Word; Windows;
    Windows 3.1; Windows 95
Microsoft Word
    creating fractions in, 90
    tracking and, 100
    typing extended characters on, 70–71
Minus Front filter
    and engraved type, 139–140
Mistral, 236
Modern 216
    font family, 201
    overview, 200
Moderns, 166, 168–169. *See also* specific
    fonts
    overview, 196
Mona Lisa
    font family, 256
    overview, 250
Multiple Masters, 62–63

negative kerning, 80–81
New Baskerville
    font family, 195
    overview, 194
NFNT resource
    of Macintosh PostScript fonts, 13
Nisus Writer, 85
    and tracking, 100
non-lining numerals. *See* Oldstyle figures

numbers
    Oldstyle figures, 100
    point size for, 101
numerals
    creating fractions with inferior and
        superior, 88–89

obliquing, 61
OCR-A
    font family, 256
    overview, 250
OCR-B
    font family, 256
    overview, 250
Offset filter
    and debossed type, 147, 148
    for drop shadows, 125
Offset Path filter
    and bevel type, 130
ogonek
    key combinatons for, 76
Olde English, 240
Oldstyle figures
    use of, 100
Oldstyles, 166, 168. *See also* specific fonts
    combining with sans serif typefaces,
        172
    leading and, 105
    overview of, 172–173
    using ligatures with, 84
opened suitcase sets, 26–27
Optima
    font family, 229
    overview, 228
Option+key, 72
Option+key, release key, 72
Option+key, release key, Shift+key, 72
Opus. *See* Optima
O slash characters
key combinatons for, 76
overdot
    key combinatons for, 76

page description language (PDL), 6
PageMaker. *See* Adobe PageMaker
    font substitution in, 53–54
    and Panose Matching, 54
Panose Matching, 54
paper
    and font selection, 162
paragraphs
    distinguishing between on-line, 115
Park Avenue, 234, 236
PC. *See also* Windows; Windows 3.1;
        Windows 95
    versus Macintosh fonts, 7
PDL. *See* page description language
period
    versus ellipses, 103
    with phone numbers, 95
permanent sets, 26
PFB files, 34
    and font conversion, 51–53
PFM files, 34
    and font conversion, 51–53
Photoshop. *See* Adobe Photoshop
Phyllis, 237
Phyllis Swash, 237
Picto, 242, 244–245
PI fonts
    overview, 242
Plakette
    font family, 257
    overview, 250
Plug-Ins. *See* graphic programs,
        extensions
point, 167
point size, 167
    of body text, 106
    for capitalized text, 98–99
    for numbers, 101
PostScript editors, 78
PostScript fonts
    and bitmap fonts, 10–11
    converting from Macintosh, 51–53

converting from TrueType fonts,
        49–50
    converting to Macintosh, 51–53
    converting to TrueType fonts,
        49–50
    curves defined in, 3–4
    hinting, 6
    icons for, 12
    on Macintosh, 13–14
    as PDL, 6
    with QuickDraw GX, 28–29
    recognizing, 10–12
    scalability of, 2–3
    storing in Windows, 41
    storing with suitcases, 20
    Type I, 2
        versus Type III, 7
    using with TrueType fonts, 48–49
    in Windows, 34
PostScript printers
    RAM in, 57
    resident fonts in, 57
PostScript RIPs (Raster Image
        Processors), 6
primes, 74, 98
printer outline file. *See also* PFM files
    of Macintosh PostScript fonts, 13
printer resident fonts, 55–57
printers
    adding hard drive to, 58
    adding RAM to, 57–58
    downloading fonts to, 57–58
        from Macintosh, 58–59
        when used by Macs and PCs, 59
        from Windows, 59
    selecting, 6
    TrueType fonts versus PostScript fonts
        on, 48–49
PSDOWN.EXE, 59
punctuation
    with quotation marks, 97
    single space after, 94–95

quadratic B-Splines, 3–4
QuarkXPress
    kerning in, 96
    letterspacing in, 99–100
QuickDraw GX, 27–29
quilted type. *See* type, quilted
quotation marks
    creating, 98
    key combinations for, 74
    with punctuation, 97
    use of true, 96–97

RAM
    adding to printers, 57–58
    in PostScript printers, 57
Random Access Memory. *See* RAM
readability, 107–108
    improving, 108–110
        with line spacing, 104–105
Reed, Chris, 50
reflective type. *See* type, reflective
Reflex
    font family, 257
    overview, 250–251
Refont, 52
registered trademark symbol, 102
ResEdit, 14
    renaming fonts with, 15
resident fonts. *See* printer
    resident fonts
ring
    key combinatons for, 76
Ripple filter
    and type in flames, 151
rivers, 108–109

Sabon. *See also* Savoy
    font family, 187
    overview, 186
Salut
    font family, 257
    overview, 251

sans serif typefaces, 166, 170. *See also*
    specific fonts
    combining with Oldstyles, 172
    leading and, 105
    overview, 210
    readability of, 163
    versus serif typefaces, 105–106
    using ligatures with, 84
    verifying, 61
Savoy, 173. *See also* Sabon
script fonts. *See also* specific fonts
    overview, 234
Script types, 171
Sean's Symbols, 242, 246–247
serif, 167
serifs
    on Moderns, 169
    on Oldstyles, 168
    on Slab serifs, 169
    on Transitionals, 168, 188
serif typefaces, 166
    readability of, 163
    versus sans serif typefaces,
        105–106
    verifying, 61
sets. *See* font sets
7-bit ASCII characters, 67
shift key, 66
Shift+Option+key, 72
Slab Serifs
    overview, 204
Slab serifs, 169
slash character, 89
small caps, 98–99
    letterspacing with, 99–100
smiloglyphs. *See* emoticons
SoftMaker
    license agreements, 50
solidus. *See* fraction bar
spacing. *See also* letterspacing; line
        spacing; word spacing
    after punctuation, 94–95

spell checkers
    ligatures and, 85
stem, 167
Stop
    font family, 257
    overview, 251
stress, 169
    Oldstyle versus Modern, 196
strokes, 168
Stuffit, 52
Suitcase, 12, 17, 23–24
    clipboard suitcase sets, 27
    closed suitcase sets, 27
    installing, 24
    installing fonts with, 24–25
    opened suitcase sets, 26–27
    permanent sets, 26
    temporary sets, 26
    using, 24–25
    working with sets, 25–26
suitcase files
    combining, 14–15
    creating new, 15
    on Macintosh, 10–12, 14–15
    and PostScript fonts, 20
    TrueType fonts versus bitmap in, 11–12
suitcases. *See* suitcase files
swash caps, 234
    Deanna, 235
symbol typefaces
    overview, 242
Syntax
    font family, 231
    overview, 230
System 7.5
    installing fonts with, 15–16

temporary sets, 26
text alignment
    justified text
        and word spacing problems, 108
    selecting, 110

text weights
    creating new, 63
Thorn characters
    key combinatons for, 77
tilde
    key combinatons for, 76
Toxica
    font family, 258
    overview, 251
tracking, 99–100
trademark symbol, 102
Transitionals, 166, 168. *See also* specific
    fonts
    overview, 188–189
TrueType fonts, 2
    and Adobe Type Reunion, 62
    and bitmap fonts, 10–12
    versus bitmap in suitcase files, 11–12
    converting from Macintosh, 50–51
    converting from PostScript fonts,
        49–50
    converting to Macintosh, 50–51
    converting to PostScript fonts, 49–50
    curves defined in, 3–4
    editing tables of, 32
    hinting, 6
    identifying in Windows 95 Fonts
        Folder, 32
    installing in Windows 3.1, 34–35
    installing in Windows 95, 36–37
    on Macintosh, 14
    organizing files of with
        FontMinder, 46
    previewing in Windows 95, 38–39
    with QuickDraw GX, 28–29
    recognizing, 10–12
    removing from Windows 95, 37
    removing in Windows 3.1, 35
    scalability of, 2–3
    storing in Windows, 41
    using with PostScript fonts, 48–49
    on Windows, 32–33

Tschichold, Jan, 186
TTConverter, 50, 51
TTF files, 32
type. *See also* specifics kinds of
    bevel, 130–131
    classification of
        overview, 166
    debossed, 146–149
    embossed, 144–145
    engraved, 138–140
    in flames, 150–151
    ghosted, 123, 134–135
    interlapping, 136–137
    with neon glow, 128–129
    on path, 126–127
    quilted, 132–133
    reflective, 141–143
TypeCaster, 155, 157
Typeface
    license agreements, 50
Type Reunion. *See* Adobe Type
        Reunion
Typewriter
    font family, 258
typography. *See* digital typography;
        e-mail typography

umlaut. *See* diaeresis
Uncials, 171. *See also* specific fonts
    overview, 238
underscoring
    guidelines for, 102
    on-line use, 116
units of measurement. *See also* points
    key combinations for, 74, 98
University Roman
    font family, 255
    overview, 251
Unsit, 52
URW Antiqua
    font family, 190
    overview, 190

URW Palladio
    font family, 185
    overview, 184

VAG Rounded Bold
    font family, 258
    overview, 251
vector fonts
    in Windows, 33
Vendome
    font family, 258
    overview, 251
virgule character. *See* slash character
Vivaldi, 237

Walbaum
    font family, 203
    overview, 202
Wind filter
    and type in flames, 150
Windows. *See also* Windows 3.1;
        Windows 95
    accessing extended characters, 245
    and ATM, 34
    bitmap fonts in, 33
    character chart, 69
    Character Map accessory, 71
    character translation, 70
    converting fonts from Macintosh, 50
    converting fonts to Macintosh, 50
    converting PostScript fonts to/from,
        51–53
    converting TrueType fonts to/from,
        50–51
    distinguishing TrueType fonts from
        PostScript fonts, 48
    downloading fonts from, 59
    expert font sets, 84
    and FontMinder, 46
    ligatures on, 84
    managing fonts in, 39–42
    PostScript fonts in, 34

storing PostScript fonts in, 41
type extended characters in, 70–72
using ligatures on, 85–86
vector fonts in, 33
Windows 3.1
    Fonts control panel
        identifying TrueType fonts, 33
    fonts on, 32
    installing TrueType fonts in, 34–35
    storing TrueType fonts, 41
    TrueType fonts on, 32–33
Windows 95
    Fonts Folder
        identifying bitmap fonts in, 32
        identifying TrueType fonts in, 32
    fonts on, 32
    installing TrueType fonts in, 36–37
    previewing TrueType fonts in, 38–39
    removing bitmap fonts from, 37
    removing TrueType fonts from, 37
    storing TrueType fonts, 41
    TrueType fonts on, 32–33
    Word Pad application, 62
WINPS.EXE, 59
WordExpress
    creating fractions in, 91
word spacing, 107–110
word stacks, 111–112
Wrefont, 52
WYSIWYG
    viewing with MasterJuggler, 23

x-height, 167
    on sans serifs, 170
    on Moderns, 169
    on Oldstyles, 168
    on Slab serifs, 169
    on Transitionals, 168
Xtras. *See* graphic programs,
        extensions

Zapf, Hermann, 184, 190

Sean Cavanaugh spends most of his days developing software, or writing about it. He's been doing this since 1984 or so. His last real job was director of typography for SoftMaker, Inc., where he oversaw the development and release of SoftMaker's *definiType* typeface library and associated products. He also wrote the *definiType* User Guides, which won acclaim, a few awards, several fans, and was the impetus for this book (his fourth).

"My love of type comes from a love for words," he says. "I find it impossible to separate the two."

Sean is thirty-three years old as he goes on living in San Diego.

Sean Cavanaugh
70471.160@compuserve.com

Ken Oyer
KAOyer@aol.com

ABOUT THE AUTHORS

PHOTOS BY K. C. ENNIS

Ken Oyer has been working in the graphic arts industry since 1978. Beginning as a typographer, he gradually focused his career on design. Ken sat down at a Macintosh in 1986 and has since worked in virtually every major graphics program known to man. Photoshop, Illustrator and QuarkXPress are his main tools, but lately he's been spending much of his time exploring 3D programs.

Ken teaches computer graphics at Platt College in San Diego, including seminars in *Advanced Photoshop* and *Digital Pre-Press*.

COLOPHON

This book was written and designed using QuarkXPress 3.31, Adobe PageMaker 6.0, Illustrator 5.5, and Photoshop 3.0 running on a Macintosh Quadra 840AV. Adobe Dimensions and KPT Vector Effects were used to create some charts and illustrations. Text was prepared in Nisus Writer 4.0 and Microsoft Word 5.1. The typeface Bergamo was used for text, running heads, and captions. Franklin Gothic was used for folios, run–ins, section headings, and captions. Both faces are available on the companion CD. In fact, with very few exceptions, every page of this book was produced using typefaces from the companion CD. ✍

mayonnaise